Maths & Music

Julia Winterson

Published by University of Huddersfield Press
University of Huddersfield Press
The University of Huddersfield
Queensgate
Huddersfield HD1 3DH
Email enquiries university.press@hud.ac.uk
Text © 2024
This work is licensed under a Creative Commons Attribution 4.0 International License

Images © as attributed
Every effort has been made to locate copyright holders of materials included and to obtain permission for their publication
The publisher is not responsible for the continued existence and accuracy of websites referenced in the text
A CIP catalogue record for this book is available from the British Library
ISBN Print: 978-1-86218-230-1
ISBN eBook: 978-1-86218-231-8
Cover design and diagrams © Simon Sellars

Acknowledgements

THE AUTHOR WOULD like to thank all those who contributed their time and expertise to the development of this book in particular Simon Sellars for his work on the illustrations, diagrams and cover design. Many thanks go to all those who helped with the proof-reading; Chris Hewison, Richard Steinitz, Mike Russ, Jessica Winterson, and in particular Elizabeth Hutchinson. The author is grateful to Christopher Fox for his insightful copy editing and to Mike and Helen Limer for their help with languages and the finer points of the music quotations.

Contents

Foreword	vii
Rhythm	xi
1 Rhythmic devices: time signatures, barlines and polyrhythms	1
2 Mathematical approaches to rhythm used in the twentieth-century	19
3 Rhythm systems in music from across the world	37
Symmetry	55
4 Symmetry in music	57
5 Frieze patterns in music	79
Scales	97
6 Diatonic scales and tuning	99
7 More scales: whole tone, octatonic, pentatonic, and scales that use microtones	113
8 Serialism and the 12-note scale	125
Forms and Structure	139
9 Canons and fugues	141
10 Proportion: Golden Section and the Fibonacci series	159
11 Randomness and chance	177
12 Fractals and chaos theory	193
13 Musical cryptography	213
14 Magic squares and Latin squares	229
15 Change ringing	249
Glossary of musical and mathematical terms	257
General index	269
Index of composers and their works	277
Popular music index	285

Foreword

THE COMPOSER IGOR Stravinsky once referred to the way in which 'musical form is close to mathematics' in terms of 'mathematical thinking and relationships'. *Maths and Music* is divided into sections, each one exploring a different mathematical aspect of music: rhythm; symmetry; scales; form and structure; and finally some musical curiosities. Musical examples are taken from across the world, from ancient and medieval music through to popular music of the twenty-first century.

Chapter 1 explores the mathematical qualities of rhythm with examples of their application in Western classical music, popular music and jazz. Several twentieth-century composers took an innovative approach to rhythm and their work is examined in Chapter 2, looking in particular at pieces by Olivier Messiaen, John Cage, Steve Reich and Conlon Nancarrow. This is followed by a discussion of some of the rhythmic devices found in popular music and jazz including the use of unusual time signatures, disco beats and the rhythmic construction of electronic dance music.

The rhythms of Western music are relatively simple in comparison with the examples given of music from around the world in Chapter 3: the irregular divisions of aksak rhythms; the *tala* of North Indian classical music; the interlocking figurations of gamelan; the polyrhythmic patterns of West African drumming; and the beat cycles of Spanish flamenco. Euclidean rhythms are also introduced, a family of cyclical rhythms whose structures are derived from the Euclidean algorithm and whose use can be found in traditional music across the world.

Much Western music has its basis in repetition and contrast, so it is not surprising, that the different types of symmetrical transformation (reflection, rotation, translation, and scale) are frequently found in music.

Chapters 4 and 5 look at the different ways in which musicians have used elements of symmetry and frieze patterns, ranging from the Medieval composer Guillaume de Machaut in 'Ma fin est mon commencement et mon commencement ma fin', to Nirvana in 'Smells like teen spirit'.

For centuries there has been much debate about different scales and tunings with many eminent mathematicians, scientists and musicians across Europe devising and analysing them. Three main systems evolved; the Pythagorean scale, just intonation and equal temperament and the mathematical and scientific principles involved are explored in Chapter 6; ratios, square roots and irrational numbers; the harmonic series and the circle of 5ths. Chapter 7 moves onto modes of limited transposition, such as the whole tone scale and the octatonic scale, along with the ubiquitous five-note pentatonic scale that is found in different forms across the world in music as diverse as the Javanese gamelan and the songs of The Smiths. The closing section of this chapter explores the use of the microtone, an interval smaller than a semitone that is used in scales which divide the octave into more than 12 notes.

Serialism with its note rows of 12 notes draws heavily on mathematical principles; it is algorithmic in its use of a strict set of procedures designed to be applied systematically; it uses symmetrical transformations in the construction of different rows and it uses combinatorics in its formulation of harmonies. These factors are explored in Chapter 8, primarily through the works of Schoenberg, Berg and Webern.

The focus then turns to form and structure, opening in Chapter 9 with two musical forms, canons and fugues, where rules and geometric transformations are central to their composition. In Stravinsky's words 'human activity must impose limits upon itself. The more art is controlled, limited, worked over, the more it is free'. Music is organized sound; an essential aspect of any musical composition is that the structure follows certain rules, but it should not be forgotten that sounds trigger an emotional response in the listener, understanding the mathematical structure does not tell us anything about the effect on the audience. Given that the set of procedures which need to be followed in a fugue could be described as an algorithm, perhaps a computer programme could be designed to fulfil this function; a discussion follows of the attempts that have been made to achieve this over recent decades.

Golden Section and the associated Fibonacci series give rise to satisfying natural proportions. Their use in music is explored in Chapter 10 with examples as diverse as that of Stockhausen's *Klavierstuck IX* and Lady Gaga's song 'Perfect illusion'. It looks in particular at the music of Mozart, Satie, Bartók, Debussy, and composers associated with the Darmstadt School, questioning whether such ratios are used consciously by composers or simply stem from an intuitive sense of proportion.

Chapter 11 explores the different ways in which composers have used randomised elements in their music from the use of rolls of dice by eighteenth-century composers to the computerised chance operation of Iannis Xenakis who coined the term 'stochastic music'. The leading composer of aleatoric music was undoubtedly John Cage who used chance procedures in almost all the music he created after 1951.

Can fractals be found in music? Chapter 12 outlines various attempts that have been made to identify these patterns in music including the use of nested sequences and self-similarity. These include the prolation canons dating from the fifteenth century and two twentieth-century composers, Tom Johnson and György Ligeti. Two questions are posed throughout the book: did the composer use ideas from maths intentionally, and can you hear the mathematical nature? Some composers consciously based their music on mathematical principles: Iannis Xenakis used random numbers and stochastic processes; John Cage used what he called square root forms; and György Ligeti used the self-similarity and nested sequences of fractals in his compositions. These were all conscious links with mathematics made by twentieth-century composers, but that does not mean to say that the music of, say, J S Bach, Mozart and Beethoven, precludes any mathematical connections. Often the links with maths were used unconsciously; perhaps the closest link to fractals can be found in the prolation canons of Johannes Ockeghem which were composed hundreds of years ago at a time when the concept of fractals did not exist.

Finally, there is a section on various curiosities, mathematical techniques which do not fit neatly into the previous sections. Chapter 13 looks at examples of musical cryptography across the centuries, from the use of the solmization system by the Renaissance composer Josquin des Prez, through the monograms of various composers to the secret messages conveyed by Pink Floyd in their album *The Wall*. A number of composers have used magic squares and Latin squares to generate material for their compositions notably the two British twentieth-century composers Peter Maxwell Davies and John Tavener whose work is examined in Chapter 14. The book closes with the extraordinary case of change ringing, the practice of ringing church bells in a methodical order. Chapter 15 shows how this system pre-empted the mathematical discipline of group theory, a theory which was not properly established until nearly a century later.

In all, the book covers over 200 pieces of music ranging from classical symphonies to electronic dance music with numerous musical excerpts given. There are clear explanations throughout along with glossaries of musical and mathematical terms.

Rhythm

1 Rhythmic devices: time signatures, barlines and polyrhythms

THIS CHAPTER OPENS by introducing some elements of music theory in order to illustrate the connections between rhythm and mathematics.[1] It then goes on to explore various rhythmic devices with examples of their application in Western classical music, notably polyrhythms, and quintuple and septuple rhythms. This is followed by a discussion of the use of barlines, the restrictions they can impose and how eventually some composers broke away from what has been described as the 'tyranny of the barline', notably Stravinsky in his ballet *The Rite of Spring*. The final section discusses some of the rhythmic devices found in popular music and jazz including the use of unusual time signatures, four-on-the-floor, and the rhythmic construction of electronic dance music.

Introduction

The word 'rhythm' describes the way that sounds are grouped together in different patterns over time. These patterns are produced by notes (sounds) and rests (silences) of different lengths.

---

1 For further information about music theory please see either *Rock & Pop Theory. The Essential Guide* (London: Faber Music and Peters Edition, 2014) or *Music Theory. The Essential Guide* (London: Faber Music and Peters Edition, 2014).

Table 1- Duration of notes

British name	American name
Semibreve	Whole note
Minim	Half note
Crotchet	Quarter note
Quaver	Eighth note
Semiquaver	Sixteenth note
Demi-semiquaver	Thirty-second note

The pulse of a piece of music is the basic beat, to which we clap along or dance. The word metre (or meter) refers to the organisation of regular pulses into patterns of strong and weak beats. Western notation is largely a divisive rhythm system where a regularly repeated unit (the bar) is divided into smaller parts (usually two, three or four beats). In contrast, an additive rhythm is one which is formed by combining small metrical units. It moves from one note (x time units long) to another note (y time units long) where the sum of x plus y forms the metrical pattern such as 2 + 3 + 4 beats. As such, the bars of additive rhythms cannot be divided in the same way.

The metre is shown by the time signature. A time signature is placed at the beginning of a composition. It denotes how many beats there are in a bar. The top number of a time signature tells us the number of beats per bar and the bottom number tells us what type of beat. Of course across the world much music is not notated, or is notated differently, and here time signatures do not exist. Most Western classical music has either two, three or four beats in a bar – duple, triple or quadruple time. The same can be said for pop music where the very large majority of songs (of whatever genre) has four beats in a bar. For this reason 4/4 is often referred to as common time and is denoted by the sign C at the beginning of a piece. Across both classical music and pop, there is a tendency to accent the first beat of the bar, and bars are usually grouped into phrases in multiples of four.

As can be seen, rhythm deals with numbers and is thus linked to several basic mathematical concepts. The time signature, for example, looks like a fraction where the top number could be denoted as the numerator and the bottom number the denominator. The duration of time is plotted along the x axis, and the rising and falling of pitch is plotted on the y axis. The sequence of the duration of notes (see Table 1 above) forms a mathematical pattern where each successive note is half the length of the previous note as is clear from the American note names – whole note, half note, quarter note and so on. This could be said to form a geometric sequence with a ratio of $r = 1/2$.

Note values and rests can be lengthened by adding dots to them. A single dot after a note adds half of its original value. So, for example, when a dot is added to a quarter note (or crotchet) it has the duration of a quarter note (crotchet) plus an eighth note (or quaver).

$$a + a/2 = b$$

Similarly, when two dots are added after a note, it has the duration of the note (a) plus half the value of a (b) plus half the value of (b).

$$a + b + b/2 = c$$

So if a double dot is added to a quarter note (or crotchet), it has the duration of a quarter note (crotchet) plus an eighth note (or quaver) plus a sixteenth note (or semiquaver).

Dots therefore follow the mathematical concept of iteration where the same process is applied repeatedly.

Polyrhythms

The word polyrhythm refers to the simultaneous use of two (or more) independent rhythms built around the same pulse. One of the most common polyrhythms to be found in Western classical music is that of two against three frequently found in, for example, the piano sonatas of Haydn, Mozart and Beethoven amongst many others. The example below is taken from the first movement of Beethoven's *Piano Sonata, Op. 14, No 2 in G* (bars 89 – 92) where the right hand plays triplet semiquavers (in groups of three) against the semiquavers grouped in twos in the left hand.

Right hand   1 2 3 1 2 3 1 2 3 1 2 3
Left hand   1 2 1 2 1 2 1 2

The table below shows the precise location of where the notes are placed. This device is based on the mathematical concept of the least common multiple (LCM). The LCM of two positive integers is the smallest integer that each number divides into evenly. Polyrhythms are always based on numbers that are relatively prime. In the example above, the integers two and three, are divided into the LCM of six showing where the first notes of the groups are heard together.

1		2		3		1		2		3		1		2		3		1		2		3	
1			2			1			2			1			2			1			2		
1	2	3	4	5	6	7	8	9	10	11	12	13	14	15	16	17	18	19	20	21	22	23	24

More complex polyrhythms are used in the piano music of Frederic Chopin (1810-1849). His Nocturnes are characterised by their use of florid melodic lines in the right hand with the left hand providing a steady harmonic accompaniment. Chopin often uses not only two against three, and five against three, but also rarer examples of polyrhythms such as eleven against four and thirteen against four as in the example below from bars 60 and 61 of his *Nocturne in C# minor*.

Here the LCM in bar 59 is 44 so to find the precise location of each note would involve dividing the second half of the bar into 44 micro-beats. Nevertheless, as is discussed in a later chapter, even such seemingly complex rhythms are relatively straightforward in comparison with those used outside Western classical music, as in, for example, West African drumming (see pages 41-5). To Western classical players, such rhythms are quite demanding to perform, but in the words of the American composer Aaron Copland '...by comparison with the intricate rhythms used by African drummers or Chinese or Hindu percussionists, we are mere neophytes.'[2] As the musicologist A M Jones wrote, 'If from childhood you are brought up to regard beating 3 against 2 as being just as normal as beating in synchrony, then you develop a two-dimensional attitude to rhythm.'[3]

Quintuple and septuple rhythms

Duple and triple rhythms are relatively common in Western classical music and pop music, but examples of music with quintuple or septuple music rhythms are rare. However rhythms based on a five-beat or seven-beat structures can be traced as far back as to the metre of ancient Greek songs and such irregular rhythms can be found in traditional music across much of Europe, Asia and Africa. The musicologist and mathematician Andrew Gustar argues that the 'scarcity of septuple time in Western music is largely attributable to the development of the time signature' which lends itself to

---

2 Aaron Copland. *What to Listen for in Music* (Philadelphia, Signet, 1953): 35.
3 A M Jones. *Studies in African Music*. (London: Oxford University Press, 1959): 102.

multiples and divisions of two and three.⁴ Both quintuple and septuple times are almost always additive: for example, a unit of three beats plus a unit of four beats, with this pattern being repeated. In quintuple time the five beats are subdivided into either 2+3 or 3+2; and in septuple time the seven beats can be grouped into various combinations of two, three and four e.g. 2+3 +2, or 3+2+2, or 4+3. As Gustar writes of septuple rhythms: 'the notation is messy; the rhythm is uncomfortable for those brought up on twos, threes and fours; and it constrains the music in ways that do not support the broader aesthetic values'.⁵ As a consequence music using quintuple and septuple time is almost absent from the Baroque and Classical periods. The American psychologist Leslie A Osborn notes that:

Conventional notation is at its best ... dealing with the prime two and its multiples four, six, and eight. It is awkward with... the number three and its multiples, but manages with a complexity of dotted and tied notes. It is extremely difficult to use with higher prime numbers, so that the possibilities of quintuple and septuple time have been rarely exploited. ⁶

Quintuple and septuple rhythms are based on the prime numbers five and seven. As Gustar points out, when we look at the next prime number in the series, eleven, it is 'virtually unknown as a musical metre in Western music before the twentieth century' and although there are Indian *tala* with eleven beats, these demand greater conscious effort on the part of both the listener and the performer, and they too are rare.⁷

Early examples of both quintuple and septuple metres can be found in the *Libro de tientos* (1626) of the Spanish composer Francisco Correa de Arauxo (1584 – 1654) where he experimented with irregular meters in the organ pieces No. 34 and No. 41. Near the end of No. 34 there is a shift to septuple time and in No. 41 there is a passage of quintuple metre. Examples from the eighteenth century are rare, although a few are to be found in Italian operas by composers such as Monteverdi, Cavalli and Handel where they are sometimes used to fit the changing rhythms of the words. At other times

---

4   Andrew James Gustar.'The Closest Thing to Crazy: The Shocking Scarcity of Septuple Time in Western Music' *Journal of the Royal Musical Association*, 2012, Vol. 137, No. 2 (2012): 351- 400.
5   Gustar,'Closest thing to crazy', 381-382.
6   Leslie A. Osborn, "Notation Should Be Metric and Representational', *Journal of Research in Music Education*, 14 (1966), 67-83.
7   Gustar,' Closest thing to crazy', 364-365.

they are there primarily for their disruptive effect. In his opera *Orlando* (1733), Handel included several bars in 5/8 in the middle of a 4/4 passage to represent his hero's madness when suffering from unrequited love. Similarly, Hector Berlioz used septuple metre for dramatic effect in his opera *Benvenutu Cellini* (1836) where two bars of seven time form part of the countdown in the duel scene of Act II.

Robert Schumann (1810-1856) uses seven-time to create an atmosphere of dreamy vagueness in the slow movement 'Eusebius' of his piano work *Carnaval* (1833).[8] Although it is notated in duple metre, it is largely in a seven-over-two cross rhythm where there are seven equal parts in the right hand and two or four in the left. As a result it is difficult to hear a pulse or a pattern of strong and weak beats. Here are the opening bars of 'Eusebius'.

More examples can be found in music from the second half of the nineteenth century; Berlioz, Brahms and Liszt all used septuple time in the 1850s and in the second half of the nineteenth-century septuple rhythms were employed by Tchaikovsky, Janacek and Debussy amongst others. In 1849, the French composer Charles Alkan (1813-1888) composed his Op. 32 No. 2 for piano. This set of pieces includes three '*Airs à cinq temps*' along with an '*Air à sept temps*' (see below for the opening bars).[9]

---

8   Eusebius was Schumann's name for the dreamy, introspective side of his character contrasting with the passionate, outgoing Florestan whom he portrayed in *Carnaval* in the '*Passionato*' movement.
9   Although today Alkan is a relatively little-known composer, in the early nineteenth century he had a burgeoning career as both a composer and concert pianist which flourished alongside those of Chopin and Liszt. His career did not thrive in the same way as theirs and his work gradually fell into obscurity. Since the 1960s, his work has attracted more attention with an enthusiastic following of aficionados.

Samuel Coleridge-Taylor (1875-1912) composed his *Fantasiestucke Op.* 5 for string quartet, a collection of five short character works for string quartet featuring cross rhythms and misplaced accents in 1895. It was described by *The Times* as a 'curious and most original work … showing the hand of a composer of real freshness [who] has something to say that is worth saying and he does so in a most original way'.[10] Here is the melody of the opening bars of the second movement, 'Serenade', which is in 5/4 time (see below).

Hemiolas

The word 'hemiola' is derived from the Greek word '*hemiolios*' which means 'half as much again'. It refers to any two quantities in the ratio 3: 2 (1½ to 1). The rhythmic device known as a hemiola is the pattern that occurs when three beats are performed in the time of two or two beats are performed in the time of three. William Byrd uses hemiola in his madrigal 'Though Amaryllis Dance in Green' (1588). The madrigal is mainly in triple time (three minim beats) but switches to duple time (two dotted minim beats) in bars 2 and 8 of the example.

---

10   *The Times*, March 14, 1895.

Hemiolas were frequently found in music up to and including the Baroque period, notably in lively dances such as the galliard and courante which included elements of 3: 2, usually alternated, but sometimes together. Hemiolas are relatively uncommon in Western art music after this period but a well-known example can be heard in the song 'America' from Bernstein's musical *West Side Story* where the first bar is divided into two main beats and the second bar is divided into three (see below).

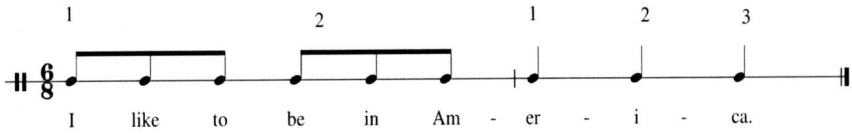

In contrast, the hemiola is central to the rhythmic scheme in the music of sub-Saharan Africa.

Folk music influence in twentieth-century classical music

In the twentieth century, composers began to draw more often from influences from outside the canon of Western classical music and both quintuple and septuple time, although still quite unusual, became more accepted as musical devices. Across the late nineteenth century and the early twentieth century there was a growing interest in national folk music. One of the first composers to use irregular rhythms was the Australian composer Percy Grainger (1882-1961) who was a pioneering folksong collector and arranger, an avant-garde thinker and an experimentalist. He was also a linguist and a philologist, fluent in 11 languages including Icelandic and Russian. Describing his early use of irregular rhythms, Grainger referred to the 'Studies in the rhythms of prose speech that I undertook in 1899 led to such irregular barrings as those in bars 69-74 of 'Love Verses' from *The Song of Solomon*, composed 1899-1900, which (as far as I know) was the first use of irregular rhythms in modern times'.[11]

As a young man in England Grainger set out to collect and record folk songs with the Edison Phonograph, one of the first folk song collectors to do so. Grainger composed in a broad spectrum of styles from highly experimental works to popular pieces such as his wind band suite *Lincolnshire posy* that he described as a 'bunch of musical wildflowers'. The movement entitled 'Lord Melbourne' is based on a song which Grainger recorded and noted down in 1906. Some of the passages are marked 'Free Time'. At the top of the score Grainger explains that in these passages the 'bandleader should slightly vary his beat-lengths with that rhythmic elasticity so characteristic of many English folksingers – and especially characteristic of George Wray, the singer of this song'. Bars 38 and 40 even have a time signature of 2½/4. 2½ over 4 is different to 5/8 because it implies a certain stress pattern that the former does not; 2½ is two and a half crotchet beats rather than the 2+3 or 3+2 beats implied by a time signature of 5/8.[12] Grainger was not, however, the first to divide the top number of the time signature in this way. 'The Alcotts', the third movement of Charles Ives' *Concord Sonata* (1912) includes a bar with the time signature of 4½/4 – four and a half crotchet beats.

Music in five and seven time was found by folksong collectors in several countries, notably Bartók (1881-1945) in the music of Bulgaria. Bela Bartók's *Six Dances in Bulgarian Rhythm* (1926-1939), for example, use asymmetrical dance rhythms. The time signatures are written as the sum of smaller groups e.g. No. 1 has a time signature of 4 + 3/8 + 3. A characteristic of much of Bartók's music is its great rhythmical energy, and he often based passages

---

11   Grainger, Percy. "Percy Grainger's Remarks about His Hill-Song No. 1 by Percy Aldridge Grainger (5-page typescript dated September 1949) located in Number 4 – 1st Edition 1982 – 2nd Edition 1997 - *A Musical Genius from Australia – Selected Writings by and about Percy Grainger* – with commentary by Teresa Balough: 85.
12   https://percygrainger.org/blog/12712906

on alternating patterns, triple then duple, or groups of five alternating with groups of three.

The early twentieth century witnessed a growing avoidance of standard patterns and regular four-bar rhythms, which more innovative composers saw as too predictable and unadventurous, characteristics which are sometimes referred to under the term the 'tyranny of the barline'. In the late nineteenth century, the maverick French composer Erik Satie (1866-1925) composed his piano pieces *Gnossiennes* in free time where, at times, he dispensed with barlines and time signatures altogether.

Igor Stravinsky (1882-1971), like Bartók, played a major role in the revitalization of rhythm in Western classical music. Amongst his first musical successes were the ballets *Firebird* and *Petrushka*, where the music had a Russian folk-music influence. The music of both ballets features intricate rhythms, sometimes using units of seven, eleven or thirteen beats, and often shifting from one metre to another which dislocate the accents. One of the effects of building patterns from irregular accents is to subvert the barline. In 1913 Stravinsky launched what Ivan Hewett describes as a 'full frontal attack' on the tyranny of the barline in his ballet *The Rite of Spring*.[13] The work portrays pagan rituals of ancient Slavic tribes evoking the return of spring when a young girl is sacrificed by dancing herself to death. Audiences were shocked by what they heard as 'primitive' dissonant music, its 'barbaric' rhythmic energy accompanying the strange movements of the dancers which seemed to defy all the rules of ballet.

Above all it was the pounding rhythms with changing time signatures, polyrhythmic effects and frequent ostinati (repeated patterns) which sounded shockingly new. In most Western classical music from the Renaissance onwards, rhythm had been subservient to melody and harmony but in *The Rite of Spring*, the music is driven by the rhythm and there are innovative rhythmic devices in every movement. Stravinsky also makes use of additive rhythms by adding or subtracting beats from a pattern as it repeats. As Gillian Moore writes in her detailed study of the work, 'there is a clear connection with folk melodies, which often freely expand or contract by a beat to fit in words'.[14][15] *The Rite of Spring* opens with a Lithuanian wedding

---

13   Ivan Hewett https://www.classical-music.com/features/articles/why-do-we-have-barlines/
14   Gillian Moore. *The Rite of Spring. The Music of Modernity* (London, Apollo, 2019): 138.
15   For more information about *The Rite of Spring* see Gillian Moore (2019).

song played in the uppermost register of the bassoon, a sinuous winding solo whose time signature changes repeatedly for the first five bars. 4/4, 3/4, 4/4, 2/4, 3/4. The effect is one where any feeling of metre is removed. In other places relatively simple musical patterns of differing lengths are layered on top of each other creating an effect of rhythmic complexity. In the 'Ritual of Abduction', for example, a polyrhythmic effect is used at Fig. 41, where the violins, violas and cellos are playing in 9/8 at the same time as the double basses play in 4/8 + 5/8 (this time signature is written on the score). The two different pulses are heard together – the upper parts play in groups of three at the same time as the basses are playing in groups of four plus five.

1 2 3 1 2 3 1 2 3
1 2 3 4 1 2 3 4 5

The final section, the 'Sacrificial Dance', is constructed from cells of from 1 - 6 notes rather than phrases in the usual way. The cells are unequal in length meaning that frequent changes of time signature are needed. The overall effect is that time is no longer measured in bars but 'marked by the individual duration of crotchet and quaver'.[16] Below is the rhythm of the final bars.

As the musicologist Paul Griffiths writes 'The rhythmic newness of *The Rite of Spring* was recognized immediately, it could hardly be mistaken… Some condemned it as a barbaric annihilation of all that musical traditions stood for …others praised it on the same grounds'.[17] As Stravinsky wrote "Mild protests against the music could be heard from the beginning…Then when the curtain opened on the group of knock-kneed and long-braided Lolitas jumping up and down, the storm broke.' The music could hardly be heard for the cat calls and cries of *'Ta gueule'* ('Shut up') but the orchestra played on until the end. Since its notorious premiere in Paris 1913, the influence of *The Rite of Spring* has been felt by generations of composers.

---

16   Paul Griffiths. *Modern Music*. (London: Thames and Hudson, 1994): 42.
17   Griffiths, *Modern Music*, 41.

RHYTHMIC DEVICES: TIME SIGNATURES, BARLINES AND POLYRHYTHMS

© Copyright 1912, 1921 by Hawkes & Son (London) Ltd. Reproduced by permission of Boosey & Hawkes Music Publishers Ltd.

Unusual time signatures and polyrhythms in popular music and jazz

Although most pop music has a straightforward four beats to the bar, there are some well-known examples which do otherwise. Pink Floyd's song 'Money' (1973) has a time signature of 7/4 and its famous bass riff follows a 3 + 4 pattern. The verses of the 1967 Beatles' song 'All you need is love' alternate bars with four beats with bars of three beats and Peter Gabriel's song 'Solsbury Hill', recorded ten years later, uses the same alternating-bars device to give a metre of seven.

Perhaps more than anyone else, the jazz musician Dave Brubeck (1920 – 2012) has been instrumental in introducing quintuple and septuple metres to mainstream Western audiences. In 1958 the Dave Brubeck Quartet took part in a US State Department tour covering parts of Europe, the Middle East and the Indian subcontinent. Whilst on tour they played with local musicians and, according to Fred Hall (Brubeck's biographer), there were times in Afghanistan, Turkey and India, when Brubeck 'immersed himself in the music of the East, that later influenced much of his composing'.18 In 1959 the Dave Brubeck Quartet released their album *Time Out* including several songs in unusual metres, the best-known is 'Take five' which is in 5/4; some bars using a 2+3 metre, others 3+2. Brubeck followed up the album with four more using non-standard time signatures. On three numbers, of which 'Unsquare dance' is the most familiar, he uses 7/4 time. Brubeck's musicians would improvise over these unusual time signatures and Brubeck observed in the liner notes to the album *Countdown: Time in Outer Space*, that '7/4 remains the most challenging for improvising, but I figure if a whole Greek culture can feel seven, we can too!'

Polyrhythms in popular music

Polyrhythms are frequently found in boogie-woogie piano music, popular during the 1920s and 1930s played by Afro-American artists such as Albert Ammons, Lux Meade Lewis and Pine Top Smith. The essence of the style is the interplay between the left and right hands. The left hand plays a driving bass line, keeping the beat and providing the chords whilst the right hand provides an embellished melody often set up in polyrhythms against the left hand. Here are some typical figurations found in boogie-woogie (see below).

Polyrhythms, although frequently found in jazz, are fairly unusual in popular music post-1950 although there are notable exceptions such as Wham's chart-topping hit 'Wake me up before you go-go' (1984) where the horn section make exciting use of two against three at its climax. The songs of the metal band Metallica frequently use polyrhythms, change time signature and make much use of metric modulation ('Enter Sandman', 1991, is a good example).[19]

---

18   Hall, Fred. *It's About Time: The Dave Brubeck Story*. (Arkansas: The University of Arkansas Press, 1996): 74.

19   Metric modulation is where there is a change in pulse rate or time signature wherein a note value from the first section is made equivalent to a note value in the second section. For example, there could be a change of time signature from 2/2 (two minims to a bar) to 6/4 (two dotted minims per bar) where the pulse remains the same by means of the tempo of the minim beat becoming equivalent to the tempo of the dotted minim beat.

Captain Beefheart too was adventurous in his use of rhythm; many examples of polyrhythms and changing time signatures can be heard on his albums such as *Trout Mask Replica* (1969). Beefheart's friend and fellow musician Frank Zappa also experimented with complex polyrhythms such as 11:17. A very effective use of polyrhythm can be heard in the 2007 song by the America rock band The National in their song 'Fake Empire' which uses a four against three pattern throughout. The song opens with solo piano playing four beats in the right hand against three beats in the left hand. When the other instruments enter, some follow the three pattern and others follow the four pattern. Because this four against three polyrhythm is heard throughout, it could be argued that 'Fake Empire' uses two time signatures simultaneously.

Four-on-the-floor in disco

One of the most basic rhythms found in pop music is known as four-on-the-floor. It is a very simple pattern where the bass drum accents each of the four beats in a 4/4 bar (see below).

The term comes from the way that the drummer had to press the foot pedal four times per bar. A constant stream of four-on-the-floor beats was prevalent in 1970s disco, it can still be heard in electronic dance music and it is not unknown for it to be incorporated into jazz. Although the reggae beat is typically characterised by the bass drum playing on beats two and four, it can also be found in some reggae songs; Carlton Barret, the drummer with Bob Marley and the Wailers, used four on the floor on songs such as 'Exodus' and 'Is this love'.

Rhythm in electronic dance music (EDM)

Electronic dance music is technology-based with DJs playing an important role in mixing and presenting tracks. The emphasis is on rhythm and timbre rather than melody and harmony. It is characterized by extensive use of samples and loops producing a layered texture made up of repeating motifs, rhythms or samples. DJs use different ways to add their own creative element to a live set, selecting, combining and manipulating sounds. The loudest most resonant sound in the texture is usually the bass drum and its sound is often referred to as the beat, a sound which can be felt as well as heard. The fundamental structural units of EDM are loops, constantly repeated rhythmic passages which together create a layered texture. As such loops make use of cyclical repetition and EDM tracks are composed largely, sometimes entirely, of them. The loops are of different lengths varying from one note to sixteen bars.

EDM embraces several different styles and these are being added to all the time. The styles can be divided into two broad categories which can be defined by their metrical characteristics. The first category is distinguished by its use of the four-on-the-floor rhythm and includes, house, garage and techno with artists such as Basement Jaxx, Mis-Teeq, and DJ Misjah & DJ Tim. Typical drum patterns are as below where all the rhythms are evenly divided.

The second category features more complex rhythms and includes drum 'n' bass, hardcore and bigbeat with artists such as Andy C, DJ Trax and the Chemical Brothers. These genres also include breakbeats where drum breaks are sampled from old funk records and speeded up, the most common samples being taken from James Brown's 'Funky Drummer' (1970) and a recording of the gospel song 'Amen Corner' by The Winstons (1969).

In breakbeat-driven genres such as drum 'n' bass, the rhythm is manipulated in various ways with other rhythmic techniques being used to add variety. These include asymmetrical divisions, some of the most common are shown below. The rhythm at the top of table is divided into 3 + 3 + 2 as is the rhythm below it where all the note values are halved (diminution).

It is interesting to note the similarity between the breakbeat rhythm above and some of the rhythms used in West African drumming (see pages 41-5).

2 Mathematical approaches to rhythm used in the twentieth-century

THE OPENING CHAPTER included an exploration of the ground-breaking rhythmic techniques used by Stravinsky and Bartók. This chapter examines the work of further twentieth-century composers who took innovative approaches to rhythm rooted in mathematics, in particular Henry Cowell, Conlon Nancarrow, John Cage, Olivier Messiaen and Steve Reich. It opens by exploring the music and writings of the American composer, music publisher and teacher Henry Cowell whose work foreshadowed some of the main developments in twentieth-century music, not least in rhythm. Cowell outlined the majority of his ideas about music in his seminal work *New Musical Resources (1938)*, and many of them were later taken up by composers in America and Europe. Nancarrow's rhythms were so complex that, inspired by the writing of Cowell, he composed most of his music for the automated player piano. Cage, a one-time pupil of Cowell, experimented with rhythm through the use of what he referred to as square root form. The next section explores Messiaen's approach to rhythm based on his principle of added values and this is followed by Reich's rhythmic transformation through phase shifting. The chapter closes with an example of hyper-complexity in the music of Brian Ferneyhough moving on to the potential of computer-generated rhythms.

Henry Cowell's experiments in rhythm

In 1919 Cowell composed *Fabric*, a short piano piece based on the interactions of various rhythmic units based on different numbers. For example, in bar one the lowest part in the left hand is written in straightforward semi-quavers (sixteenth notes) whilst above it the middle part uses a rhythmic unit of five and the top part is divided into two units of three. In the preface to this piece Cowell (1897-1965) includes an 'Explanation of New Rhythms and Notes' in which he advocates a new system of rhythmic notation that he had expounded on in his book *New Musical Resources*[20]. Rather than always subdividing note lengths by two (whole note, half note, quarter notes and so on) he proposes that irregular time values 'be called by their correct names according to the part of a whole note they occupy'. Thus triplets would be referred to as third notes, quintuplets would be fifth notes and so on up to fifteenth notes. In order to be able to distinguish these new types of notes, the note heads would be different shapes, the third note series, for example, would have triangular note heads and the fifth notes series would have square note heads.

Cowell completed two quartets around the same time, *Quartet Romantic* (1917) and *Quartet Euphometric* (1919). Both were rhythmic experiments, the first in its extreme rhythmic complexity and the second in its use of 'implied or actual polytempo or polymeter'. In his prefatory notes Cowell described them as 'totally impractical works at that time' which, because of their rhythmic complications, could only be performed by 'electronic means'. He looked forward to a time when a keyboard instrument could be devised which would be able to control more complex rhythms.[21] Ten years later he met the electrical engineer Leon Theremin, now best known as the inventor of his namesake instrument the *Theremin* which he had recently created. Together Cowell and Theremin invented the Rhythmicon an instrument that could play triplets against quintuplets, or any other combination of up to sixteen notes in a group.[22] When a single note was held down a steady rhythm was produced whereas holding down multiple notes produced polyrhythms. The instrument was operated by a keyboard producing a percussive almost drum-like sound. The rhythms were related to the corresponding frequency of the vibrations so, for example, quintuplets would be sounded on the fifth harmonic, and nonuplets on the ninth harmonic. All of this meant that Cowell had to create a new system of notation for its use. By the end of 1931

---

20   Henry Cowell. *New Musical Resources*. (New York: Alfred a Knopf, 1930): 58.
21   David Nicholls and Joel Sachs. 'Henry Cowell' in *Grove Music*.
22   For further details of this instrument please see Leland Smith. 'Henry Cowell's Rhythmicana' in *Anuario Interamericano de Investigacion Musical*, Vol. 9 (1973): 134-147.

he had written *Rhythmicana*, a four-movement piece for rhythmicon and orchestra. For various reasons, *Rhythmicana* did not receive its premiere until 40 years later when it was performed by the Stanford Symphony Orchestra in 1971 using a computer.[23]

Rather confusingly, Cowell produced a four-movement piano work with the same name in 1938. *Rhythmicana* for piano provides a further illustration of Cowell's rhythmic experimentation. The first two movements have the time signature of 1/1 and the third has a time signature of 5/4 in the left hand and 3/4 in the right hand meaning that the barlines in the left and right hand staves are in different places. There are examples of conflicting polyrhythms throughout.

Conlon Nancarrow and the player piano

Much of the early piano music of the American-Mexican composer Conlon Nancarrow (1912-1997) was so rhythmically complex that it was almost impossible to perform. When Nancarrow came across a copy of Cowell's *New Musical Resources* (1930), he read that some rhythms 'could not be played by any living performer; but these highly engrossing rhythmic complexes could easily be cut on a player-piano roll.'[24] In 1947 Nancarrow travelled to New York where he bought one of the instruments and had a roll-punching machine built. From then on Nancarrow composed music with highly intricate rhythmic designs for the auto-playing piano. His *Studies for Player Piano* comprise 50 pieces covering a range of rhythmic techniques, mostly derived from four basic rhythmic ideas: ostinato, isorhythm, tempo canon and acceleration.

Nancarrow was a jazz trumpeter and much of his music has a jazzy feel. His first pieces, the group known as Study No. 3, were extremely fast jazz pieces, influenced by Art Tatum and Earl Hines. In Nos. 1, 2, 3, 5 and 9, ostinatos are set against each other at different speeds. Nos. 6, 7, 10, 11 and 20 use the medieval technique of isorhythm with multiple repetition of the same

---

23   One of the original machines can be found in the Smithsonian Institute, Washington, DC but it is no longer operational. An operational model is housed at the Theremin Centre for Electroacoustic Music in Moscow.
24   Cowell, *New Musical Resources*, 65.

rhythm against different pitch patterns, sometimes played at lightning speed.

Tempo canons are used in Nos. 13–19. The word canon refers to a form or a compositional technique (see pages 141-52). Canons are based on the principle of imitation, in which an initial melody is imitated at a specified time interval by one or more parts and in a tempo canon the same idea is used at different speeds. Nancarrow takes a melody or block of texture and superimposes it upon itself at varying tempo ratios, so for example a ratio of 4: 5 could indicate that one melody, going at a speed of 100 beats per minute (bpm), is played with the same melody superimposed at a speed of 125 bpm. At some point the melodies converge at the same point in their material, so for example, in No. 14 the convergence point falls at the mid-point of the piece. In Nancarrow's later canonic studies the ratios became more complex: in No. 33 the ratio is $\sqrt{2}: 2$ and in No. 40 it is $e: \pi$ (e being the base of natural logarithms), so in other words roughly 2.718: 3.142.

Studies 8, 21, 22, 23, and 27 to 30 are based on different rates of acceleration and deceleration; in No. 27 for example, the voices of the canon accelerate and decelerate at rates of 5%, 6%, 8% and 11%. Notes are shortened to achieve different rates of acceleration; an 11% acceleration would mean that each note is 11% shorter than its predecessor. Nancarrow combined these various rhythmic ideas in his later studies and also utilised other features that the player piano was capable of such as the extremely fast glissandi and arpeggios in No. 27 and, at the climax of No. 25, 1028 notes whizz past in 12 seconds.[25]

John Cage and square root form

For a brief period in 1933, Cage studied with Henry Cowell whom he described as "the open sesame for new music in America" a reference to both Cowell's pioneering ideas about music and his role as a music publisher promoting new composers.[26] It has been argued that from Cowell Cage

---

25   Kyle Gann. 'Conlon Nancarrow' in *Grove Music*.
26   John Cage. *Silence. Lectures and writings by John Cage.* (Hanover, New England: Wesleyan University Press, 1973): 67.

'inherited a spirit of musical adventurousness'.[27]

In the 1930s Cage began to experiment with the form of his pieces, believing that the structure of a piece should be defined by rhythm rather than harmony and melody. He was later to write:

> Sound has four characteristics: pitch, timbre, loudness and duration. The opposite and necessary coexistent of sound is silence. Of the four characteristics of sound, only duration involves both sound and silence. Therefore a structure based on durations (rhythmic: phrase, time, lengths) is correct (corresponds with the nature of the material), whereas harmonic structure is incorrect (derived from pitch, which has no being in silence).[28]

This led to his concept of the micro-macrocosmic rhythmic structure in which each part of a composition (microstructure) was divided into the same proportions as those of the piece as a whole (macrostructure). Cage sometimes referred to this as 'square root form'. In his piece *First Construction (in Metal)* (1939) the structure is 4: 3: 2: 3:4, a total of 16 units where each unit is represented by a bar of 4/4. The 16-bar structure is heard 16 times.

Cage's one-time teacher Cowell experimented with the piano strings being plucked, scratched and manipulated in other ways in, for example, his solo piano piece *Banshee*. Cage started similar experiments, discovering that by placing a variety of objects (for example metal screws, bolts, washers and nuts, plastic and cloth) between the strings the piano could be made to sound more like a percussion ensemble.

In 1945 he composed *Three Dances for Two Prepared Pianos*, a virtuoso piece for two amplified prepared pianos.[29] The piano preparation in *Three Dances* involves 36 notes on each piano, and uses a variety of materials including screws, pennies, rubber, plastic, weather stripping, and various bolts and nuts. The piece was premiered in New York in 1945 where it was

---

27   Ed. David Nicholls. *The Cambridge Companion to John Cage*. (Cambridge: Cambridge University Press, 2002): 16.
28   Cited in *The Cambridge Companion to John Cage*, 246.
29   A piano which has been prepared by altering the pitches, timbres and dynamic responses of individual notes by means of bolts, screws, mutes and/or other objects inserted at particular points between or next to the strings.

used as the music for a dance piece, 'Dromenon', by Cage's lifelong partner the choreographer Merce Cunningham. Dance No. 1 is 30 x 30 bars long with a rhythmic structure where the 30 bars are divided as follows - 2 : 5 : 2 : 2 : 6 : 2 : 2 : 7 : 2. These divisions are marked by boxed numbers. The piece uses many repetitions, and the sections and phrases are differentiated by changes in timbre and shifts from one rhythm to another. In addition, the proportion for each dance is defined for a particular tempo with a change in tempo causing change in the proportion. Dance No. 1 has a tempo of 88 minim beats per minute whereas Dance No. 2 has a tempo of 114 minim beats per minute; the ratios are adjusted proportionately so that there are 39 x 39 bars with a rhythmic structure of 3 : 6 : 3 : 3 : 7 : 3 : 3 : 8 : 3.

Rhythmically *Three Dances* is very intricate. In the polymetric opening bars, for example, where the two pianos use a different metre; Piano 2 has four crotchet beats in the left hand and off beat quavers in the right hand, whereas Piano 1 is made up of groups of three quavers which go across the bar line and do not fall on any of the main beats. The percussive sounds and fast interlocking patterns are reminiscent of the Indonesian gamelan (see pages 45-7).

Cage wrote several pieces for the prepared piano over the 1940s and 1950s including the large-scale concert work *Sonatas and Interludes*. Here, for the first time he used rhythmic structures using fractions. *Sonata 1* is made up of 7 x 7 bars where the units are arranged according to the proportions 1 ¼ : ¾ : 1 ¼ : ¾ : 1 ½ : 1 ½.[30]

Olivier Messiaen and his use of rhythm

'Let us not forget that the first, essential element in music is rhythm, and that rhythm is first and foremost the change of number and duration', said Olivier Messiaen in his lecture at the 1958 'Conference de Bruxelles' echoing Cage's words on the importance of rhythm.[31] In Messiaen's book *The Technique of My Musical Language* (1944 he outlines his compositional methods.[32]

---

30   Nicholls, *The Cambridge Companion to John Cage*, 82.
31   These words are taken from a lecture given by Messiaen at the 'Conferences de Bruxelles' in 1958.
32   Olivier Messiaen. *Technique of My Musical Language* (Paris: Alphonse Leduc, 1944).

He devotes a large part of his writing to rhythm with chapters on Hindu rhythm, rhythms with added values, augmented and diminished rhythms, nonretrogradable rhythms, polyrhythm and rhythmic pedals. His interest in rhythm stemmed from his student days in the 1920s, a significant moment being his discovery of a table of 120 *decitalas* – Hindu rhythms which had been transcribed by the thirteenth-century Hindu theorist Carngadeva.[33]
[34]Messiaen was fascinated by the characteristics of these *talas* (repeated cyclical rhythmic patterns) and the ways in which they were used. As Julian L Hook explains in his article about rhythm in the music of Messiaen

> Indian rhythms do not arise by elaboration of an underlying pulse in the manner of Western rhythms, but by accumulations of small rhythmic values. The concept of a beat is replaced, in effect, by a smallest note value …of which all other rhythmic values are multiples, often in irregular groupings.[35]

In the opening section on rhythm in *The Technique of My Musical Language* Messiaen takes one of these rhythms - *ragavardhana* - and uses it to demonstrate some of the qualities he had found in Hindu music. Here is the *tala* in its original form.

---

33 Messiaen found these Hindu rhythms in Lavignac's *Encyclopedie de la musique*.
34 A *tala* is a repeated cyclical rhythmic pattern.
35 Julian L. Hook. 'Rhythm in the Music of Messiaen: An Algebraic Study and an Application in the "Turangalîla Symphony"'. *Music Theory Spectrum*, Vol. 20, No. 1 (Spring, 1998): 97-120.

Here is *ragavardhana* in reverse.

Messiaen points out that when *ragavardhana* is reversed, it contains the equivalent of (A) three crotchets (quarter notes) and (B) three quavers (eighth notes) and that B is an inexact diminution of A with the addition of a half-value (dot) on the second note (see below).

From this he derives the principle of 'added values' whereby a value can be added to a note by either lengthening it, or adding a short note-value or rest. Thus his approach to rhythm arises from an extension of durations (additive) rather than from a division of time (divisive).[36] As he observes, 'We can conclude [that] it is possible to add to any rhythm whatsoever a small brief value which transforms its metric balance'.[37] He went on to adapt these characteristics for use in his own music, altering, elaborating and superimposing them to create his own rhythmic language. Sometimes he used *ragavardhana* itself as in the organ piece *Les corps glorieux* and *Visions de l' Amen* for two pianos.

---

36   Robert Sherlaw Johnson. *Messiaen* (London, Omnibus Press, 2009).
37   Messiaen, *Technique of My Musical Language*, 14.

During World War II Messiaen was called up for military service and in 1940 he was captured and interred in a prisoner-of-war camp at Görlitz in Silesia. It was there that he completed the *Quatuor pour la fin du temps* (Quartet for the end of time) and performed it: Messiaen played the piano part, alongside three of his fellow inmates, a violinist, cellist and a clarinettist. In the Preface to this piece Messiaen describes the sixth movement, 'Danse de la fureur, pour les sept trompettes', as the most rhythmically characteristic movement. This is evident in its use of augmentations and diminutions, added values and the use of a series of non-retrogradable rhythms. Here is the rhythm of the first four bars which are played in unison, or at the octave, by the quartet (see below).

941 Editions Durand, a catalogue of Universal Music Publishing Classics & Screen. *International Copyright Secured. All Rights Reserved.* Reprinted by kind permission of Hal Leonard Europe BV (Italy)

Rather than constantly changing time signatures Messiaen abandons them altogether, only adding barlines to break up the blank succession of durations. The time signatures have been added in the quotation above for clarity, but they are not in the original score; the movement deliberately avoids a sense of metre. The note values do not follow conventional groupings, another device used to avoid the placement of accents and any consequent metrical implications. Each of the bars is of a different length but is based on the same rhythmic motifs, various combinations of quavers and semi-quavers. Bar 2 could be regarded as an inexact diminution of bar 1 in terms of the number of notes, whereas bar 5 is an inexact augmentation of bar 1.

Messiaen was fascinated by what he referred to as the 'charm of impossibilities', musical devices which included non-retrogradable rhythms and modes of limited transposition (see pages 113-16). In his own words, the charm of impossibilities 'resides particularly in certain mathematical impossibilities [in] the modal and rhythmic domains' describing the rhythms as those 'which cannot be used in retrograde, because in such a case one finds the same order of values again'.[38] The first seven notes of bar 1 of 'Danse de la fureur' form a non-retrogradable rhythm – they are the same backwards as forwards.

In his *Technique of My Musical Language* Messiaen states that '[Canons] may exist without the presence of any melodic canon' and goes on to discuss examples of rhythmic canons by augmentation and diminution, along with nonretrogradable rhythms.[39] In 'La Bouscarle' (Cetti's Warbler) from Book 5 of his piano work *Catalogue d'Oiseaux* he uses a rhythmic canon in bars 20-24 where the left hand enters a semi-quaver beat after the right hand. The left hand part is an augmentation of the right hand part by a semi-quaver. Messiaen also used rhythmic canons in 'Regard du Fils sur le Fils' the fifth movement of *Vingt Regards sur l'enfant-Jésus* and the last movement of his song cycle *Harawi*.

In 1931 Messiaen heard a Balinese gamelan at the Exposition Coloniale in Paris. Gamelan is a term applied to both Indonesian orchestras, largely comprising gongs and metallophones, and to the music composed for them based on the overall effect of interlocking rhythms (see pages 45-7). The sound of the gamelan later prompted him to compose pieces for tuned percussion ensembles and was an important element of his ten-movement work *Turangalîla-symphonie* (1948). *Turangalîla* uses a huge battery of percussion instruments along with piano and *ondes martenot* (an early electronic instrument). Again there were influences from Indian classical music: the word *Turangalîla* itself is derived from Sanskrit vocabulary and can be loosely translated as 'love song', and three of the movements were originally subtitled *tala*. Most striking is his treatment of the percussion instruments which are used in the manner of the gamelan, not only in the gamelan-like sonorities produced by the tuned percussion (piano, glockenspiel, celeste and vibraphone) but also in the intricate textures; superimposed layers involving many simultaneous rhythmic processes.

---

38   Messiaen, *Technique of My Musical Language*, 16.
39   Messiaen, *Technique of My Musical Language*, 63.

György Ligeti, *Poème Symphonique* and 100 metronomes

In 1962, the Hungarian composer György Ligeti (1923-2006) completed his *Poème Symphonique* where 100 mechanical metronomes are set to different speeds – between the metronome markings MM 144 and MM 50 - and then wound up for 'four half turns'.[40] They are then set in motion as 'simultaneously as possible' and the 'performers' leave the stage, leaving the metronomes to wind down. The LCM of the fastest speed (144 beats per minute) and the slowest speed (50 beats per minute) is 3600. This means that the first time the two metronomes will be heard together is on beat 3600. This takes place 25 minutes into the piece. Ligeti writes in the set of instructions which form the score:

> The overall design of the piece consists of a single long phrase which could be characterized as a rhythmic diminuendo: at the outset the number of metronomes ticking is so large that, heard together, the sound appears to be continuous. As the first metronomes come to rest, the static uniform sound thins and it gradually becomes possible for complex rhythms to be carved out of the now crumbling sound block. These rhythmic structures become increasingly clear as more and more instruments wind down: as the complexity is reduced, the rhythmic differentiation increases… towards the end of the work with the rhythmic differentiation further reduced, the rhythmic pattern becomes more regular… until only one metronome is left ticking.[41]

Or as Alex Ross puts it 'as the faster metronomes wind down and stop, spiderwebs of rhythm emerge from the cloud of ticks'.[42]

---

40   A metronome is a device used to indicate the tempo of a composition by sounding regular beats at different speeds. Metronome markings are given in the score and indicate the number of beats per minute (bpm) for a specified note value e.g. a crotchet at MM = 120 would signify 120 crotchet beats per minute. The original metronomes were pyramid shaped, operated by clockwork and based on the principle of a double pendulum. Nowadays they are commonly digital electronic devices. The metronome was invented in 1814 by Dietrich Nikolaus Winkler (c.1780-1838) in Amsterdam. Two years later Johann Nepomuk Maelzel, an inventor of mechanical gadgets, copied the idea and patented it under his name. Beethoven was a fan of metronomes and was the first significant composer to adopt metronome markings.
41   Ligeti's programme notes from the score of *Poème Symphonique*.
42   Ross, Alex. *The Rest is Noise*. (London: Fourth Estate, 2008): 119.

Steve Reich and phase shifting

The musical style known as Minimalism originated in America in the 1960s with composers including Terry Riley (see page 185), Steve Reich and Philip Glass. Minimalist music features constantly repeated patterns that are subjected to gradual processes of melodic and rhythmic transformation as the piece unfolds. It often uses interlocking repeated phrases and rhythms, addition and subtraction (where notes are added to or taken away from a repeated phrase), a layered texture and diatonic harmony. Central to Minimalism is a musical device known as phase shifting, constantly repeated patterns that are subjected to gradual changes, one part repeats constantly and another gradually shifts out of phase with it. The effect of phase shifting can be almost hypnotic. Phase shifting can be seen in terms of a mathematical translation or shift (see pages 30-4). By taking a periodic graph function (a function which repeats regularly in cycles such as a sine wave) and shifting it either horizontally or vertically a new function is created where although the general shape does not change, the point at which the wave starts does change. This type of transformation is known as phase shift.[43] The scientist Philip Ball, author of *The Music Instinct*, describes how

> ... the voices interlock into distinct rhythmic patterns at different stages, which then dissolve and crystallize into new ones ..we form an interpretation of what the rhythmic pattern is, only to have to keep revising it as a new structure emerges.[44]

Ball goes on to compare this process with the Moiré patterns generated by overlapping grids. Moiré patterns are produced by two identical grids one of which is rotated relative to the other. As the rotation proceeds we see a series of regular geometric patterns formed from the grid lines that move in and out of phase with one another.[45]

---

43   Gareth Roberts. *From Music to Mathematics {Exploring the connections}*. (Baltimore: John Hopkins University Press, 2016): 269.
44   Philip Ball. *The Music Instinct: How Music Works and Why We Can't Do Without It*. (London: Vintage, 2011): 223.
45   Ibid.

Steve Reich was born in New York in 1936 and started work as a composer in the 1960s. As a young man he became interested in the music of Africa, initially through A.M. Jones's work *Studies in African Music*. He was struck by the methods of music organisation which were radically different from those in the West.[46] He noted in particular the use of short repeating patterns played simultaneously but without their downbeats coinciding and the 'many rhythmic ambiguities inherent in subdivisions of 12.'[47]

Reich made his first forays into phase shifting in the 1960s in *It's Gonna Rain* (1965) and *Come Out* (1966) which both use recorded speech. He takes a single phrase or sentence and repeats it against versions of itself, looped and played at different speeds. On the *Come Out* tape, a Harlem teenager recounts being brutalized by officers for a crime he did not commit. Because he was not visibly bleeding he was turned away when he went to hospital for treatment. In his words "I had to, like, open the bruise up, and let some of the bruise blood come out to show them." Reich re-recorded the four-second fragment "come out to show them" on two channels. They begin in unison then slip out of sync to produce a phase shifting effect, the discrepancy widening to become at first a reverberation before splitting into four, then eight, until the words become unintelligible. Reich wrote "by not altering its pitch or timbre, one keeps the original emotional power that speech has while intensifying its melody and meaning through repetition and rhythm."[48] In 1967 he composed *Piano Phase* (1967) for two pianos (or piano and tape) which used a similar method in which the second player gradually makes slight rhythmic shifts with occasional re-alignments of the twelve notes against each other.

In 1971 Reich made a field trip to Ghana to study African drumming. On his return home he described the impression that the trip had had on him, saying that it 'turned out to be confirmation of gradually shifting phase relations between identical repeating patterns that I had used in *Piano Phase*.' Inspired by what he had learnt in Africa he went on to write *Drumming* (1971) which he described as the 'final expansion and refinement of the phasing process'. *Drumming* has one basic rhythmic pattern throughout

---

46   A M Jones. *Studies in African Music*. (London: Oxford University Press, 1959).

47   https://stevereich.com/composition/drumming/

48   Steve Reich wrote this in the liner notes to his album *Early Works, 1987*, which includes *Come Out* and *It's Gonna Rain*.

with the pattern undergoing changes of phase position, pitch, and timbre. In Reich's words the piece

> begins with two drummers building up the basic rhythmic pattern of the entire piece from a single drum beat, played in a cycle of 12 beats with rests on all the other beats. Gradually additional drumbeats are substituted for the rests, one at a time, until the pattern is completed. The reduction process is simply the reverse where rests are gradually substituted for the beats... until only a single beat remains.[49]

Clapping Music (1972) is one of Reich's most performed and discussed pieces. It too uses phase shifting: two performers clap the same short 12-quaver phrase in unison as the piece opens. While one performer claps the same rhythm throughout the piece, the other claps the same sequence, but after 12 repetitions per bar, Player 2 shifts the emphasis by starting one quaver later, gradually moving through the whole pattern, quaver by quaver, and shifting further out of phase until eventually the parts come together again. The effect is one of huge rhythmic diversity. Here are the opening bars.

© Copyright 1980 by Universal Edition (London) Ltd., London/UE16182. Reproduced by permission. All rights reserved.

As he writes in the directions for performers, Reich has deliberately not included a time signature to avoid metrical accents. Rather he writes that the second player should always place their downbeat on the first beat of the new pattern and that no other accents should be made. This means that it is difficult to discern a clear downbeat at the beginning of each bar.

The original rhythm pattern has been carefully chosen in order that it has certain characteristics. Each bar of *Clapping Music* contains 12 'beats'.

---

49   https://stevereich.com/composition/drumming/.

Player 1 repeats the same bar throughout but with Player 2 the rhythm undergoes a cyclic shift or phase shift. In the second bar, the entire pattern is moved by a quaver to the left and the first note is placed at the end. The bar-long pattern could be denoted by the numbers 3, 2, 1, 2 (3 quavers, a rest, 2 quavers, a rest, 1 quaver, a rest and 3 quavers, a rest). This means that the fundamental pattern is asymmetric so that each new bar created by the shifting transformations is different to each other bar including the original. This creates 12 distinct patterns for Player 2 each having a different relationship with the original. So, for example, when Player 2 moves to the first shift, Players 1 and 2 combined results in eight quaver notes without any rests.

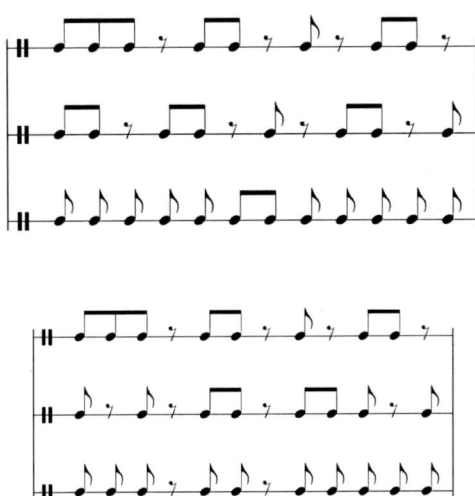

In contrast, a different musical character is produced when the rests coincide, for example bar 6.

Here the combined rhythm of the two players is quite different with what could be described perhaps as a dance-like feel.

Although the original rhythm pattern is asymmetric, the 12 new patterns produced by phase shifting produce symmetries with the original. So, for example, bar 4 which produces the pattern 2, 1, 2, 3, is a retrograde of the original (3, 2, 1, 2). In fact there are six further retrograde pairings to be found in the piece.[50]

Brian Ferneyhough and rhythmic complexity

The British composer Brian Ferneyhough, whose music belongs to the genre sometimes referred to as 'New Complexity', consistently uses highly complex rhythmic textures. The term New Complexity is used to categorize the aesthetic and formal characteristics of Ferneyhough's music as well as that of Michael Finnissy and a number of younger British composers. In the words of Christopher Fox 'they sought to achieve … a complex, multi-layered interplay of evolutionary processes occurring simultaneously within every dimension of the musical material…Microtonal pitch differentiations, ametric rhythmic divisions and the minutiae of timbral and dynamic inflection were all painstakingly notated….'.[51] Ferneyhough has referred to his use of complex rhythmic textures as shapes within shapes or hyper-rhythms. Here he explains his approach:

> Rhythm, metre and density are all different aspects of the disposition of events in time. If you have a set of measures, let's say 5/8, 3/8, 4/8, I may in the 5/8 measure take subdivisions of 5, 3 and 4. That set of proportions then anticipates the sequence of measure lengths (5, 3, 4) on the larger scale. Inside that 5, 3 and 4 it's possible to embed 5, 3 and 4, so that I have three levels of 5, 3 and 4. Even the additions of rests, for instance: …I say, 'Take five notes, leave out the next three notes, play four notes, leave out the next five notes', I am creating a hyper-

---

50   The American mathematician Joel K Haack set out a series of mathematical problems to be used in the classroom in his article 'Clapping Music-A Combinatorial Problem' in *The College Mathematics Journal* of San Jose State University, Vol 22, No 3, May 1991.
51   Christopher Fox in 'New Complexity' in *Grove Music*.

rhythm.⁵²

The rhythmic complexity of Ferneyhough's music makes it very difficult to perform, hence the number of its performances is limited. As the composer Curtis Roads writes in *Rhythmic Processes in Electronic Music* (2014), 'In the late 20th century, rhythmic notation evolved over time into hyper-complexity, testing the limits of readability and playability. However, at the same time, the 'technology of electronic music made the design of complex rhythms ever more accessible.' He argues that 'technology has changed the paradigm of rhythmic theory and organization' facilitating 'the exploration of polyrhythmic grids and fields' which have led into 'uncharted rhythmic territories'.⁵³ In doing so it has spawned a multitude of new styles from contemporary art music (such as electroacoustic) to pop music (such as electronic dance music EDM with artists such as Andy C and Roni Size). In breakbeat-driven genres such as drum 'n' bass, for example, the rhythm is manipulated in various ways including asymmetrical rhythm divisions made possible by computer-driven technology (see pages 16-17). This does not mean that electronic music has replaced instrumental or vocal music, rather it has opened up a new set of possibilities.

This chapter has explored rhythmic innovations created by some of the leading twentieth-century composers of contemporary art music in the West. In several cases their influences have been drawn from other parts of the world, in particular India and Africa. The chapter which follows looks at North Indian classical music and West African drumming in more detail, along with music from other regions of the world, each with a singular approach to rhythm rooted in mathematics.

---

52   The words of Brian Ferneyhough cited in Michael Oliver. *Settling the Score: A Journey Through the Music of the Twentieth Century.* (London: Faber and Faber, 1999): 119).
53   Curtis Roads. *Rhythmic Processes in Electronic Music* Proceedings ICMC|SMC|2014 14-20 September 2014, Athens, Greece.

3 Rhythm systems in music from across the world

THIS CHAPTER SPANS the music of several seemingly disparate countries and regions. What they have in common is that each has a unique approach to rhythm whose fundamental mathematical principles differ from those found in most Western music. It opens by introducing the concept of Euclidean rhythms; a family of cyclical rhythms whose structures are derived from the Euclidean algorithm and whose use can be found in traditional music across the world, not least in over 40 time lines. It then moves on to the time lines and rhythmic complexities of West African drumming. One of the underlying structural principles of Indonesian gamelan music, and indeed Balinese monkey chant, is its interlocking figurations. Much Afro-Cuban music also uses interlocking rhythms, here the rhythmic foundation is provided by the clavé, another Euclidean rhythm. The metric framework of *tal*, the repeating rhythm pattern found in North Indian classical music, is intrinsically linked to numbers and their complex manipulations, as too are the *palo* beat cycles of Spanish flamenco.

Euclidean rhythms

This section describes the way in which the structure of the Euclidean algorithm can be used to define a family of rhythms, known as 'Euclidean rhythms', many of which are found in traditional music across the world. The rhythms are cyclic: phrases or patterns that are repeated throughout a piece. Many of these are time lines that serve as rhythmic reference points in different musical traditions. The concept of the Euclidean rhythm in music was first written about by Godfried Toussaint in 2004 in his paper

'The Euclidean Algorithm Generates Traditional Musical Rhythms' where he showed that the structure of the Euclidean algorithm may be used to generate a large family of rhythms used as time lines (ostinatos) in sub-Saharan African music in particular, and world music in general.[54]

The Euclidean algorithm for computing the greatest common divisor (GCD) of two integers is one of the oldest known algorithms (circa 300 B.C.). It was first described by Euclid in Proposition 2 of Book VII of *Elements*. It is a systematic repetitive procedure whereby two numbers are taken, the smaller number is subtracted from the larger one, and next the smaller number is subtracted from the difference then repeatedly replaced until both numbers are equal. This final number is then the GCD.

For example, consider the numbers 5 and 13. First, $13 - 5 = 8$;

then $8 - 5 = 3$;
next $5 - 3 = 2$;
then $3 - 2 = 1$;
and finally $2 - 1 = 1$.

This means that the GCD of 5 and 13 is 1; in other words, 5 and 13 are relatively prime.

Toussaint discovered, through the work of Erik Bjorklund, an unexpected connection to timing systems in neutron accelerators; the same type of algorithm could be used to produce a binary string with a specified number of zeroes and ones. Bjorklund's algorithm, a version of the Euclidean algorithm, provided a means of visualising binary sequences which could also be considered in terms of a family of rhythms.[55] The GCD of two numbers was used by Toussaint to give the number of beats and silences in a rhythm; this generated many rhythms found in music across the world. Musical rhythms (and scales) can be seen as two-way infinite binary sequences. In a rhythm,

---

54   G.T. Toussaint, 'The Euclidean Algorithm Generates Traditional Musical Rhythms', Conference: In Proceedings of BRIDGES: Mathematical Connections in Art, Music and Science, 2004: 47–48.

55   For more details of Bjorklund's method see E. Bjorklund, 'A metric for measuring the evenness of timing system rep-rate patterns', SNS ASD Technical Note SNS-NOTE-CNTRL-100, Los Alamos National Laboratory, Los Alamos, USA, 2003.

each bit represents one unit of time (for example, the length of a quaver or eighth note) and a zero bit represents a silence (for example, a quaver or eighth note rest) and the offset (or rotation) defines the starting pulse of a Euclidean rhythm.

In the Euclidean rhythm $E(k,n)$, k is the number of ones (onsets), and n (the number of pulses) is the length of the sequence (zeroes plus ones). So for example,

$E(5, 13) = [1001010010100]$.

The second representation is the box-like representation, also known as the Time Unit Box System, a sequence of n 'x's and ' · 's where 'x' represents an onset and ' · ' denotes a silence. This notation is popular in the field of ethnomusicology. Using box notation, the rhythm above would be written as

$E(5, 13) = [x..x.x..x.x..]$

This type of notation does not distinguish between the relative lengths of notes; rather it shows where the main notes of the rhythm, the onsets, appear. As Toussaint, and later others, discovered there are surprising numbers of Euclidean rhythms where k and n are relatively prime (numbers that are relatively prime have no common factors other than 1). Here are a few examples. The Euclidean rhythm $E(5, 8)$ can be found in the traditional music of Egypt, Korea, West Africa and Latin America.

$E(5, 8) = [x · xx · xx ·]$

It is the basis of, for example the Cuban *cinquillo* pattern.[56]

---

56 Cited in Erik D. Demaine, Francisco Gomez-Martin, Henk Meijer, David Rappaport, Perouz Taslakian, Godfried T. Toussaint, Terry Winogradf and David R. Wood. 'The distance geometry of music'. Computational Geometry 42 (2009): 429–454.

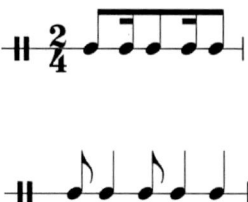

When it is started on the second onset it forms the rhythmic pattern of the Spanish tango.

Aksak rhythms

Euclidean rhythms are closely related to what are known as *aksak* rhythms. Aksak rhythms are commonly found in the rhythmic structure of the folk music of the Middle East and the Balkans, for example. They are characterized by combinations of those meters that use units of durations two and three, and no other durations. The Hungarian composer Bela Bartók referred to these as Bulgarian rhythms and used them frequently in his music (see pages 10-11). During the twentieth century *aksak* rhythms found their way into the works of a number of other twentieth-century composers, notably Stravinsky.

In 2004, the ethnomusicologist Simha Arom created an inventory of all the theoretically possible *aksak* rhythms for values of n ranging from 5 to 29 and listed all those that he found used in music across the world, these include the following.

$E(2, 5) = [\text{x} \cdot \text{x} \cdot \cdot] = (23)$ (Greece, Macedonia, Namibia, Persia, Rwanda).
$E(3, 7) = [\text{x} \cdot \text{x} \cdot \text{x} \cdot \cdot] = (223)$ (Bulgaria, Greece, Sudan, Turkestan).
$E(4, 11) = [\text{x} \cdot \cdot \text{x} \cdot \cdot \text{x} \cdot \cdot \text{x} \cdot] = (3332)$ (Southern India rhythm).
$E(5, 11) = [\text{x} \cdot \text{x} \cdot \text{x} \cdot \text{x} \cdot \text{x} \cdot \cdot] = (22223)$ (Bulgaria, Northern India, Serbia).
$E(5, 13) = [\text{x} \cdot \cdot \text{x} \cdot \text{x} \cdot \cdot \text{x} \cdot \text{x} \cdot \cdot] = (32323)$ (Macedonia).
$E(6, 13) = [\text{x} \cdot \text{x} \cdot \text{x} \cdot \text{x} \cdot \text{x} \cdot \text{x} \cdot \cdot] = (222223)$ (Macedonia).
$E(8, 17) = [\text{x} \cdot \text{x} \cdot \text{x} \cdot \text{x} \cdot \text{x} \cdot \text{x} \cdot \text{x} \cdot \text{x} \cdot \cdot] = (22222223)$ (Bulgaria).

$E(8, 19) = [× \cdot\cdot × \cdot × \cdot × \cdot\cdot × \cdot × \cdot × \cdot\cdot × \cdot] = (32232232)$ (Bulgaria).
$E(9, 23) = [× \cdot\cdot × \cdot × \cdot\cdot × \cdot × \cdot\cdot × \cdot × \cdot\cdot × \cdot × \cdot\cdot] = (323232323)$ (Bulgaria)[57]

Euclidean rhythms can also be found in pop music. E(5, 8) is commonly found in rockabilly music and jazz, for example. In his article 'Kid Algebra: Radiohead's Euclidean and Maximally Even Rhythms', Brad Osborn identifies the use of Euclidean rhythms in various songs by the UK band. As he writes 'Radiohead uses Euclidean rhythms ... that range from almost completely banal rotations of E(5,16) in 'Codex' to the jarring E(3,7) opening groove of '2+2=5' to the non-isochronous yet smooth E(4,10) recurring grooves in both 'Morning Bell' and '15 Step.'[58]

Rhythm in West African drumming

Africa is a huge continent with a wide variety of musical styles. The music played by West African drum ensembles is rhythmically very complex: multiple patterns are played at the same time creating many-layered rhythms which, in combination are built into complex and subtle constantly developing sound structures. Usually the music is not written down but passed on through oral tradition. Its complex rhythms are difficult to capture accurately in Western notation, partly because the concept of bars and the consequent strong and weak beats within the bar, is unknown in West African music. Although references are made to bars throughout this analysis, this is not a concept that would be perceived by the performers.

West African drumming uses a time line - a short repeated rhythm which is either clapped or played by a single or double bell. The performers follow the time line which effectively holds the piece together orienting time for the musicians and dancers as well as the audience. The African musicologist and composer Joseph Kwabena Nketia first used the term time line in 1963 describing it as 'a constant point of reference by which the phrase structure

---

57   Simha Arom. 2004. "L'aksak: Principes et typologie". *Cahiers de Musiques Traditionnelles* 17 (Formes musicales): 11–48.
58   Brad Osborn. 'Kid Algebra: Radiohead's Euclidean and Maximally Even Rhythms'. *Perspectives of New Music*, Vol. 52, N0. 1, (Winter, 2014): 81-105.

of a song as well as the linear metrical organisation of phrases are guided'[59] Here is one of the most common time lines found in sub-Saharan Africa, sometimes referred to by ethnomusicologists as the 'standard pattern'.

As a Euclidean rhythm it could be classified as

$E(7, 12) = [× . . × . . × × . . × . .× . .x]$

The rhythmic structure of African drumming is divisive (rather than additive, see page 2); it often uses eight and twelve pulse patterns but these may be divided into both four groups of three and three groups of four, or into the irregular divisions of 7+5 or 5+7. Several different rhythms are played at the same time, and rhythm patterns interlock and overlap to form polyrhythmic patterns and cross-rhythms.[60] The rhythmic scheme of West African drumming could be described as polymetric where more than one metre is used at the same time. Philip Tagg refers to sub-Saharan rhythms as being 'composite' because 'two metres operate together as one'. The cross-rhythms are 'ongoing and continuous, not a temporary feature of the music'.[61] There are many different divisions of the twelve pulse pattern in 'Agbekor Dance' – the sogo part (the time line) is in groups of three whereas the atsimevu uses many different divisions.

---

59   Joseph Kwabena Nketia. African Music in Ghana. Evanston, IL: Northwestern University Press, 1963.
60   Polyrhythms occur when two or more different types of rhythm are heard together against the same pulse, such as one drum in triple time playing against another in quadruple time. A cross rhythm is the effect produced when two conflicting rhythms are heard together using different metres. The terms polyrhythm and cross-rhythm are often confused.
61   Philip Tagg. *Music's Meanings a modern musicology for non-musos* (New York and Huddersfield: The Mass Media Music Scholars' Press, Inc., 2013): 457 citing J M Chernoff. *African rhythm and African sensibility, aesthetics, and social action In African musician idioms.* (Chicago and London: The University of Chicago Press, 1979).

The examples used below are taken from 'Agbekor Dance', a traditional Ewe battle dance from Ghana as recorded by the master drummer and ethnomusicologist Mustapha Tettey Addy. There are three instruments playing in the fast dance: the gankogui (bell) which plays the time line; the sogo drum; and the atsimevu played by the master drummer. The gankogui opens the playing with the time line which continues throughout the performance. The master drum then opens with a simple rhythm followed by the sogo whose entry creates a complex three-part polyrhythmic texture (see below).

The master drummer has the most elaborate part in a drum ensemble and often plays solos. Part of their role is to lead the drum ensemble by giving musical cues in the form of rhythm patterns. As one of the pioneers of African music studies, A M Jones, wrote, 'The master drummer... has a number of standard patterns at his disposal ...what he does having first established the pattern, is to play variations on it ...besides being able to play the patterns at will, he can also play them in any order and need not play them at all.'[62] As the piece unfolds the patterns increase in complexity and virtuosity. Sometimes entries are staggered as below creating interesting cross rhythms. The parts operate in different metres and could be described as polymetric (see below).

---

62   A M Jones. *Studies in African Music*. (London: Oxford University Press, 1959): 80.

The rhythms get increasingly complex as the piece goes on as can be seen below in the final bars. The rhythms operate on three different strata each of the players using different figurations. The master drummer improvises complex figurations riding on the two levels above and with little use of repetition. As the battle dance closes all three players come together on the final three notes (see below).

Much Afro-Cuban music also uses interlocking rhythms. Here the rhythmic foundation is provided by the clavé, the main rhythmic organizing principle, not only in music from Latin America but across the world in, for example, Central Africa, Cuba, the Middle East and the United States. In Spanish clavé means key or keystone. The clavé rhythm is often played by a pair of small wooden sticks which are struck together and are known as claves. There are two versions of the standard clavé rhythm – forward (3 +2) and reverse (2 + 3). The commonly used clavé patterns are Euclidean rhythms which could be classified as E(5, 16) = [324222] in the forward rhythm and E(5, 16) = [24334] (counting from the first onset) in the reverse version. Here is the forward clavé rhythm.

Here is the reverse clavé rhythm.

The clavé is similar in function to the West African time line in the way that it serves as a rhythmic reference point, holding the players together; its patterns determining how dancers move to the music.

The Indonesian gamelan

On first hearing live gamelan music in Bali, the Canadian composer and ethnomusicologist Colin McPhee (1900-1964) wrote of its interlocking rhythms:

> Gradually the music revealed itself as being composed, as it were, of different strata of sound. Over a slow and chantlike bass … the melody moved in the middle register, fluid, free, appearing and vanishing in the incessant shimmering arabesques that rang high in the treble as though beaten out a thousand little anvils. Gongs of different sizes punctuated this stream of sound, divided and subdivided it into sections and inner sections, giving it meter and meaning. Through all this came the rapid

and ever-changing beat of the drums, throbbing softly or suddenly ringing out with sharp accents. They beat in perpetual cross rhythm …Tiny cymbals pointed up the rhythm of the drums, emphasized it with their delicate clash, while the smallest of bells trembled as they were shaken, adding a final glitter…[63]

Gamelan is the word used to describe an Indonesian ensemble made up mainly of tuned percussion instruments such as metal chimes and gongs of different sizes. A typical ensemble will usually have around 25 performers who work very closely together. Although there are a number of different gamelan traditions in Indonesia, they tend to share certain musical principles, such as polyphonic stratification, cyclical time structures and the complex construction of melodies that are shared seamlessly between two or more performers to produce a single strand of music. The basis of the music could be described as a core melody, a melodic outline around which other instruments perform closely interrelated variants at the same time creating an uninterrupted melody varying in complexity and density. In the words of the ethnomusicologist Leslie Tilley, 'One often cannot discern which musician has performed which note in an interlocking passage: the perceptual effect is of a group of musicians each playing the entire passage, in perfect synchrony, much faster than humanly possible'.[64] McPhee described the effect thus

> The brilliant, interlocking two-part figuration that is a unique feature in Balinese gamelan music is an ingenious and sophisticated elaboration of a primitive technique, in which a group of performers create rhythmic or melodic patterns by each man sounding in turn a single tone, so that a more or less unbroken continuity results.[65]

A form of this interlocking rhythmic device can be found in *katak* music, sometimes referred to as the Balinese monkey chant. Here a large chorus of

---

63   Colin McPhee. *A House in Bali* (Hong Kong: Periplus, 2002): 40-41.
64   Leslie Tilley. 'The draw of Balinese rhythm' in *The Cambridge Companion to Rhythm*. Eds. Russell Hartenberger and Ryan McClelland. (Cambridge: Cambridge University Press, 2020): 270.
65   Colin McPhee. 'The five tone gamelan music of Bali', *The Musical Quarterly*, Vol. 35, No. 2 (April, 1949): 272.

RHYTHM SYSTEMS IN MUSIC FROM ACROSS THE WORLD

men, sometimes over 100, chant the syllable 'chak' in a syncopated pattern. One of the most common patterns used is known as *cak telu* a 3 + 3 + 2 rhythm made up of three notes (the rests are part of the count). Each of the three vocal lines enters a single note after the one before, creating a constant interlocking stream of notes which repeats many times (see below).

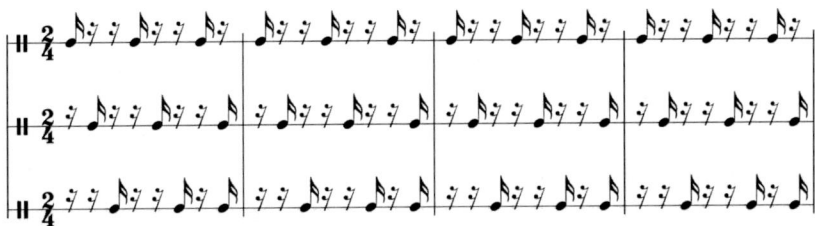

Gamelan has a colotomic structure where specified instruments are used to mark off established time intervals at numbered points.[66] Gongs of different sizes are used to mark the main divisions of cycles of music known as *gongan*. The Balinese, *bapang*, for example, is a common 8-beat structure where the medium-sized gongs (*kempur*, abbreviated as P) and small high-pitched gongs (*klentong* 't') form a symmetric pattern with *gong ageng* (G). They create a cyclic structure together as follows - G – P – t – P – G.[67] Thus the music is conceived in terms of articulated points rather than in terms of duration between points. Because the largest gong provides accents at the ends of gongan, this means that the music is end-weighted, rather than having accents at the beginning of bars and phrases as in much western music. Other examples of colotomic structure can be found in the *gagaku* (court music of Japan) where divisions are marked by a drum and hanging gong, and in the pi phat (percussion and wind instrument) ensembles of Thailand.

Rhythm in North Indian classical music

Rhythm is highly developed in music across the Indian subcontinent whether in the classical music of the North (Hindustani music), the South

---

66 In a colotomic structure, specific instruments (such as gongs) mark the beginnings and ends of rhythmic cycles.
67 Tilley, *Cambridge Companion*, 263.

(Carnatic music), or devotional or popular genres. This section focuses on North Indian classical music, the Indian musical tradition most familiar in the West. Other forms of Indian music, such as film music and Qawwali, borrow heavily from this tradition in terms of rhythm as well as form and instrumentation.

North Indian classical music ensembles have only a handful of players and most instruments are played while seated on the floor. The group will usually have the same three elements: a soloist, either a singer or an instrumentalist performing the melody; percussion, usually tabla; and a drone, either a harmonium or a tanpura. *Raga* and *tala* are the basic structural principles of Indian classical music essentially a linear melody over a cyclical rhythm. A *raga* (also spelled as *rag* in Northern India) is a pattern of notes that forms the melodic basis of an entire piece. Each *rag* has a particular ascending and descending pattern and is associated with a different time of the day, a season, particular mood or a special occasion.

The *tal* is a repeating rhythm pattern, usually played by the tabla (small drums). *Tal* can be traced back through musicological treatises over a period of approximately 2,000 years of continuous development. The South Indian or Carnatic tradition has its own *tal* system, which diverged from that of the North around 300-400 years ago.[68] The concept of *tal* is intrinsically linked to numbers. *Tal* are usually between six and sixteen beats long, although some are much longer. They have names and distinctive characteristics e.g. their length and specific divisions into subsections. The recurring patterns of beats are manifested in hand claps, waves, finger counts and drum strokes. In Hindustani music about 20 *tals* are commonly used, the most prevalent being *tintal* – four beats, each beat lasting for four counts.[69] The repetitive beat patterns are cyclic with smaller cyclic patterns embedded within them. They differ from typical Western music in that they do not include regularly recurring strong and weak beat functions, rather they are arranged in an abstract hierarchy according to whether they are indicated with a clap, a wave or a finger count. As such, *tal* is based on additive rhythm principles rather than the divisive principles used in Western music.

The metric framework of *tal* defines the rhythmic structure of the music. The beats are grouped into small sections within the pattern. So, for instance,

---

68   Martin Clayton. *Time in Indian music: Rhythm, Meter and Form in North Indian rag.* (Oxford: Oxford University Press, 2000): 11.
69   Clayton, *Time in Indian music*, 43.

tintal has sixteen beats (4 + 4 + 4 + 4) but this should not be thought of as the equivalent of 4/4. The beginning of the first, second and fourth sections is marked by a clap, but the beginning of the third section is weaker and this is shown by a wave of the hand. The sections are known as *vibhag* and the beats are known as *matras*. The tabla uses different strokes (*bols*) to mark the different beats. The framework of the stroke patterns is known as *theka*. Each *tal* has a particular *theka*. X marks the *sum* – the first beat of the cycle. 0 indicates silence and is usually marked by the wave of the hand with the palm turned upwards. These points are known as *khali vibhag* and are important reference points.

X			2				0			3				
> clap			> clap							> clap				
1	2	3	4	5	6	7	8	9	10	11	12	13	14	15	16

Every *tal* has a different identity. There are different ways in which the same number of beats can be grouped, as can be seen in the 14-beat *tals*, *jumhra* and *dhamar* below.[70]

Jumhra

X			2				0			3			
>			>							>			
1	2	3	4	5	6	7	8	9	10	11	12	13	14

=

Dhamar

X					2		0			3			
>					>					>			
1	2	3	4	5	6	7	8	9	10	11	12	13	14

---

70   Gerry Farrell. *Indian Music in Education*. (Cambridge: Cambridge University Press, 1990): 29-35.

There can be more than one *khali* in a *tal* as in *sultal* below.

Sultal

X			0		2		3		0	
>					>		>		>	
1	2	3	4	5	6	7	8	9	10

The *khali* may also occur on sum as in *rupak* below.

Rupak

X (0)			2		3	
			>		>	
1	2	3	4	5	6	7

Bols imitate the various stroke patterns on the tabla, their meaningless syllables are used to help memorise compositions. They can also be used as a means of notation. The *theka* for tintal is as follows.

X				2				0				3			
>				>								>			
1	2	3	4	5	6	7	8	9	10	11	12	13	14	15	16
dha	dhin	dhin	dha	dha	dhin	dhin	dha	dha	tin	tin	ta	ta	dhin	dhin	dha

Each tal has a particular *theka*.

Jumhra

X							2			0			3			
>				>						>						
1	2	3	4	5	6	7	8	9	10	11	12	13	14
dhin	dha	tirakitja	dhin	dhin	dhage	tirakitja	tin	ta	tirakitja	dhin	dhin	tirakitja	dhin

Rupak

X (0)		2		3		
		>		>		
1	2	3	4	5	6	7
tin	tin	na	dhin	na	dhin	na

The tabla player is therefore manipulating several layers of metrical information: the basic outline of the *tal*; the framework of stroke patterns in the *bols*; and the distribution of the different strokes across the different *vibhag*. Numerous variations are possible within this framework and part of the table player's skill is in the ability to manipulate the rhythm within this. The basic structure of the *tal* remains intact but a musician can choose to disrupt these smaller patterns by contradicting them, eventually bringing the music back to the fundamental pattern of cyclical beats, usually on *sum*, the first beat of the cycle. *Sum* marks the beginnings and ends of improvisations so it is often accented. Some improvisations end with a thrice repeated short rhythmic pattern.

The rhythmic structure of Spanish flamenco

Just as North Indian classical music incorporates the hands into its rhythmic structure (in the form of hand claps, waves, and finger counts) so too does Spanish flamenco, a musical tradition in which hand claps are integral to the form. Flamenco is the generic term applied to a particular ensemble art form, mostly coming from Southern Spain, that utilises song (*cante*), dance (*baile*) and guitar music (*toque*). The musical accompaniment is provided by guitar along with a rhythmical backbone where hand-clapping, stomping, and finger snapping are important elements. The flamenco *cante* uses a rhythmic structure in which the accented beats are distributed in a particular pattern in a short sequence that repeats at regular intervals. There are two kinds of *palmas* (hand clapping) used in accompaniment.

> Flamenco *palmas sordas* ('deaf *palmas*') have a dull sound and are made by cupping the palms at right angles to each other; they are used in quieter sections, during singing or melodic playing... *Palmas fuertes/ secas/claras* ('strong/ dry/clear *palmas*') have a sharp, crisp sound and are made with three fingers in the tensed palm of the other hand with both hands roughly aligned in the same direction; they are used during loud stomping, during the faster parts of accelerations... [71]

Flamenco pieces are usually in *palo* form, the most common *palos* being *bulerías*, *alegrías* and *soleá*. Each *palo* is distinguished by its basic metrical form and rhythmic structure (*compás*), along with its harmony and mood. A flamenco performance will usually contain several different *palos*. The compás is marked through various techniques such as the guitarist strumming, picking and tapping the soundboard, hand clapping (*palmas*) and finger snapping (*palillos*).

The most common beat cycle for *palos* is 12. The 12 beats are usually formed from a mixture of 6/8 + 3/4 bars. A common pattern used has bars of 6/8 followed by 3/4 which results in alternating groups of two and three beats.

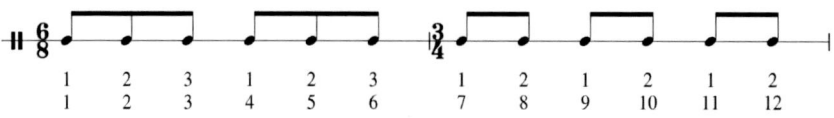

---

71 Mariana Maduell and Alan M Wing. 'The dynamics of ensemble: the case for flamenco'. *Psychology of Music* Vol 35(4): 591-627.

However, the accents do not correspond to the downbeats as found at the beginning of bars in Western classical music. Notes are accented at different points and it is the placing of these accents which differentiate the *palos*. The lively 12-beat *palo Alegrías* originated in Cadiz. Its beat pattern is as follows, the accented notes are shown in bold:

1 2 **3** 4 5 **6** 7 8 **9 10** 11 **12**

The divisions corresponds with the **1** 2 3 **1** 2 3 **1** 2 **1** 2 **1** 2 pattern above but the accents do not fall on the downbeats.

One of the most popular *palos* is the bulerias, a fast flamenco rhythm made up of a 12 beat cycle where the emphases are placed at certain points in the two general forms shown below. Notice how, in both cases, the pattern begins on the 12th note of the cycle.

12 1 2 **3** 4 5 **6** 7 **8** 9 **10** 11

12 1 2 **3** 4 5 **6** 7 8 **9 10** 11

The accompanying *palmas* are played in groups of six beats resulting in numerous counter-rhythms.

As has been illustrated, flamenco performances are closely tied to a strict rhythmic structure, but, in common with North Indian classical music, improvisation takes place within this and is seen as a measure of the performer's skill.

This chapter has illustrated a number of the rhythm systems found in music across the world. It has pointed out the differences between their foundations and those of Western music; a divisive system where bars and barlines are fundamental to the metrical structure and time signatures divide the beats, usually into groups of two, three and four with an accent on the first beat. In contrast, most of the music in the systems explored is not divided into bars, and time signatures (and indeed staff notation) are unknown. The rhythms of Western music are relatively simple in comparison with the given examples of music from around the world: the irregular divisions of aksak rhythms; the *tala* of North Indian classical music; the interlocking figurations of gamelan; and the polyrhythmic patterns of West African drumming. Some systems are additive rather than divisive (North Indian music for example) and numbers, although featuring prominently in several styles, perform different functions: they form the basis of Euclidean rhythms; they define the *matras* and *thekas* of different *tals*; they are central to the colotomic structure of Indonesian gamelan; and they define the beat cycles of Spanish flamenco. Furthermore, unlike in most Western music, improvisation is integral to several of the musical styles described.

Symmetry

4 Symmetry in music

A GEOMETRIC OBJECT or shape is symmetric if it can be divided into two or more identical parts and is invariant under transformation. In other words, it can be transformed by moving individual pieces whilst keeping the same overall shape. There are several different types of transformation; the main types are reflection, rotation, translation, and scale. Much Western music has its basis in repetition and contrast so it is not surprising, given that symmetry is a form of repetition, that it is frequently found in music. As Arnold Schoenberg (1874-1951) wrote in *Fundamentals of Musical Composition* (1967) 'A melody, classic or contemporary, tends towards regularity, simple repetitions and even symmetry.'[72] The repetition of ideas helps bind music together. One idea is not enough, but if there are too many ideas following each other with no unifying factor then the music may sound shapeless and without a sense of direction. Symmetry is a way of creating unifying factors. This chapter looks at the different ways in which musicians have used symmetry as a formal element from the Medieval composer Guillaime de Machaut (c 1300-1377) in 'Ma fin est mon commencement et mon commencement ma fin' to Nirvana in 'Smells like teen spirit'.

---

72 Arnold Schoenberg. *Fundamentals of Musical Composition* (London: Faber & Faber, 1982): 103.

Reflection

When an object has reflectional symmetry it can be divided into two pieces which are images of each other. The dividing line is known as the axis of symmetry. This could be the on the horizontal x axis or the vertical y axis. The letters B, C, D, E and K all reflect along the x axis. This is known as a vertical reflection. Or the reflection could be along the vertical y axis. This is referred to as horizontal reflection and it is sometimes referred to as temporal reflection symmetry. The letters A, M, T, U, V, W, M and Y all reflect along the vertical y axis. Melodies can therefore be reflected in two ways: along the x axis and along the y axis.

Inversion

When music is reflected along the x axis, what went up goes down and vice versa. This is known in music as inversion. It can be done in two different ways or a combination of both.

1. The intervals are inverted so that only the numbering of the interval is preserved: E down to C (a falling 3rd) becomes E up to G (a rising 3rd).

2. The exact intervals are inverted so that a major 3rd down becomes a major 3rd up. E down to C (a falling major 3rd) becomes E up to G# (a rising major 3rd).

Reflection is clear to see in the outer parts of the left hand (LH) and right hand (RH) of Bartók's piano piece *Mikrokosmos No. 141*. Béla Bartók (1881-1945) wrote *Mikrokosmos* in 1939. It is a series of 153 piano pieces ranging in difficulty from easy to advanced with each one featuring a different scale or mode, rhythmic or melodic feature. In No. 141 'Subject and Reflection' the LH part is an exact reflection of the RH part (see below). In this example the theme and its inversion are played simultaneously.

In the first bar Bb up to C in the top part (a major 2nd) becomes Bb down to Ab (a major 2nd), then C up to Eb in the upper part (a minor 3rd) becomes Ab down to F (a minor 3rd). Notice how the number of this piece, No. 141 is also symmetric. Although virtually all of No. 141 demonstrates this simultaneous reflection, later on in the piece there are a few bars where one of the notes in the inner parts is deleted, a compromise to fit in with Bartók's harmonic scheme.

In the third movement *of Symphony No. 1* (1876) by Johannes Brahms (1833-1897), a different approach is taken where the second half (bars 6 - 10) of the opening clarinet melody is a mirror image of the first half (bars 1 – 5) (see below).

In the first bar, Eb down to Db (a major 2nd) becomes C to D (a major 2nd) in the sixth bar, then Db down to C (a minor 2nd) becomes D natural to Eb (a minor 2nd) and so on. Notice how D flat has to become D natural in order to maintain the same intervals.

One of the most famous examples of the use of inversion can be found in the *Rhapsody on a Theme of Paganini* for piano and orchestra by Sergei Rachmaninov (1873-1943). The work is a set of 24 variations based on Niccolò Paganini's 24th *Caprice* for solo violin. Here is the main theme which is heard in the strings towards the beginning of the piece (see below):

Original   Variation XVIII

A to C - up a minor 3rd   Ab to F - down a minor 3rd
C to B - down a minor 2nd   F to Gb - up a minor 2nd
B to A – down a major 2nd   Gb to Ab – up a major 2nd
A to E – up a perfect fifth   Ab – Db – down a perfect fifth

Variation XVIII is based on an inversion of the main semiquaver – quaver figure found in the first bar of the main theme with all the intervals preserved (see above). The tempo is slowed down and there is a change of key. The result is a complete change of character where the original spritely theme is transformed into a languorous romantic melody.

The transformation is very effective, but it is difficult to discern by the ear alone.

In contrast, the inversion used by Franz Schubert (1797-1828) in his Fantasia Op. 15[73] is easily discernible: the descending scale becomes an

---

[73] Schubert's Fantasia Op. 15 is often known as the *Wanderer Fantasia* because of its use of the melody taken from his lied 'Der Wanderer'.

ascending scale and the chords move from the bass part to the treble part (see below).

Franz Schubert (Wanderer) Fantasia Op. 15 (bars 83-84)

Franz Schubert (Wanderer) Fantasia Op. 15 (bars 90-91)

There is often an element of compromise in the use of inversion – or indeed any of the symmetrical devices. This is because of the musical constraints imposed by tonal music and functional harmony. In order to avoid unwanted dissonance or tonal ambiguity, precise intervals are not always used: a major third may become a minor third, for example.

The question remains as to whether composers were consciously using points of symmetry in their works. It is not always possible to know their intentions. In the above examples it is fair to assume that Bartók was consciously using inversions, given the title 'Subject and Reflection'.

J S Bach (1685-1750) makes extended use of inversion in the Gigue of his *English Suite No. 6 in D minor* and it would appear that this was intentional. When the second section is compared with the first, we can see that the latter is a mirror version of the former (see below). This is all the more impressive because of its chromatic nature.

J S Bach- English Suite No. 6 in D minor - Gigue (opening)

J S Bach- English Suite No. 6 in D minor - Gigue (opening of second section)

Furthermore this mirror image is maintained for most of the second part of the Gigue. This cannot have been an accident: it must have been intentional. Further evidence of this is given by Bach's treatment of the form. During the Baroque period, the gigue was one of the most popular instrumental dances and a standard movement of the suite. Most gigues were in binary form. One of the features of two-section binary form is that the first section, the A section, opens in the tonic key (in this case D minor) and closes in another key, usually the dominant or the relative major (in this case A major). The B section opens in the new key and modulates back to the tonic. In order to comply with the conventions of binary form, Bach inserts eight extra bars which do not follow the mirror pattern shortly before the end of the piece.

Retrograde

In horizontal reflection, the last note becomes the first and the notes appear in reverse order, back to the first. Sometimes the rhythm is retained, at other times the rhythm is abandoned. When music is reflected along the vertical y axis the notes form a kind of palindrome. This is known in music as retrograde.

Béla Bartók uses retrograde motion in the fourth movement of his 1936 work *Music for strings, percussion and celesta*. Here the piece is in a Bulgarian folk style with a rhythm pattern of 2 + 3 + 3 beats. Quavers and crotchets are used for both the opening melodic line (A G# F# E D# C# B, notes 1 – 7) and its reflection (B C# D# E F# G# A notes 7 – 13) but the notes fall on different strong or weak beats (see below).

The use of retrograde was very popular in Medieval and early Renaissance music when it was sometimes known as *cancrizans*, the Latin form of crab (although it should be noted that crabs walk sideways most of the time). One of the most famous examples is by the Medieval French composer Guillaume de Machaut. In his three-voice setting of 'Ma fin est mon commencement et mon commencement ma fin' (My end is my beginning and my beginning is my end) the *triplum* part was created by reading the *cantus* line in reverse. Here are the opening bars....

... and the closing bars where the last four bars of the cantus are an exact reversal of the first four bars of the triplum in terms of both pitch and rhythm.

How does this this sound? As the musicologist William Drabkin observes of the passage, it has been 'admired more for the finesse with which the technique is used than for the chanson's other artistic merits'.[74]

In 1597 Thomas Morley (1557-1602) published his famous musical treatise *A Plaine and Easie Introduction to Practicall Musicke* which includes instructions on how to compose a palindromic piece for voices. He writes '... you may make eight partes in foure (or fewer or more as you list) which may be sung backward and forward, that is, one beginning at the beginning of every part, and another at the ending, and so sing it quite through' He goes on to set out some (rather confusing) rules. He warns against using dotted notes because although 'in singing the part forward, it will go well' when coming backwards it 'will make a disturbance in the music because the singer

---

[74] William Drabkin. 'Cancrizans' in *Grove Music*.

SYMMETRY IN MUSIC

will be in a doubt to which note the dot belongeth'. He includes an example of an eight part canon (for more about canons see pages 141-52) and then writes 'If you desire more examples of this kind, you may find one of master Byrd, being the last song of those Latin Motets which under his and master Tallis his name were published'.[75] The piece Morley refers to is the eight-voice motet *Diliges Dominum* (1575) by the composer William Byrd (1540-1623) who had once taught Morley.[76] It is a musical palindrome for double choir where one four-part choir (soprano, alto, tenor, bass) sings the same music as the other choir, exactly in reverse; at the halfway point the two voices of each pair exchange parts and present them backwards. Here are the four opening bars of the 'bassus primus' part – the bass in choir 1.

... and here are the four closing bars of the bassus secundus part - the bass in choir 2. The bassus primus part of the opening is now sung in reverse order by the bassus secundus, and the opening notes of the bassus secundus are sung in reverse order by the bassus primus.

---

75 Thomas Morley. *A Plaine and Easie Introduction to Practicall Musicke* (London, 1597): 175-6.
76 *Diliges Dominum* is part of the Cantiones Sacrae (Sacred Songs), a collection of works by William Byrd and his teacher Thomas Tallis dedicated to Queen Elizabeth I.

It has been argued that the retrograde used here was in response to the text and that the exhortation to 'love thy neighbour as thyself' occasioned the reprise to bring the music full circle.[77]

Nearly 200 years later C P E Bach (1714-1788) composed his Minuet in C (1770) for keyboard. This is made up of two eight-bar sections where the second section is reversal of the first.

The piece is short and simple and is largely built on two chords, C and G, (the tonic and dominant/dominant 7th in the key of C). This means that when played in reverse the chords and harmony stay the same, a means of avoiding unwanted dissonances or tonal ambiguity.

Two years later Joseph Haydn (1732-1809) included a 'Menuet al Reverso' (minuet in reverse) in his Symphony No. 47 in G hence the symphony's nickname 'The Palindrome'. The second half of the minuet is identical to the first, but it is played in reverse - backwards. The trio has a similar palindromic construction. It is no accident that both C P E Bach and Haydn both chose to use a minuet to employ this palindromic device. Minuets during this period were usually light-hearted dance movements, less sophisticated in terms of both harmonic rhythm and texture in comparison with the more serious musical business taking part in the first and second movements of the symphonies and sonatas that they often formed part of.

Haydn arranged the Minuet and Trio from his Symphony No. 47 for his Piano Sonata No. 26 in A. Here it is easy to see the vertical reflection,

---

77   Brian Newbould. 'A Schubert palindrome'. *19th-Century Music* Vol. 15, No. 3, 1999): 207-214.

between bars 10 and 11 in what he now names the 'Menuetto al Rovescio'. In the same way as that of C P E Bach, Haydn's harmonic scheme for both the Menuet and Trio is firmly centred on the chords of A and E/E^7 major the tonic and dominant/dominant 7th. This means that when played in reverse, the harmony stays the same (see below).

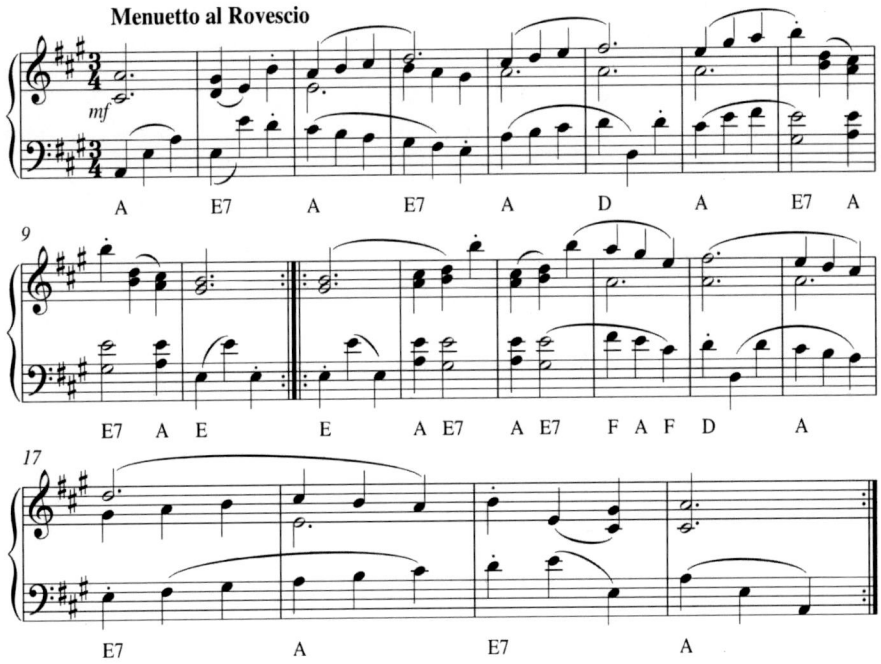

The Trio uses a similar combination of tonic and dominant seventh chords (see below). Notice how both the left and right hand parts play their parts backwards. The point of symmetry is between bars 12 and 13 (see below).

Another famous example of the use of retrograde can be found in the fugue of the fourth movement of the *Hammerklavier Sonata, Op. 106* by Ludwig van Beethoven (1770-1827) which was composed in 1818. Here is the first announcement of the theme:

Ludwig van Beethoven· *Hammerklavier Sonata Op. 106* Movt. IV (bars 16-21)

In the earlier examples by C P E Bach and Haydn, the retrograde version of the theme follows the original immediately whereas the retrograde version of Beethoven's theme appears 137 bars later. The backward rhythm is exact, but it is now in B minor rather than Bb major. Any problems with the harmonic scheme are avoided by the fact that the first appearance, unlike the second, is not harmonised (although there is inevitably some implied harmony in the first).

Ludwig van Beethoven, *Hammerklavier Sonata Op. 106* Movt. IV (bars 153-158)

In his article 'A Schubert Palindrome', the musicologist Brian Newbould writes with surprise of his discovery of what he considers to be the most ambitious example of a nineteenth-century musical palindrome. It is a passage in Schubert's little-known opera-melodrama *Die Zauberharfe* (The Magic Harp, 1820). The passage is long and surprisingly complex given that it comes from the pen of a composer who compositional process is often considered as 'intuitive' with 'finitely shaped gems' arriving in 'an instant'. As Newbould writes 'Schubert is one of the least likely perpetrators of the cerebral deed'.[78] The passage can be found near the opening of No. 3 with the retrograde version following the original 309 bars later.[79] Newbould describes it as a 'technical tour de force' where the 'harmonic thinking is far more venturesome

---

78 Newbould, 'A Schubert palindrome', 214.
79 *Die Zauberharfe* was not a critical success and after only eight performances it disappeared from the repertoire. However, after Schubert's death the overture was published as the overture to *Rosamunde*.

than that in the Haydn minuet'. Furthermore it is written for large Romantic orchestral forces and, at 19 bars long, is significantly longer than the C P E Bach and Haydn examples. At the same time Newbould notes that in order to comply with tonal constraints, Schubert used a certain amount of licence in the ordering of pitches and rhythms within a bar or half-bar. There are two main ways in which he deviates: firstly, at times the reversal of pitches is not accompanied by the reversal of rhythm; and secondly, sometimes the two halves of a bar may change places, but the original order of notes (rather than the reverse order) is retained within each half bar. Nevertheless, as Newbould writes, although the palindrome is not exact 'only the most keen-eared and thoughtful listener would detect the deviations from exactitude.'[80] Bars 7 – 25 are found in retrograde in bars 334 – 353. Here are the string parts for bars 21- 24 followed by the retrograde version found in bars 335 – 338 (see below).

---

80   Newbould, 'A Schubert palindrome', 211.

SYMMETRY IN MUSIC

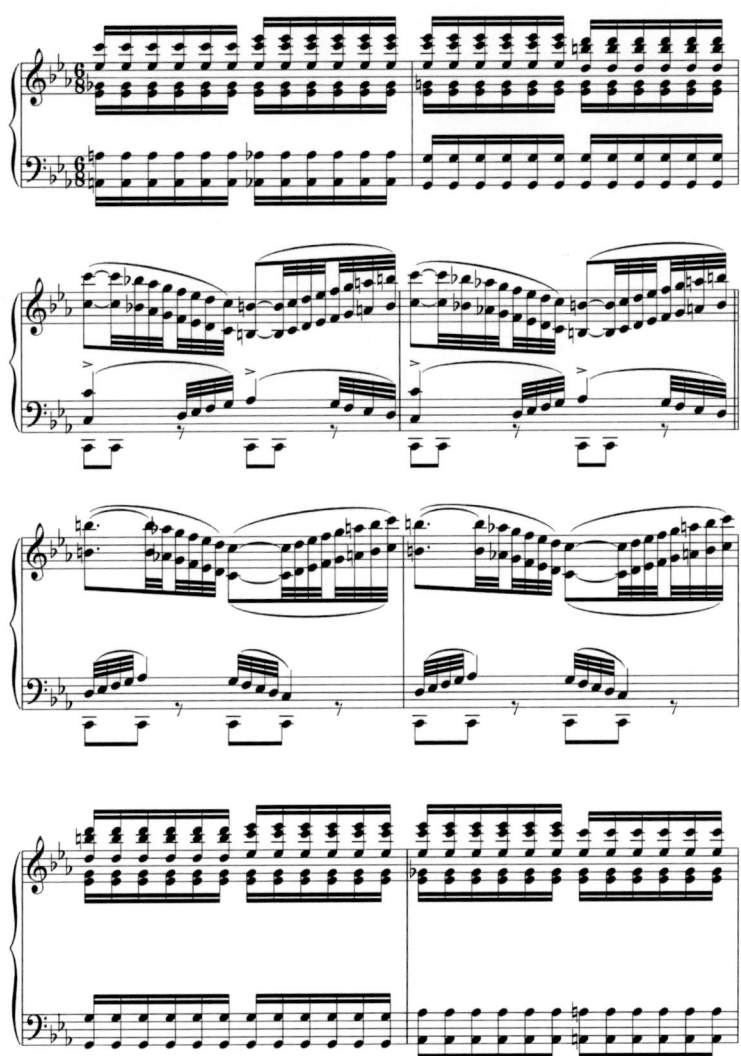

Franz Schubert, *Die Zauberharfe*, No. 3 (strings, bars 21-24 followed by strings bars 335-338)

As we have seen, diatonic music and functional harmony can impose certain musical constraints when using retrograde devices, so, for example, both Haydn and C P E Bach restricted the harmony of their retrograde pieces to little more than two chords. The twentieth century however heralded new approaches to harmonic schemes and consequently more freedom for composers when using palindromes. This was particularly evident in the music of the Second Viennese School where tonality was largely abandoned to make way for twelve-tone techniques as we will see in Chapter 8. For composers such as Arnold Schoenberg (1874-1951), Alban Berg (1885-1935) and Anton Webern (1883-1945) the advent of serialism considerably eased the strict harmonic demands of palindromic music.

Rotation

When an object has rotational symmetry it can be turned about a fixed point whilst keeping the same overall shape. One way this can be done is by reflecting the figure across both axes. Reflection across the x axis results in inversion and reflection across the y axis results in retrograde, so when the two types of reflection are put together the result is retrograde inversion. Some composers combine both inversion and retrograde – the music is both backwards and upside down. This is known as retrograde inversion. Its geometric equivalent is $180°$ rotation.

Paul Hindemith's 1942 piano work *Ludus Tonalis* ('Tonal Play') is subtitled 'Studies in Counterpoint, Tonal Organization and Piano Playing'. The Tonal Play of the title could well refer to the way that the composer plays with symmetries: different types of reflection and a symmetrical layout. It is one of few pieces to use rotation. The work opens with a three-part Praeludium and ends with a Postludium. The Postludium is a rotated version of the opening movement: visually it is an exact retrograde inversion of the Praeludium (with an added final chord). That is, the Postludium is the Praeludium turned upside down and played backwards.

SYMMETRY IN MUSIC

If we focus on the first bar of the Praeludium we can see that the equivalent bar of the Postludium is played backwards in terms of note values, so that:

quaver triplet, semi-quaver sextuplets, eight demi-semi-quavers then two quavers *becomes* -
two quavers, eight demi-semi-quavers, semi-quaver sextuplet then quaver triplets.

The melodic inversion here however, is visual rather than musical. Rather than strictly inverting the intervals used, the notes are selected according to how they look upside down on the page and in the bass clef (allowing adjustment for the accidentals which must come before the note). In order for the movement to work, there were several things to take into consideration. We know this from the numerous sketches that Hindemith (1895-1963) made for this movement. It needed to make musical sense rather than simply be a technical exercise so, for example, dynamics and marks of expression had to remain appropriate in the visual retrograde inversion. Also, as Hindemith discovered, there were only five scales – C, C# and Cb major, and the Phrygian mode on C and C# - that would resemble a mirror image when the pitches were inverted and placed in the bass clef. As can be seen below, the note F# spoils the mirror image pattern in the scale of G.

Mirror images of the scales of C major and F major

Retrograde inversion is much more uncommon than the other transformations used in music composed before the twentieth century, but it is an important element of the compositional technique known as serialism or twelve-tone technique (see Chapter 8) which first appeared in the 1920s.

Translation

When an object has translational symmetry it can be shifted a fixed distance in a fixed direction whilst keeping the same overall shape. This can happen in two ways.

1. It can be shifted from left to right – horizontal translation   *   *   *
OR
2. It can be shifted upwards or downwards – vertical translation.
*
*
*

Horizontal translation is essentially repetition and there are many examples in music where the same bar is repeated one or more times. A well-known example can be found in the repeated snare drum pattern used in the orchestral piece *Bolero* by Maurice Ravel (1875-1937) (see p.84). Electronic Dance Music (EDM) makes much use of horizontal translation and is largely based on tape loops of short repeated rhythms. A feature of pop music in general is its use of repeated chord progressions, drum patterns, and riffs. A riff is a short, repeated melodic or harmonic pattern usually of two or four bars' duration, although it may be heard at different pitches to fit in with the harmony, it is often simply repeated over and over as in the famous opening riff of the Nirvana song 'Smells like teen spirit' (1991). 'Smells like teen spirit' uses basically the same riff and chord progression (F- Bb – Ab – Db) throughout; the structure is primarily defined by differences in instrumentation and dynamics with the pattern of quiet verses building to loud, powerful choruses.

When an extended sequence of notes is taken and each note is shifted by the same interval, up or down in vertical translation, then this can result in a key change or modulation, something that happens all the time in music. A common device in pop music is to raise the key a tone or a semitone higher for the last verse or chorus of a song. This gives a sense of climax and allows the singer to hit higher notes. Michael Jackson's 'Man in the Mirror' (1988), for example, features a semitone key change at the repeat of the final chorus. Ella Fitzgerald takes this to new extremes in the famous 1960 recording of the Kurt Weill song 'Mack the Knife', where she forgets the words. The songs opens in the key of G and then each verse is taken up a semitone (G – Ab – A – Bb – B – C) and finally ending in the key of Db.

On a smaller scale, a short melody or harmonic progression can be repeated (more or less exactly) at a different pitch either higher or lower. This is termed a 'sequence' and is used in countless pieces of music. One of the most famous examples of the use of sequence is in the first movement of Beethoven's Symphony No. 5.

This repeated four-note cell or motif unifies the movement and propels it along in its different guises of repetition, inversion, transposition and variation.

For more on the use of translation see the following chapter on Frieze Patterns.

Scale

An object has scale symmetry when it can be expanded or contracted whilst keeping the same overall shape.

The one-bar rhythm above can be transformed through scale symmetry in two ways: augmentation and diminution. The note values can be expanded – made longer - through augmentation. In this example the note values have been doubled.

SYMMETRY IN MUSIC

The note values can be contracted – made shorter - through diminution. In this example the note values have been halved.

Augmentation and diminution are musical devices which are often found, though not exclusively, in fugues and canons (ssee Chapter 9). Here is an example of augmentation taken from J S Bach's Fugue No. 2 in C minor from Book II of the *Well-Tempered Clavier*. The fugue opens with the subject made up of quavers and semi-quavers:

In bar 14 the note values of the subject are doubled, the quavers become crotchets and the semi-quavers become quavers:

This is how it appears in the music as an inner-part.

Here is an example of diminution. This is again taken from Book II of the *Well-Tempered Clavier*. Fugue No. 9 in E major opens with the subject in the bass. The first note values are a semibreve and four minims (see below).

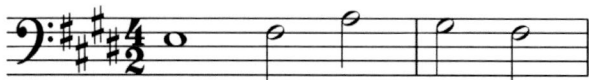

In bar 28 it is heard in diminution – all the note values are halved.

Here it is *in situ* in an inner part.

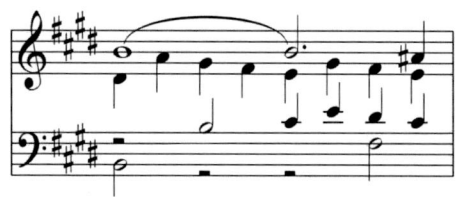

Further examples of augmentation and diminution can be found in the chapters on 'Canons and fugues' and 'Serialism' where they are common features.

The next chapter looks at another aspect of symmetry; frieze patterns, plane figures with a symmetric pattern bounded by two infinite parallel lines.

5 Frieze patterns in music

FRIEZE PATTERNS ARE repeating patterns of elements arranged along a line or in a strip. They have existed for centuries as decorative adornments and occur frequently in architecture and decorative art. They often appear as borders; the term 'frieze' comes from architecture where it is used to refer to a decorative carving or pattern running horizontally just below a roofline or ceiling.

In mathematical terms a frieze pattern can be described as a plane figure with a symmetric pattern bounded by two infinite parallel lines. The patterns are repetitive in one direction according to the symmetries of the pattern. Frieze patterns can be classified in terms of their groups of symmetries, hence the mathematical study of frieze patterns focuses on group theory. Group theory is a branch of abstract algebra, which looks at the main features of a group, from both the point of view of its elements and its group operations. Symmetrical patterns are classified according to the types of symmetry which are used. There are exactly seven different frieze symmetry types. All frieze patterns have translation symmetry i.e. you can slide a horizontal frieze pattern along a fixed distance (to the left or right, up or down) and it will appear unchanged. As well as translational symmetry, the other six types also have different combinations of rotational, horizontal, vertical and glide symmetry. This chapter looks at the way that the symmetries of the seven different frieze patterns can be found in music.

Here is a list of the frieze patterns along with the International Notation.

Frieze pattern	Description	International notation
TYPE 1	Translation.	p111
TYPE 2	Translation and glide symmetry.	p1a1
TYPE 3	Translation and reflection along the horizontal line.	p1m1
TYPE 4	Translation and reflection along the vertical line.	pm11
TYPE 5	Translation and 180° rotation.	p112
TYPE 6	Translation, 180° rotation, horizontal and vertical symmetry.	pmm2
TYPE 7	Translation, 180° rotation, glide, and reflection along the vertical line.	pma2

Guide to the international notation. The second symbol refers to reflection along the vertical line – where this exists the letter 'm' is used, otherwise there is a 1. The third symbol refers to reflection along the horizontal line – where this exists the letter 'm' is used, otherwise there is a 1. If there is a letter 'a', this means that there is glide symmetry (where the figure is reflected (inverted) and then translated by being shifted horizontally). Where the fourth symbol is 2 this means that there is rotational symmetry, otherwise there is a 1.

In the 1970s, the mathematician John Conway created names relating to footsteps for each of the frieze groups. The footsteps represent the following symmetries.

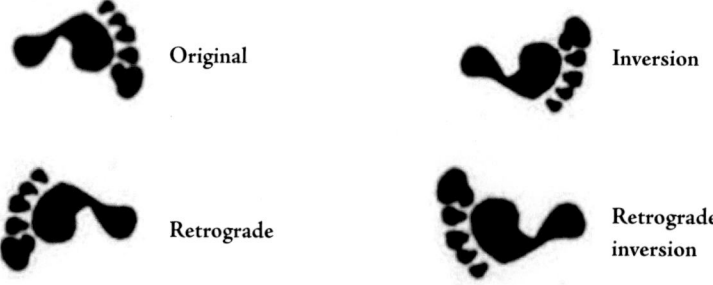

These can be seen in the table below along with a musical illustration of each frieze pattern. In each case a simple musical motif has been used to illustrate the symmetric pattern.

FRIEZE PATTERNS IN MUSIC

The seven frieze patterns with musical illustrations

HOP translation.

TYPE 1 p111

STEP translational and glide symmetry.

TYPE 2 p1a1

JUMP translation and reflection along the horizontal line.

TYPE 3 p1m1

SIDLE translation and reflection along the vertical line.

TYPE 4 pm11

SPINNING HOP translation and 180^0 rotation.

TYPE 5 p112

SPINNING JUMP translation, 180^0 rotation, horizontal and vertical symmetry

TYPE 6 pmm2

SPINNING SIDLE translation, 180^0 rotation, glide, and reflection along the vertical line

TYPE 7 pma2

TYPE 1 HOP Translation

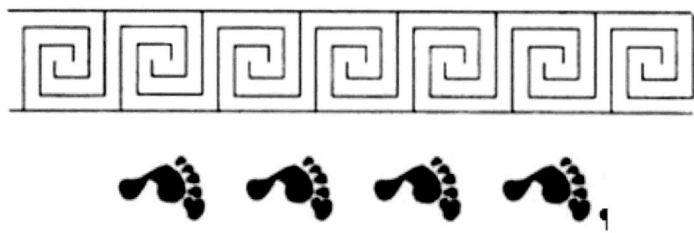

The Type 1 frieze pattern is the most common. It is based on translation in a horizontal direction - it is simple repetition. Repetition is the easiest symmetry for the listener to perceive and as listeners we are often attracted to repetition; repeated ideas become familiar, they set up expectations, allowing us to anticipate and thus to reap the reward. As Arnold Schoenberg (1874-1951) wrote in *Fundamentals of Musical Composition* (1967): 'Intelligibility in music seems to be impossible without repetition.'[81] The repetition of ideas helps bind music together. One idea is not enough, but if there are too many ideas following each other with no unifying factor then the music may sound shapeless and without a sense of direction.

Schoenberg went on to write 'While repetition without variation can easily produce monotony, juxtaposition of distantly related elements can easily degenerate into nonsense, especially if unifying elements are omitted'. The French composer Erik Satie (1866 – 1925) risked potential monotony with his 1893 piece *Vexations*. The music is only half a page long and the piece bears the inscription *In order to play the theme 840 times in succession, it would be advisable to prepare oneself beforehand, and in the deepest silence, by serious immobilities.* It was 70 years before anybody took up the challenge of a 'full' performance.[82] In 1963, the American composer John Cage (1912-1992) organised a team of players for the first performance at the Pocket Theater

---

81 Arnold Schoenberg. *Fundamentals of Musical Composition* (London: Faber & Faber, 1982): 103.

82 In his study of performances of *Vexations*, Gavin Bryars writes that the first performance of the piece that he knows of was given in 1958 by Richard David Hames at his school when he was 13 years old. For a list of most of the performances of this work up to 1979, see Gavin Bryars, "Vexations and its Performers," Contact 26 (1983): 12-20.

in New York. In the event there were twelve pianists and the performance lasted eighteen hours and forty minutes.[83] From then on there have been several marathon performances by teams of players. Here is the theme on which it is based. It uses every note of the chromatic scale other than G#/Ab and is marked 'Tres lent' (very slow).

The theme is then harmonised by a series of chromatic chords mostly unresolved, consequently any sense of the harmonic progression, normally found in Western classical music, is absent. The musicologist Robert Orledge believes that this was not Satie's intention.

> Satie was not concerned with through-composition and the normal perception of music "getting somewhere" through functional forms and harmonies. [...] His concern lay in the way our perception of time could be expanded and telescoped, and how music could function as a spatial element in time.[84]

This reinforces Cage's response to his involvement in its performance. He recalled that after about 90 minutes 'we all realised that something had been set in motion that went far beyond what any of us had anticipated'.[85]

Constant repetition can be used for dramatic effect. In *Stay On It* (1973 the African-American composer Julius Eastman (1940-1990) repeats the opening seven-note theme throughout most of the 24-minute work. The memorable ostinato stays the same, but the dramatic effect comes from the way the music around it changes. For the first half of the piece the ostinato

---

83   The twelve pianists were: John Cage, David Tudor, Christian Wolff, Philip Corner, Viola Farber, Robert Wood, MacRae Cook, John Cale, David Del Tredici, James Tenney, Howard Klein and Joshua Rifkin. Gavin Bryars, "Vexations and its Performers," Contact 26 (1983): 12-20https://gavinbryars.com/work_writing/vexations-and-its-performers/

84   Robert Orledge, *Satie the Composer* (Cambridge: Cambridge University Press, 1990), 142-43.

85   Luckett. *Every Day is a Good Day. The Visual Art of John Cage*. (London: Hayward Publishing, 2010).

stays in the same form but eventually improvised licks are heard around it until the piece descends into exuberant chaos and the ostinato briefly collapses. For a few bars it is no longer there, but it is still firmly imprinted on the mind. When, after a few bars, it returns it is more a disfigured shadow of itself.

A frequently played piece that uses much repetition is the one-movement orchestral work *Bolero* by Maurice Ravel (1875-1937). The opening two-bar snare drum ostinato is repeated throughout the 17-minute work (see below). An ostinato is a short musical pattern repeated throughout a section or complete piece. In *Bolero* two alternating melodies are passed around the instruments above the relentless rhythm.

Before its first performance Ravel 'issued a warning' to the effect that' the piece was an exercise in orchestration with 'no contrasts, and practically no invention except the plan and the manner of execution'.[86] The interest lies in the brilliant orchestration, the hypnotic power of the unflagging rhythm, and the steady crescendo which leads to an exciting climax. The piece was an instant success with audiences. Ravel, however, once described it wryly to his friend the composer Arthur Honegger as 'a masterpiece…without any music in it'.[87]

There are, loosely speaking, two types of repetition used in music. These are the repetition of short units (a few bars, a theme or a motif, for example) and repetition of large sections of a piece of music as a structural device (in binary, ternary and sonata form, for example). Repetition allows themes to be heard again and for patterns to be displayed.

The Italian composer Domenico Scarlatti (1685 – 1757) wrote over 500 keyboard sonatas, originally intended to be played on harpsichord or fortepiano. Virtually all the pieces are written in simple binary form. However, they are abundant with musical ideas, interesting rhythms and harmonies, remote keys (for the time) and unprepared modulations. One

---

86 *Daily Telegraph*, July 11, 1931.
87 A. Honegger, *Incantation aux fossils* (Lausanne: Editions d'Ouchy Lausann, 1948): 91–2.

FRIEZE PATTERNS IN MUSIC

of the musical characteristics found in many of the sonatas is the use of repetitions of the same musical phrase, one after the other – as in the Type 1 frieze pattern. Here is an example taken from his Keyboard Sonata K 27 (bars 11-16) where the same two bars are played three times consecutively.

A commonly found use of repetition popular in Baroque music is the ground. A ground is a recurring melody, usually in the bass, accompanied by continuous variation in the upper parts. The term 'ground' may refer to the bass line, or to the entire musical scheme including the harmonies and upper voices. A ground bass is a repeating bass line which forms the basis of a set of continuous melodic and/or harmonic variations. The bass line repeats many times whilst the variations usually get more and more complex as the piece goes on. It was particularly popular during the Baroque period in music and often formed the basis for the passacaglia and the chaconne.[88] The bass line of the famous *Canon for three violins and continuo* by Johanne Pachelbel (1653-1706) has only eight notes forming a two-bar phrase (see below). This is repeated throughout the piece – 28 times in all.

---

88 The passacaglia is typically in triple time, in a minor key with a four-note pattern descending by step. The chaconne, although usually minor, sometimes uses a major key.

Clearly, if all the parts simply repeated, then the music would soon become rather dull. What Pachelbel does instead is to write a canon for the three violins with each section becoming increasingly rhythmically complex as the piece goes on (see Chapter 9). Probably the most famous use of ground bass can be found in the aria 'Dido's Lament' from *Dido and Aeneas* by Henry Purcell (1659-1695).

Contemporary use of the ground can be heard in the soundtrack to Peter Greenaway's film *The Draughtsman's Contract*. In creating the score, the English composer Michael Nyman (b. 1944) researched the music of Purcell and set out to use Purcell's grounds as a starting point to 'signify a kind of Baroque prototype'[89].[90] The well-known opening sequence, 'Chasing sheep is best left to shepherds' is based on the Prelude to Act III from Purcell's *King Arthur* (see below).

Although Purcell's original was not conceived as a ground, Nyman takes the music and fashions his own ground from the opening bars, creating a series of layers out of the given music, each one being treated differently in terms of rhythm, texture and melody. Nyman's pitches stay more or less the same as those of Purcell, but the rhythm changes. The resulting 15-bar sequence

---

89 Pwyll ap Siôn. *The Music of Michael Nyman: Texts, Contexts and Intertexts*. (London: Routledge, 2007).
90 In 'An eye for optical theory' Nyman unwittingly chose a composition by William Croft, a lesser-known contemporary of Purcell.

is heard four times each time the repetition is varied with changes in texture and instrumentation.

The work of Minimalist composers such as Steve Reich (b 1936), Philip Glass (b 1937) and John Adams (b 1947) features constantly repeated patterns that are subjected to gradual processes of melodic and rhythmic change (transformation) as the piece unfolds. Such transformations include phase shifting (or phasing) where one part repeats constantly and another gradually shifts out of phase with it (see pages 30-4).

Pop music in general makes much use of repeated chord progressions, drum patterns, and riffs not mention whole sections, such as the verse and chorus. Many pop songs are built on riffs - short, repeated melodic or chordal patterns which may be heard at different pitches. Riffs first came to prominence in jazz, swing and rhythm and blues. They formed the basis of the song's structure where musical variants took place above them. In his definition of riffs, the pop musicologist Richard Middleton notes their structural importance, describing them as 'short rhythmic, melodic, or harmonic figures repeated to form a structural framework'.[91] Certain riffs are typical of the blues style. The pattern below, for example, would be repeated through the song with the same shape being built on the different chords of the 12-bar blues.

Amongst songs including the best-known riffs are Led Zeppelin's 'Whole lotta love' (1969), 'Sweet Child O' Mine' (1987) by Guns 'N' Roses and 'Seven Nation Army' by the White Stripes (2003). What they have in common is that they are both memorable and catchy, so much so that the 'Seven Nation Army' riff with its roots in garage blues was transformed into a political anthem sung to the words 'Oh, Jeremy Corbyn' when he was leader of the UK Labour party. Thousands joined in with the chant at the Glastonbury Festival in 2017.

In 1977 Donna Summer and Georgio Moroder collaborated on the disco song 'I feel love'. Combining Moroder's incessant synthesizer bass-line, swirling

---

91   Middleton, Richard. *Studying Popular Music*. (Philadelphia: Open University Press, 1990)..

chords and programmed drums with Summer's ecstatic vocal floating over it, the song was to serve as a blueprint for house and techno, two of the earliest forms of Electronic Dance Music (EDM).[92] A simple one-bar pattern in the synthesizer is repeated over and over, for nearly six minutes (roughly 350 repetitions), helping to create a trance-like state. Here is the synth bass line.

In the 1980s technology opened up different ways of creating music. The short, repeating patterns (or ostinati) of house music were facilitated by the new technology available which meant that they did no longer have to be played live. Most EDM songs are based on loops of short repeated rhythms. DJs have different ways to manipulate these sounds in order to add variety - cutting up tracks, mixing, scratching, beat-matching, and pitch-shifting, adding these to the creative mix. The ostinati are then layered on top of each other, dropping in and out of the mix.

The rhythmic foundation of much Afro-Cuban music is provided by the clavé – repeated interlocking rhythms with a metronomic pulse underlying the music and keeping all the players together. The clavé rhythm is made up of several one- or two-bar patterns creating a layered texture made up of melodic and rhythmic ostinati (see pages 44-5). Here is a typical clavé pattern as used in 'Se Quema la chumbamba' played by Familia Valera Miranda (see below).

In many styles of African music the bell functions much like the clavé of Afro-Cuban music. It sets the foundation with all other instruments weaving around the pattern. The Ewe musicians of Ghana, for example, often use the

---

92   Julia Winterson. *Pop Music The Text Book* (London: Peters Edition, 2013).

FRIEZE PATTERNS IN MUSIC

following bell pattern (see below). Its role is vital in maintaining the flow, energy and clarity of the entire ensemble. L and S refer to long and short strokes (see pages 41-2 for more detail).

L L S L L S   L L S L L S   L L S L L S   L L S L L S

TYPE 2 STEP Translation and glide symmetry

The Type 2 frieze pattern uses glide symmetry which means that the figure is reflected (inverted) and then translated by being shifted horizontally to the right.

The next two examples, Types 2 and 3, are both taken from Igor Stravinsky's score *Petrushka*. *Petrushka* is a ballet in four scenes which tells the story of three puppets who are brought to life. It is scored for large orchestra with a prominent piano part and was first performed by the impresario Diaghilev's *Ballets Russes* in Paris in 1911.

The following extract is taken from the first scene in the section titled 'Russian Dance'. For ease of reading, the music below has been written using treble clefs. The top two staves are the Bb clarinets and the lower two staves are the viola parts. In both instruments, the music on the second beat is an inversion of the rising arpeggio figure on the first beat. The Type 2 frieze pattern uses glide symmetry which means that the arpeggio figure is reflected (inverted) and then translated by being shifted horizontally to the right.

© Copyright 1912 by Hawkes & Son (London) Ltd. Revised Version © Copyright 1948 by Hawkes & Son (London) Ltd. U.S. Copyright Renewed. Reproduced by permission of Boosey & Hawkes Music Publishers Ltd.

There are many other examples of uses of musical symmetry in this score. Did Stravinsky (1882-1971) make a conscious decision to use such musical devices? We know from his writings that the answer is almost certainly yes. As well as being a composer, Stravinsky was an influential thinker about music and he wrote much on the subject. His work *Poetics of Music in the Form of Six Lessons* (1942) is considered to be a landmark of twentieth century musical aesthetics. In this he writes at length about his own compositional process.

The creator's function is to sift the elements he receives from her, for human activity must impose limits upon itself. The more art is controlled, limited, worked over, the more it is free.[93]

TYPE 3 JUMP Translation and reflection along the horizontal line

---

93   Igor Stravinsky. *Poetics of Music in the Form of Six Lessons*. (London: Harvard University Press, 1942).

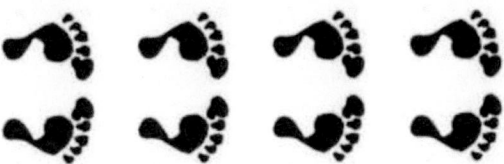

The Type 3 frieze pattern uses translation and reflection along the horizontal line. This means that the descending scale figure in the example below is reflected along the horizontal line (inverted). The bars of music below are taken from the harp part of 'The Shrove – tide fair'.

© Copyright 1912 by Hawkes & Son (London) Ltd. Revised Version. © Copyright 1948 by Hawkes & Son (London) Ltd. U.S. Copyright Renewed. Reproduced by permission of Boosey & Hawkes Music Publishers Ltd

TYPE 4 SIDLE Translation and reflection along the vertical line

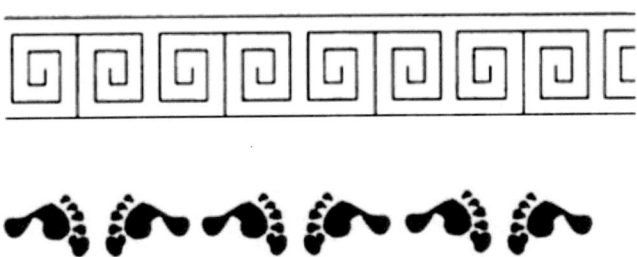

The Type 4 frieze pattern uses translation and reflection along the vertical line. This means that in each pair of footprints the motif is reflected along the vertical line (played backwards).

The following examples illustrate the ways in which two composers from different centuries have used this type of frieze pattern in their keyboard music. The first example is from the eighteenth century where Domenico Scarlatti uses the device in his Keyboard Sonata K. 514 in C (see below).

Notice how the second half of the bar in the left hand is a retrograde (backwards) version of the first half of the bar in the right hand.

The second example is taken from the twentieth century. The way that the French composer Claude Debussy (1862–1918 wrote for piano altered the way in which the instrument was perceived; he often used the extreme registers, with widely spaced chords and parallel movement as well as taking a new approach to pedalling which produced subtle blending effects. *Estampes* (1903) is a set of three pieces for piano. The first piece *Pagodes* evokes the Javanese gamelan which Debussy had heard played at the 1889 Exposition Universelle in Paris (for bars 26 – 29, see below).

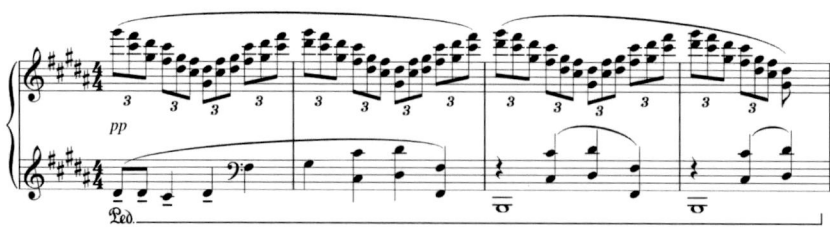

In this example above, the Type 4 frieze pattern is found in the right hand: the second half of the bar is a retrograde version of the first half with the first quaver of the third triplet acting as the point of reflection.

TYPE 5 SPINNING HOP Translation and 180⁰ rotation

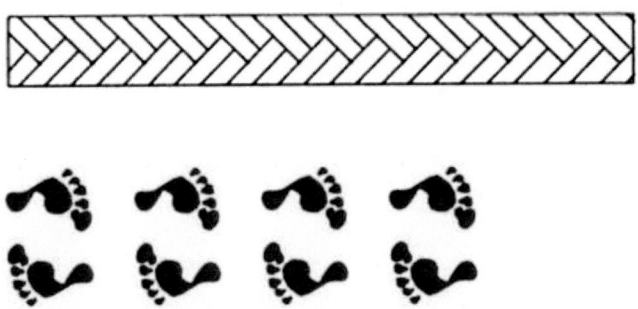

The Type 5 frieze pattern combines translation with 180⁰ rotation (retrograde inversion). The original musical idea is combined with the retrograde inversion. Béla Bartók (1881-1945) uses the Spinning Hop frieze pattern in the fifth and final movement (Allegro molto) of his *String Quartet No. IV* (for bars 329-331, see below).

Here is the first violin part with its 180° rotation immediately underneath it.

The rotation is played by the viola in the first bar of the example and by the cello in the second and third bars.

TYPE 6 SPINNING JUMP Translation 180° rotation, horizontal and vertical symmetry

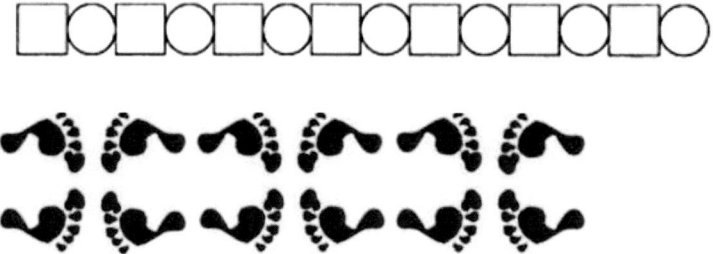

The Type 6 frieze pattern is one of the most complex in its construction. It combines translation with 180° rotation along with reflections about both the x and y axis. The upper stave is formed by alternating the original with a retrograde of the original. The lower stave is an inversion of the upper stave.

Musical examples of Type 6 are very difficult to spot. The example below from Beethoven's *Diabelli Variations* is almost, but not quite, there. Conway's footprints shown below correspond with the middle complete bar of the Beethoven in terms of the overall shape. The original motif in Variation XXVI is followed by the retrograde version in both staves, and the lower stave is an inversion of the upper stave (bars 9-11). However, strictly speaking the notes on the second beat in the R H should be C D E rather than C# D E. Similarly the C D E of the L H should be followed by E D C (rather than G F E).

FRIEZE PATTERNS IN MUSIC

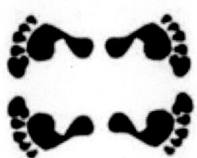

TYPE 7 SPINNING SIDLE Translation 180° rotation, glide, and reflection along the vertical line

The Type 7 frieze pattern is similar to Type 4 in that it uses translation and reflection along the vertical line. This means that in each pair of footprints the motif is reflected along the vertical line (played backwards). In Type 7 this is combined with 180° rotation and glide as can be seen in the middle pair of footprints.

The example below is taken from a keyboard suite by Handel. This is the Prelude, the opening movement of *Suite No. 1* marked *quasi fantasia*. Such improvisatory flourishes were typical of Baroque keyboard music particularly in the opening bars of toccatas and preludes.

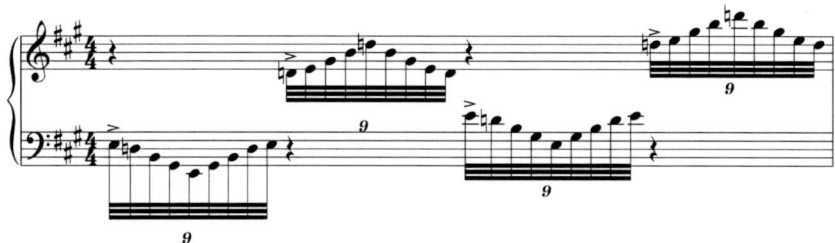

This chapter has shown how the symmetries of each of the seven frieze patterns can be found in music. Chapter 9 looks in more detail at the ways in which symmetries are fundamental to the musical structure of two musical forms in particular, the canon and the fugue.

Scales

6 Diatonic scales and tuning

THIS CHAPTER DESCRIBES various scales, intervals and systems of tuning. Most of the scales are commonly used, some of them less so. It opens by introducing the music theory involved; the diatonic major scale, intervals and the concept of consonance and dissonance. For centuries there has been much debate about different scales and tunings with many eminent mathematicians, scientists and musicians across Europe devising and analysing scales. What follows focuses on the three main systems that evolved; the Pythagorean scale, just intonation and equal temperament. It covers the mathematical and scientific principles involved such as ratios, square roots and irrational numbers, the harmonic series and the circle of 5ths.

The diatonic major scale, intervals, consonance and dissonance

A scale is a pattern of notes arranged in order of pitch from low to high (or vice versa) with specified distances or intervals between them. An interval is the distance between two notes and, in Western music, these are usually measured in numbers of tones or semitones. In this way from C up to D or down to B is a 2nd, another step from C up to E or down to A makes a 3rd, and so on.

Major and minor scales are known as diatonic scales and are built on a pattern of seven notes within an octave span. All major scales are built on the following pattern

The semitones come between the 3rd and 4th degrees of the scale and the 7th and octave. Here is the scale of C major. It uses only the white notes on the keyboard.

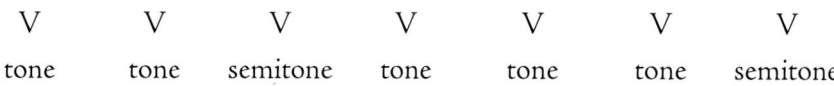

The major scale can be reproduced at any pitch i.e. it can start on any note. The following shows the names of all the intervals found between the tonic (key-note) of a major key and the other degrees of the scale. This serves as a useful standard by which other intervals can be worked out.

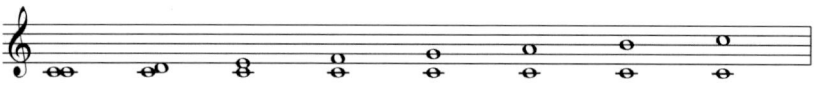

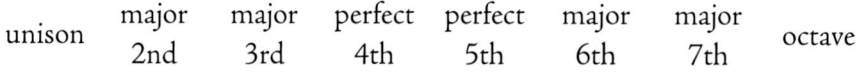

The character of different intervals is often referred to in terms of consonance and dissonance. Consonant intervals feel relatively stable and do not need to resolve to another interval. Major and minor 3rds and 6ths, perfect 5ths and octaves are all consonant intervals. Two voices producing the same pitch are said to be in unison. Dissonant intervals feel somewhat unstable, as though one of the notes needs to move up or down to resolve into a consonance. The major 7th, for example, feels as though it needs to resolve upwards, and the minor 7th feels as though it needs to resolve downwards. Major and minor

2nds, perfect 4ths, major and minor 7ths and all augmented and diminished intervals are dissonant. Consonance is often loosely defined as being pleasing to the ear, dissonance being the antithesis, unstable and needing resolution. These definitions, however, should be treated with caution: the pleasing/displeasing notion depends on aesthetic preferences and implies a psychoacoustic judgment, whereas the notion of resolution of tension depends upon a familiarity with Western tonal harmony.

The Pythagorean scale

One of the earliest recorded musical scales was the Pythagorean scale. Pythagoras, the Greek mathematician and philosopher lived in the second half of the 6th century BCE. Although the system of construction of this scale existed long before his time, the term Pythagorean scale came about because of his theoretical justification in mathematical terms. Apparently, in passing a blacksmith's forge, Pythagoras heard different musical intervals in the striking of hammers against the anvils. Hammers of different weights struck simultaneously produced different consonant and dissonant intervals, so, for example, a hammer weighing half as much as another, a ratio of 2:1, produces a note an octave higher. Pythagoras went on to deduce from this that there was a relationship between consonant sounds and simple ratios and investigated further by carrying out a series of experiments with other bodies; water-filled glasses, strings, bells and pipes. The results pointed to unchanging relationships between the dimensions of the instruments used and the notes they produced. The ability to express these relationships numerically made it possible to analyse scales.

Using a monochord, a single-string instrument said to have been his invention, Pythagoras discovered that when a string is stopped half way the shorter string vibrates with twice the frequency and sounds an octave higher. Several intervals can be identified in the ways that they correspond to simple ratios of sound wavelengths or frequencies. So, for example, an octave is identified by the ratio 2:1 because the frequency of the upper note is twice that of the lower note, the interval of a 5th can be produced by the ratio 3:2 and a 4th by the ratio 4:3 From this the Pythagorean scale can be constructed by taking a note and producing others related to it through simple whole number ratios.[94]

In order to find the ratios of further intervals, Pythagoras multiplied two ratios together. As we have seen, an octave uses the ratio 2:1 and a 5th uses the ratio 3:2. Going up an octave and then down a 5th produces a 4th. We know that the 4th uses the ratio 4:3 and it follows that this can be calculated by 1/2 x 3/2 = 3/4. Using this principle, other degrees of the scale can be determined (see Table 1). So for example, if $W = 9/8$, then $1/1 \times W = 9/8$, $9/8 \times W = 81/64$ and so on. Table 1 shows the ratios used in the Pythagorean scale.

Table 1 – Ratios of each note to the lowest note used in the Pythagorean scale

Degree of scale	Interval	Ratio
1	Unison	1
2	Major 2nd	9/8
3	Major 3rd	81/64
4	Perfect 4th	4/3
5	Perfect 5th	3/2
6	Major 6th	27/16
7	Major 7th	243/128
8 = 1 - C	Octave	2/1

Table 1 gives the ratio of each note to the lowest note, the fundamental. In order to calculate the ratio between the notes, that is the intervals between them, we take the ratio of each note to the one preceding it. The result can be seen in Table 2.

---

[94] This rests on the theory of numerical ratios presented in books 7–9 of Euclid's *Elements*.

Table 2 – Ratios of each note to the one preceding it in the Pythagorean scale

Degree of scale	Interval	Ratio
1		
2	tone	9/8
3	tone	9/8
4	semitone	256/243
5	tone	9/8
6	tone	9/8
7	tone	9/8
8	semitone	256/243

There is an elegant simplicity in the way that this use of simple ratios leads to the construction of the diatonic scale. This simplicity accords with the ideals of the philosophy promulgated by Pythagoras and many of his contemporaries which sought to explain the nature of the universe through numbers, ratios and proportions. Music theory too was mathematically based dealing with ratios, proportions and number relations. However, there are several flaws within this Pythagorean method of calculation: not all of the intervals of the scale can be produced accurately by strict Pythagorean methods; they do not satisfy the properties of the circle of 5ths (see Figure 1); and the intervals do not always match the acoustical properties found in the harmonic series.

Taking each of these problems in turn, Table 1 shows us that all five steps of a tone are in the ratio of $W = 9:8$ and the two semitones are in the ratio of $H = 256:243$. However, two half steps in this Pythagorean tuning do not add up to one whole step.[95]

$$H^2 = 256/243 \times 256/243 = 2^{16}/3^{10} \neq 3^2/2^3 = W$$

---

[95] Gareth Roberts. *From Music to Mathematics {Exploring the connections}*. (Baltimore: John Hopkins University Press, 2016): 121.

This discrepancy is referred to as the 'Pythagorean comma', defined as the gap between one whole step and two half steps. It can be found by dividing the ratio for a whole step by the ratio for two half steps.

$W/H^2 = 3^{12}/2^{19} \approx 1.013643265$

This means that raising the pitch by two half steps produces a slightly smaller interval than raising it by one whole step.

The next problem with the Pythagorean scale is related to the circle of 5ths. The circle of 5ths is represented by a circular diagram demonstrating the relationship between different keys (see Figure 1).

Circle of 5ths

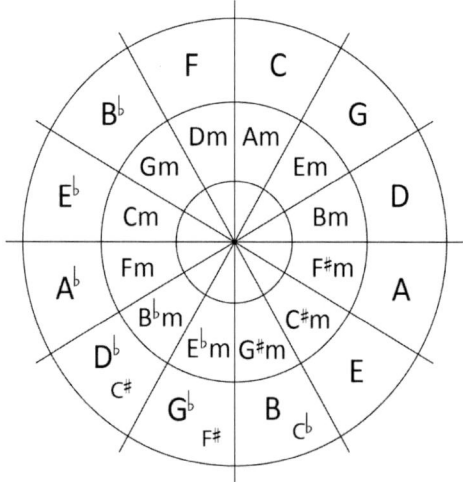

It shows a series of chords whose roots are each a 5th higher than the previous chord e.g. C-G-D-A (see Figure 1). From any starting note the pitch is raised repeatedly until the starting point is returned to and the circle closes. This is the equivalent to raising the pitch by seven octaves. However, using the specified Pythagorean ratios, the span of seven octaves is not equivalent to twelve 5ths and there is a need to introduce a new note for each octave to fill the gap. This means that rather than returning to the starting point and closing the circle, the figure becomes an ever-increasing spiral (see Figure 2). The shaded area denotes the Pythagorean comma.

Spiral of 5ths

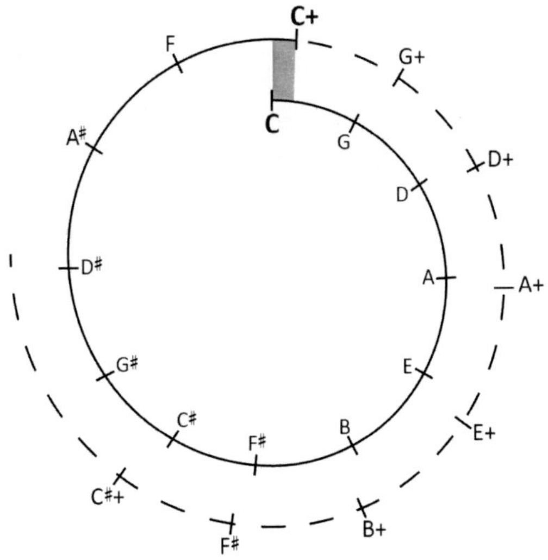

The harmonic series

Another problem lies in the correlation of the Pythagorean scale with the harmonic series. When a vibrating object, such as a string, is set in motion, it vibrates both as a whole, with a frequency called the fundamental (the lowest note or the first harmonic) and, with lesser intensity, in other sections as well. The harmonics (or overtones) generated may be represented in an ordered series called the harmonic series, a set of frequencies which are successive integer multiples of the fundamental (see Figure 3).

Figure 3 – The harmonic series

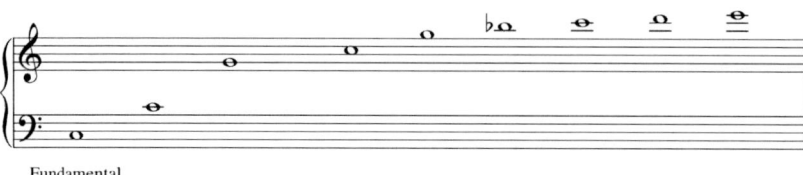

Fundamental

The frequencies are related by simple whole number ratios. In general, the nth harmonic of a series has a frequency which is n times the fundamental frequency. The harmonic series defines many of our intervals. As we have seen, the calculations used to make the Pythagorean scale were very limited and they missed out some of the most important ratios found in the harmonic series such as the major 3rd (5:4) and the minor 3rd (6:5). In this way the Pythagorean scale was out of sync with the laws of acoustics.[96]

Nevertheless, use of the Pythagorean scale persisted for hundreds of years. Another system of tuning known as equal temperament avoids the Pythagorean comma, but it was many years before it was in common use. The evolution of polyphonic music from the twelfth century onwards led to experimentation with alternative systems of tunings. Polyphony used several instruments or voices and music became more complicated harmonically; music was no longer largely restricted to the predominant use of three harmonic intervals - the octave, 4th and 5th – and 3rds and 6ths were gradually adopted.

Just intonation

Just intonation is based upon the first six notes of the harmonic series, the word 'just' used because this alignment is considered to be more acoustically pure or true. The ratios used are based on smaller numbers than those of the Pythagorean scale (see Table 3). The just major 3rd uses a ratio of 5:4, rather than 81:64, which is more consonant than its Pythagorean counterpart. Similarly the just major 6th is 5:3 (rather than 27:16) and the major 7th is 15:8 (rather than 243:128).

---

[96] Eli Maor. *Music by the Numbers*. (Princeton: Princeton University Press, 2018): 19.

Table 3 – Ratios used in just intonation

Degree of scale	Interval	Ratio
1	Unison	1
2	Major 2nd	9/8
3	Major 3rd	5/4
4	Perfect 4th	4/3
5	Perfect 5th	3/2
6	Major 6th	5/3
7	Major 7th	15/8
8 = 1	Octave	2/1

The idea of using the ratio of 5:4 was first suggested by two medieval British theorists, Theinred of Dover and Walter Odington and in ensuing decades there was much debate about different tunings by leading scientists and mathematicians across Europe, both the German mathematician Johannes Kepler (1571-1630) and the English mathematician Isaac Newton (1642-1727) devised scales. Kepler devised a scale derived from the ratios of planetary orbit minimum and maximum speeds and Newton devised a seven note diatonic scale based on the seven colour spectrum of the rainbow.[97] The French polymath Marin Mersenne (1588-1648) is credited with being the first to formulate rules governing vibrating strings, and the first to discern the nature of harmonics related to a fundamental note. In the search for a more consonant scale, the eighteenth century Swiss mathematician, Leonhard Euler, developed an elaborate mathematical theory which was based upon just-intonation ratios.

Although just intonation conforms more closely to the laws of acoustics than the Pythagorean scale, it is not without problems; the circle of 5ths is still not closed and there are two different ratios for the whole step within the scale. The ratio for the step between the first and 2nd degrees (a tone) is 9:8 whereas the step of a tone between the 2nd and 3rd degrees has a

---

[97] Neil Bibby. *Music and Mathematics. From Pythagoras to Fractals.* (Oxford: Oxford University Press, 2003).

ratio of 10:9. The gap between these two different steps (9/8 x 10/9) is the ratio 81/80 which is known as the 'syntonic comma'.[98] Although this is not discernible to all listeners and does not pose a problem for instruments that have a continuous range of notes such as violins, for instruments with fixed keys or holes it makes playing in more than one key often difficult and sometimes impossible. Keyboard instruments were particularly problematic in this respect. The celebrated German/Viennese piano maker Johann Jakob Könnicke (1756-1811) attempted to solve this problem when in 1796 he invented the 'Harmonie-Hammerflügel', a keyboard instrument with six diatonic manuals that divided the normal 12-key octave into 31 notes to enable a purer tuning. Unfortunately it was difficult to build, as well as difficult to keep in tune and to perform on.[99]

Equal temperament

The answer to this problem was to be found in equal temperament tuning. The word tempered refers to the fact that just intonation has been adjusted or compromised. It is so named because the scale is divided into 12 equal semitones. In this system, the circle of 5ths is closed. This means that there are no discrepancies between different keys, all the intervals across keys are equivalent, making it possible to play music with multiple key changes and chromatic harmony.

Rather than using the whole number ratios found in the Pythagorean scale and just intonation, the Flemish mathematician Simon Stevin (1548-1620) came up with the idea of letting the half step (semitone) equal $\sqrt[12]{2}$, the 12th root of 2 which can also be written as $2^{2/12}$. In other words, when multiplied by itself 12 times, $2^{2/12} = 2$. This is an irrational number in contrast with the rational numbers used in the aforementioned systems. The Pythagoreans were strong believers in the importance of rational numbers, those numbers which are either integers or can be written as a ratio (or quotient) of two integers. An irrational number is a real number which cannot be expressed as

---

98   Roberts, *From Music to Mathematics*, 129.
99   Michael Latcham. 'Könnicke, Johann Jakob' in Grove Music online.

an integer or as a quotient of two integers. Irrational numbers have infinite, non-repeating decimals.

Having established $2^{2/12}$ as the interval for a half step, Stevin went on to define all the other intervals by multipliers of this step (see Table 4). The numbers in the 3rd column are easily found by calculating the number of half steps in each interval.

Table 4 – Ratios used in Stevin's equal temperament

Degree of scale	Interval	Ratio
1 - C	Unison	1
2 - D	Major 2nd	$2^{2/12}$
3 - E	Major 3rd	$2^{4/12}$
4 - F	Perfect 4th	$2^{5/12}$
5 - G	Perfect 5th	$2^{7/12}$
6 - A	Major 6th	$2^{9/12}$
7 - B	Major 7th	$2^{11/12}$
8 = 1 - C	Octave	2

Marin Mersenne (1588-1648) made an important contribution to the theory of tuning and was an advocate of equal temperament. He also reassessed the nature of consonance and dissonance. The most famous early work to use the system and exploit all 24 keys is J S Bach's *Well-Tempered Clavier* – the two books were written in 1722 and 1738-1744 each comprising a prelude and fugue in each major and minor key. It took a long time for equal temperament to be adopted across Western music; as late as 1851, not one of the British organs at the Great Exhibition was equally tempered.[100] Equal temperament is now widely thought of as the normal tuning of the Western 12-note chromatic scale. Table 5 compares the frequencies of notes in a scale of A major according to the ratios of the Pythagorean scale and the equal tempered scale measured in Hertz.

---

100   Bibby, Music and Mathematics, 27.

Frequency expresses the number of repetitions during a certain length of time. It is measured in time units, usually seconds, and called Hertz after the German physicist Heinrich Hertz (1857–1894). A tuning fork that vibrates 440 times back and forth in one second, concert A, has a frequency at 440 Hz.[101] The set of frequencies 100, 200, 300, 400, 500 Hz ... is a harmonic series whose fundamental is 100 Hz and whose 5th harmonic is 500 Hz.

Table 5 – A comparison of frequencies used in equal temperament and the Pythagorean scale

	A	B	C#	D	E	F#	G#	A
Equal temperament	220.0	246.9	277.2	293.7	329.6	370.0	415.3	440.0
Pythagorean scale	220.0	247.5	278.4	293.3	330.0	371.3	417.7	440.0

Table 6 shows the approximate differences in frequencies for a whole step (tone) and half step (semitone) used in the equal tempered scale and the Pythagorean scale.

Table 6 – A comparison of the frequencies for a tone and a semitone used in equal temperament and the Pythagorean scale

	tone	semitone
Equal temperament	$2^{1/12} = 1.122$	$2^{2/12} = 1.0595$
Pythagorean	$9/8 = 1.125$	$256/243 = 1.0535$

Another commonly used way of measuring the intervals in different tuning systems is through the use of cents. Cents are based on a logarithmic scale and there are 100 cents in an octave. The system was introduced in the late nineteenth century by the English mathematician Alexander Ellis (1804-90). In his analysis of the scales used in various European musical traditions, he showed that the diversity of different systems could not be explained by a single physical law.

---

101   Concert A is the standard tuning note in the UK and USA. Until the nineteenth century musical pitch was not standardized and the levels varied widely across Europe. Nowadays ensembles which specialise in music of the Baroque period have agreed on a standard of A = 415 Hz.

DIATONIC SCALES AND TUNING

Table 7 gives a comparison of the three tuning systems discussed so far measured in cents. It can be seen that although equal temperament is a close approximation to the perfect 5th is significantly sharper than a major 3rd in equal temperament.

Table 7 – A comparison of the frequencies used in the Pythagorean scale, equal temperament and just intonation measured in cents

Scale degree	Interval	Pythagorean scale	Equal temperament	Just intonation
1	Unison	0	0	0
2	Major 2nd	203.9	203.9	200
3	Major 3rd	407.8	386.3	400
4	Perfect 4th	498.0	498.0	500
5	Perfect 5th	702.0	702.0	700
6	Major 6th	905.9	884.4	900
7	Major 7th	1109.8	1088.3	1100
8 = 1	Octave	1200	1200	1200

Moving away from the seven-note diatonic major scale with its use of tones and semitones, the next chapter goes on to look at a variety of other scales using a different number of notes and often including the interval of a microtone.

7 More scales: whole tone, octatonic, pentatonic, and scales that use microtones

THIS CHAPTER OPENS by describing modes of limited transposition, such as the whole tone scale and the octatonic scale, giving examples of their use in Western classical and pop music. It then moves on to the ubiquitous pentatonic scale, the five-note scale which is found in different forms across the world. The next section looks at some of the scales formed by dividing the octave into more than 12 semitones, made possible through the use of microtones, intervals smaller than a semitone. It discusses the long history of experimentation with equal temperament systems, notably the 19-note, 31-note and 53-note scales, and describes some of the instruments devised to accommodate them. The chapter concludes by looking at two twentieth-century composers who have used microtonal material in their music; the Czech composer Alois Hába was one of the first and went on to establish a department of microtonal music in Prague. Sometime itinerant hobo, the American Harry Partch, was similarly devoted to the cause of microtonal music, he rejected Western scales and invented his own, one of which was made up of 43 notes to the octave.

Modes of limited transposition

Olivier Messiaen was the first to use the term modes of limited transposition to denote scales which can be transposed a limited number of times before the original set of pitches reappears. The symmetry inherent in these modes means that no note can be perceived as the tonic they lend themselves to static harmony or what Messiaen described as containing "the charm of impossibilities".[102]

---

102   Messiaen, Olivier. *Technique of My Musical Language* (Paris: Alphonse Leduc, 1944): 58.

The two most common examples of modes of limited transposition are the whole tone scale and the octatonic scale (both of which were already in existence before Messiaen coined the term).

Whole tone scale

The whole tone scale is made up of six whole tones starting on either C or Db (its only transposition).

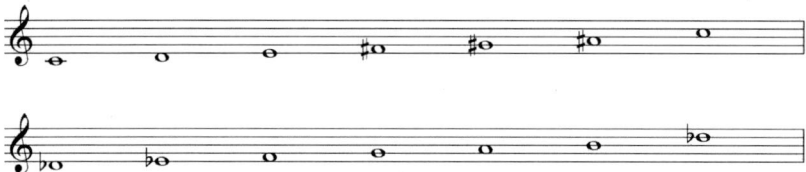

Messiaen refers to this as his first mode of limited transposition. Another French composer, Claude Debussy (1862-1918), uses the whole tone scale in 'La soirée dans Grenade' from his piano suite *Estampes*. In this languid movement, Debussy evokes images of Spain through strumming guitar sounds and a *habanera* rhythm. From bar 23 onwards he uses notes from the whole tone scale below to evoke the exotic atmosphere.

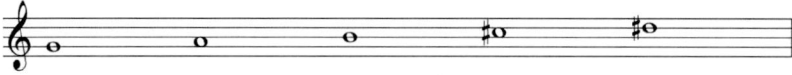

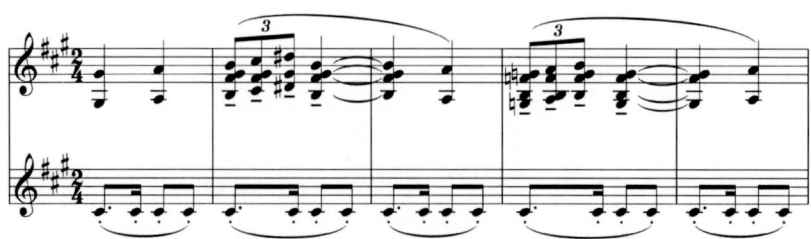

This corresponds with the second whole tone scale shown above, but using enharmonic equivalents for Db (C#) and Eb (D#).[103]

The whole tone scale is not often found in pop music but Stevie Wonder uses the scale in the Intro to 'You are the sunshine of my life' and it is found relatively frequently in jazz, by performers including John Coltrane, Thelonius Monk and Art Tatum.

Octatonic scale

The octatonic scale is made up of eight notes alternating tones and semitones. Each octatonic scale has two versions or modes; one starting with a whole step (tone) and the other starting with a half step (semitone). So, for example, starting on C the two modes are

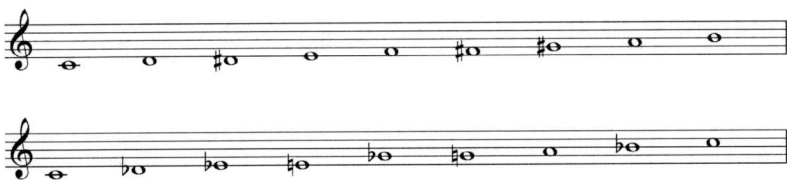

The octatonic scale can start on any note, but in all, because the same series of notes appears with different starting notes, it is limited to three different patterns. As well as the two above, the remaining pattern is as follows.

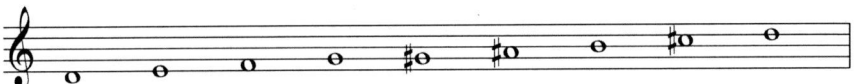

Messiaen refers to this as his second mode of limited transposition. Instances of the octatonic scale are generally fairly rare although, as Allen Forte notes

---

103 Notes that sound the same but are written (or 'spelt') differently are said to be enharmonic e.g. Db and C# where Db is the enharmonic equivalent of C#.

in his article about Debussy's use of the octatonic scale, '…it should be emphasised that '… octatonicism was "in the air" during the early twentieth century'. Along with works by Debussy (including the opera *Pelléas et Mélisande*), Forte goes on to cite Strauss's opera *Elektra* (1908), the second of Webern's *Four Pieces for Violin and Piano* (1910), and Ravel's song 'Surgi de la croupe et du bond' (1913) from the *Trois poèmes de Mallarmé*.[104] Scriabin's *Sixth Sonata, Op. 62* for piano (1911) could be added to this list as could its use in Stravinsky's ballets *Petrushka* and *Rite of Spring* and several pieces in Bartók's *Mikrokosmos* including 'From the island of Bali'. A rare example to be found in pop music is the intro to the Radiohead song 'Just'.

Pentatonic scales

All the scales discussed so far are predominantly found in Western classical music and most have seven notes. In contrast, the most widespread scales, both geographically and historically, are pentatonic scales formed of five pitches. They can be found in traditional music across the world from the British Isles, to China, Japan, Lapland, Hungary, West Africa and in the music of the indigenous people of the Americas. There are also examples in Western classical music through the centuries, from Gregorian chant to the piano music of Debussy and they can be heard in some blues, gospel and rock music. Three well-known examples of songs using pentatonic scales are 'Amazing grace', 'Nobody knows the trouble I've seen' and 'Auld Lang Syne'. Pentatonic scales are useful when improvising because they work well over several chords and have a major/minor ambiguity. They are not uncommon in pop music, 'Shape of you' by Ed Sheeran, is an example as are several songs by The Smiths including 'Heaven knows I'm miserable now' and 'There is a light that never goes out'.

Pentatonic scales can be categorized as either hemitonic (with semitones) or anhemitonic (without semitones). The formation varies from country to country, and region to region. Two of the most well-known forms are found below. The first example uses only the white notes of the piano, whereas the second uses only black notes.

---

104   Allen Forte. 'Debussy and the Octatonic'. *Music Analysis*, Vol. 10, No. 1/2 (1991): 159.

Note that each of these contains the circle of 5ths. In the first example, for instance, C-G-D-A-E

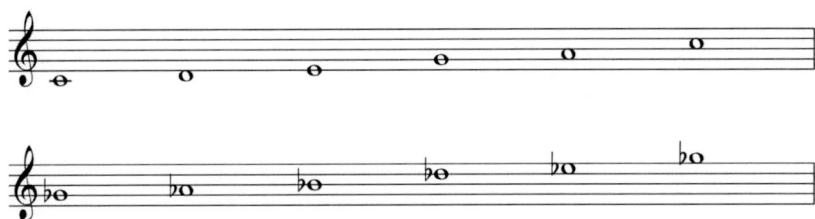

Slendro, an anhemitonic pentatonic scale, is one of the two major tunings in Javanese gamelan music, the other is pelog, a seven note scale. The five notes of slendro approximate those shown below.

At first sight the intervals employed in slendro seem to equate to the pentatonic scale on the black keys, a mixture of whole tones and minor thirds which are easily distinguished by ear. However, the five notes of slendro are more or less equally spaced, the resultant intervals lie somewhere between a whole tone and a minor third although this is not standardized and differs from one gamelan to another – the intervallic structure is known as *embat* and this marks out the personality of the gamelan.[105]

In 1889 Debussy attended the Exposition Universelle in Paris where he was particularly impressed by a Javanese gamelan with its ensemble of tuned percussion, gongs and metallophones of different sizes. In his evocative piece 'Pagodes', from the piano suite *Estampes*, he attempted to capture some of the Javanese gamelan sound partly through his use of the pentatonic scale which he uses to emulate the slendro scale. Here is the melody line in bars 3 - 4.

---

105   Neil Sorrell. *A Guide to the Gamelan.* (London: Faber and Faber, 1990): 56.

A preponderance of consonant intervals can be formed from the pentatonic scale. The nineteenth-century physician Hermann von Helmholtz (1821-1894) explained the relative consonance and dissonance of musical intervals in terms of the extent of the beating between the two notes when they are heard simultaneously. He discovered that notes whose fundamental frequencies are related by small whole number ratios have reduced beating because of the coincidences between the frequencies of the harmonics involved. Thus a perfect 5th, with a frequency ratio of 3:2, is a smooth/consonant interval with low beating because the 3rd harmonic of the lower note coincides with the 2nd harmonic of the upper note. In his study of the relative number of consonant and dissonant intervals formed by pairing notes in different scales, David Huron discovered that the pentatonic scale exhibited an optimum number of consonant intervals. He argued that the

> frequency of occurrence of various interval given pitch-class set can be correlated with corresponding perceived consonance for each interval class. If one of the composer's aesthetic goals is to generate predominantly consonant music, an appropriate choice of palette would maximize the availability of consonant harmonic intervals while minimizing the presence of dissonant harmonic interval'.[106]

It is difficult to give reasons for the ubiquity of the pentatonic scale, but it may be connected with the fact that it can be generated from the circle of 5ths and what has been described as optimum consonance.[107] Another reason may be its harmonic adaptability when improvising. However, the extent of the influence these features account for in terms of ubiquity is merely speculative.

---

106 David Huron. 'Interval-Class Content in Equally Tempered Pitch-Class Sets: Common Scales Exhibit Optimum Tonal Consonance' Source. *Music Perception: An Interdisciplinary Journal*, Spring, 1994, Vol. 11: 289-305.
107 Huron, 'Interval-Class Content', 301.

Scales that divide the octave into more than 12 notes

Most of the scales described so far divide the octave up into 12 semitones. The next section looks at some of the scales formed by dividing the octave into more than 12 divisions. This is made possible by the use of microtones, intervals smaller than a semitone. The term quarter tone is sometimes used, but this is not always accurate given that the interval may be larger or smaller than a quarter tone.[108] Since antiquity mathematicians and musicians have experimented with such equal temperament systems, notably the 19-note, 31-note and 53-note scales. The interval tunings that arise from these divisions are often closer to those found in the harmonic series (just intonation) rather than in 12 note equal temperament.[109]

19-note, 31-note and 53-note systems

Interest in the 19–note and 31-note systems dates from the sixteenth century when such systems were explored by various mathematicians. Könnicke's 'Harmonie-Hammerflügel' use of six diatonic manuals to divide the normal 12-key octave into 31 notes has already been mentioned (see page 108).[110] This was not the first instrument to experiment with this system. In 1637 Mersenne described a keyboard instrument utilising the 31-note scale in his treatise *Harmonie Universelle*, an outline of his theoretical and practical ideas on music. The instrument functions by having alternative keys for some notes, the tunings for these alternatives differing by the syntonic comma.[111] The Dutch mathematician and astronomer Christiaan Huygens (1629- 1695) took a different approach; he used logarithmic measurements of intervals to ascertain the equal division of the octave into 31 parts. His

---

108   Microtones are commonly used in contemporary near Eastern musical traditions such as those found in some Turkish, Arabic, Persian and Greek music.
109   In their study of microtones and projective planes, Wilson and Gamer compare the number of cents found in various intervals across scales using just ratios, 12 notes, 19 notes, 31 and 53 notes. See Robin Wilson and Carlton Gamer 'Microtones and projective planes' in John Fauvel, Raymond Flood, and Robin Wilson. *Music and Mathematics*. (Oxford: Oxford University Press, 2003): 148.
110   Michael Latcham. 'Könnicke, Johann Jakob' in *Grove Music*.
111   Neil Bibby. *Music and Mathematics. From Pythagoras to Fractals*. (Oxford: Oxford University Press, 2003): 22-23.

ideas are summarised in his *Lettre touchant le cycle harmonique* (1691) which includes a description of an imaginary transposing harpsichord, with 31 strings to the octave and a shifting keyboard of 12 notes which used various selections from the 31-note set.

Interest in the 53 note system can be traced back to antiquity. It originated from the fact that a series of 53 perfect 5ths equates very closely to 31 octaves. The difference between the two was calculated as $3^{53}/284$ by Nicholas Mercator (1620-1687) hence its name, the Mercator comma. Although conventional staff notation can be adapted for the 19-note and 31-note systems, this proves difficult with 53 notes, as does performance.

Indian classical music and the 22-note system

Indian music uses just intonation and the use of equal temperament is unknown. In Hindustani (North Indian) classical music, an octave is called *saptak* and has seven notes called *swara*. These can be further divided into 22 notes known as *sruti* or *shruti*. The seven notes are sa, re, ga, ma, pa, dha, ni (similar to the Western do re mi fa so la ti). The notes of the Indian scale are as follows.

Shadja (Sa), *Rishabha* (Re), *Gandhara* (Ga), *Madhyama* (Ma), *Panchama* (Pa), *Dhaivata* (Dha), *Nishada* (Ni).

The 22 note system was developed from early experiments in ancient and medieval times based on the fact that the highly concordant notes *panchama* and *madhyama* have ratios of 3:2 and 4:3 respectively. Further research was undertaken to determine the other ratios.

Table 1 – Ratios used in the Indian scale

Degree of scale	Ratio
Sa	1
Re	9/8
Ga	5/4
Ma	4/3
Pa	3/2
Dha	5/3 or 27.16
Ni	15/8
Sa	2/1

The research examined both the cycle of 4ths and the circle of 5ths (see pages 104-5). It was found that the 12th note of the cycle in one case and the 11th and 12th notes in the other case were higher or lower by a small interval, again this gap was found to be in the ratio 81/80, equivalent to the 'syntonic comma' but known as the *praman* or *pramana sruti* in Indian music theory. Using *srutis*, precisely tuned microtones, the scale can be further divided into 22 notes.[112] The first and fifth notes (sa and pa) have only one variant, whereas all the other degrees of the scale (re, ga, ma, dha, and ni) have two variants each. There are ten pairs of notes and these along with the sa and pa give the 22 *srutis* of the Indian musical scale, these are mainly used in ornamentation. The two notes constituting each pair are found to be uniformly separated by the 81/80 interval of a comma or *pramana sruti*. The notes re, ga, dha, and ni have natural and flat variants, while ma has a natural and a sharp variant.

Microtonal material used in twentieth century classical music

During the twentieth century a number of Western classical composers incorporated microtonal material into some of their music, notable examples

---

112 P. Sambamurthy. *South Indian Music Book V. (Chennai: The Indian Music Publishing House, 1963).*

including Charles Ives 'Three Quarter-Tone Pieces' (1925) for two pianos tuned a quarter tone apart, and Karlheinz Stockhausen, whose electronic piece *Studie I* (1953) uses 25 equal-tempered intervals within each span of two and a half octaves but the most notable pioneers of microtonal music were perhaps Alois Hába and Harry Partch.

Alois Hába

The Czech composer Alois Hába (1893-1973) could be credited as the first to use quarter tones and sixth tones in Western art music. His parents were both folk musicians and his mother, a singer, taught him peasant songs from Moravia. These could be characterised by their use of microtones to heighten the expressive effect, the major mode using quarter-tone and sixth-tone sharps, the minor by quarter-tone flats. In 1917 he composed his Suite for string orchestra, his first composition to use quarter-tones and went on to write a great many microtonal works from piano pieces to an opera. In 1923 he established a department of microtonal music at the Prague Conservatory. In order to perform microtonal music Hába constructed special instruments: three types of quarter-tone piano, a quarter-tone and a sixth-tone harmonium, and a quarter-tone clarinet, trumpet and guitar. The opera *Matka* ('The Mother', 1929) is arguably Hába's masterpiece.[113]

Harry Partch, *U. S. Highball (A Musical Account of a Transcontinental Hobo Trip)*

The American composer, instrument maker and philosopher Harry Partch (1901 – 1974) rejected Western scales and invented his own, one of which was made up of 43 notes to the octave. His work was inspired by ancient Greek music theory and the work of Herman von Helmholtz.[114] Partch describes

---

113   Jiří Vysloužil. 'Hába, Alois' in *Grove Music.*.
114   Herman von Helmholz. *On the Sensations of Tone as a Physiological Basis for the Theory of Music*, 1865 (London: Dover, 1954).

how he arrived at this scale and others in his book *Genesis of Music* (1949).[115] The scale is based on a 'tonality diamond'; an arrangement of ratios in a diamond shape where the diagonals sloping in one direction form 'Otonalities' and the diagonals in the other direction form 'Utonalities'. Partch's tonality diamond is similar to the diamond devised by Max Friedrich Meyer some 50 years earlier.[116] Having devised the 43-note scale, Partch devoted his time to implementing this system, creating new instruments that could be tuned to this new scale and then training performers to play them.

In 1935 at the height of the Great Depression he began a transient existence in the western states, jumping trains, sometimes living in boxcars in train yards, and picking up work occasionally. For several years he kept a small notepad that he used to transcribe fragments of conversations, writings on the sides of boxcars, names of stations and thoughts. These notes became the basis for *U.S. Highball*, a piece for speaker and Partch's instruments. In 1943 he started work on the first draft using the motley assortment of instruments he had built at that point. These included the Adapted Guitar (a guitar with new frets to accommodate his tuning system), the Chromelodeon (a re-tuned foot-pump harmonium), and the Kithara (his own version of the ancient Greek stringed instrument but now with 72 strings). New instruments were added for the second version including a set of marimba-based instruments; a smaller version of the 72 string Kithara (Surrogate Kithara), and a collection of tuned artillery shells and Pyrex water containers. Partch took the comments he had recorded in his notebook and turned them into melodies including quotes from hoboes such as "Hey, don't sleep with your head against the end of the car! You'll get your neck broke when she jerks!" With the small intervals in his new system of tuning applied to both voice and instruments, sliding steam whistle sounds and occasionally rhythmic percussive sounds, *U. S. Highball* has a surreal atmosphere, but it is oddly reminiscent of a train journey.

This chapter and the preceding one have outlined some of the mathematical and scientific thinking behind the creation and analysis of common and less common scales. This field encompasses a vast area of research which has

---

115   Harry Partch. *Genesis of a Music: an Account of a Creative Work, its Roots and its Fulfillments* (Madison: WI, 1949, enlarged 2/1974).
116   For more detail of the tonality diamond see Chris Forster. *Musical Mathematics. On the Art and Science of Acoustic Instruments*. (San Francisco: Chronicle Books, 2010).

attracted many leading musicians, mathematicians and thinkers over the centuries including J S Bach and Messiaen, Pythagoras, Newton, Kepler, Mersenne, and Hertz, so that inevitably the surface has only been scratched both historically and geographically. In the twenty-first century, technological advances mean that electronic music facilitates any kind of tuning without the need for retuning or the construction of customised instruments.

8 Serialism and the 12-note scale

PERHAPS MORE THAN any other technique of composing, serialism is rooted in mathematical concepts. It is algorithmic in its use of a strict set of procedures to generate a note row and it uses symmetrical transformations in the construction of different rows. This chapter looks at the procedures of serialism in the music of its originator, the Austrian composer Arnold Schoenberg (1874 – 1951) focussing on his *Variations for Orchestra*. It goes on to examine the different compositional approaches of the other two members of what is known as the Second Viennese School[117] - Alban Berg (1885 – 1935) and Anton Webern (1883 – 1945). The next sections look at extensions of serial approaches: rhythmic serialism where patterns of durations are ordered, and total serialism where algorithms are applied to further elements of the music such as dynamics and attack. The chapter ends with a more detailed exploration of both mathematical and musical considerations with a discussion of whether the two can be reconciled.

The twelve-note system of serialism (sometimes known as dodecaphony) follows strict mathematical rules in the form of an algorithm. First of all a note row (or series) is composed - this uses all of the 12 notes of the chromatic scale and is the basis of the whole composition. None of the notes are repeated in the note row (also known as the prime order or prime series). The note row can exist at each of the transpositional levels, as can each of the inversion, retrograde and retrograde inversions. This means that the row

---

[117] The Second Viennese School is an umbrella term for the composers Schoenberg, Berg and Webern. It is sometimes understood to include other pupils of Schoenberg. It is based on the tenuous notion that there was a First Viennese School which might have included Haydn, Mozart, Beethoven and Schubert.

can be used in any of its 48 forms. It can also be transformed through scale symmetry in two ways: augmentation and diminution. The durations of the original notes can be lengthened (augmentation), or shortened (diminution). The original notes can also be used in another octave (octave displacement). There are four main permutations of the row, each of these is rooted in symmetrical transformation. They are often referred to as the prime order, inversion, retrograde and retrograde inversion.

Here are the four permutations of the note row used in the first movement (Introduction and Theme) of Schoenberg's *Variations for Orchestra*, Op. 31 (1928), his first twelve-tone composition for a large ensemble.

Prime order – P

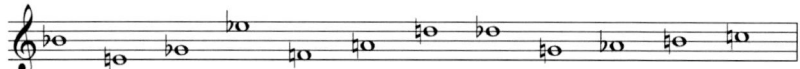

Inversion – I uses horizontal reflection, each of the intervals is turned upside down

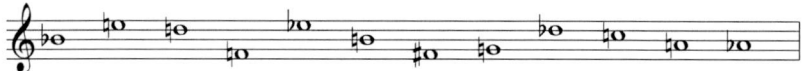

Retrograde - R uses vertical reflection where the note row is played backwards

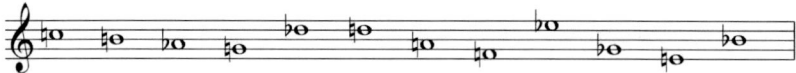

Retrograde inversion – RI. The inversion can be played backwards. In other words it undergoes a $180°$ rotation.

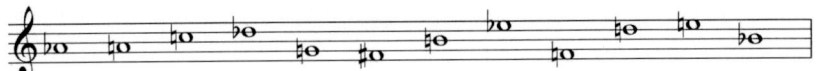

All the material of the *Variations for Orchestra* is derived from the four versions of the row. Following the 'Introduction', the second section of the *Variations for Orchestra*, 'Theme' (bars 34-57) presents four linear statements of the theme in the order P, RI, R, I. Schoenberg marks this with the word 'Haupstimme', a term he used to denote the principal part in a complex texture.

In addition to the symmetrical aspects, the notes of the row can also be used vertically to make chords (sometimes known as verticalisation). Schoenberg excluded the use of consonant chords because of their tonal qualities. It can be seen from the examples below that the Prime row and the Retrograde Inversion (in transposition) are both made up from the same two hexachords – Bb E Gb Eb F A and D Db G Ab B C.

Prime order – P

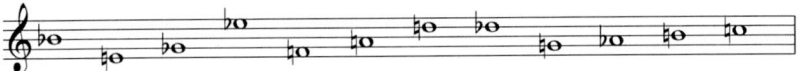

Retrograde inversion – RI in transposition

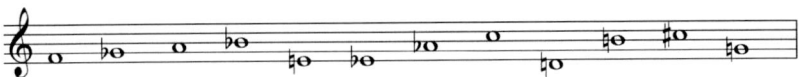

Together these two hexachords form a 12-note aggregate. The series is therefore said to show the property of 'combinatoriality', a technique found in twelve-note compositions whereby a collection of pitch classes (in this case P) can be combined with a transformation of itself (in this case RI) to form an aggregate of all 12 pitch classes. The term 'combinatorics' has been borrowed from mathematics where it refers to the study of the enumeration, combination and permutation of sets of elements and the mathematical characteristics of their properties.

Alban Berg

Each of the three members of the Second Viennese School took a different approach to serialism. Alban Berg, a pupil of Schoenberg, was quite free in his use of the note row reconciling twelve tone procedures and tonal harmony. His music tends not to keep to a single series, even within a movement. He also incorporated tonal elements into the twelve-tone language, notably in his Violin Concerto (1935) where the original row uses eight ascending thirds followed by a note row and consequently spells out two major and two minor chords

1 + 2 + 3 = G minor, 3 + 4 + 5 = D major, 5 + 6 + 7 = A minor, and 7 + 8 + 9 = E major.
8 – 12 = five notes of a whole tone scale.

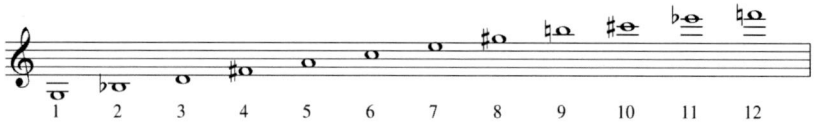

The Violin Concerto also uses a Bach chorale taken from his Cantata No. 60 and a Corinthian folk tune, both tonal in nature.

Anton Webern

Webern, who also studied with Schoenberg, took a much stricter approach to the dodecaphonic rules: unlike Berg, he always used a single series for each composition and suppressed all repetition of material. He constantly exploited the possibilities of the note row with much use of concentrated motivic working and symmetrical structures. In his *Concerto Op. 24* (1934) this symmetry can be seen within the row itself where the notes 1 - 6 and similarly 7 – 12 can be reflected along the middle to give a mirror image where the same order of intervals appears forwards as well as backwards (see below).

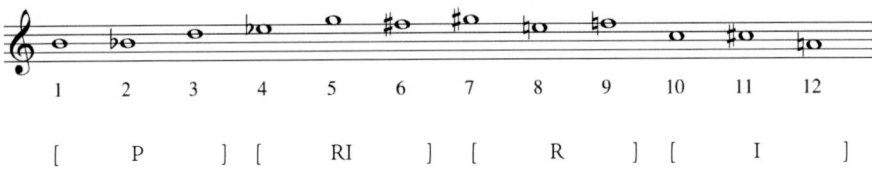

The order of intervals between the first six notes is as follows

B to Bb (semitone) Bb to D (major 3rd) D to Eb (semitone) Eb to G (major 3rd) G to F# (semitone)

In reverse order (retrograde) the notes F# G Eb D Bb B follow the same pattern - semitone, major 3rd, semitone, major 3rd semitone.

Furthermore if the notes 1- 3 are regarded as a microcosmic Prime version, then 4- 6 is the Retrograde Inversion, 7 – 9 is the Retrograde and 10 – 12 is the Inversion.

Here are the opening bars of Webern's *Concerto Op. 24* which illustrate how Webern has used the row in harmony in his composition. The parts enter in this order – oboe (P), flute (RI), trumpet (R) and then clarinet (I). The piano enters in bar 4 where the overlapping parts follow this order – P (retrograde), RI (retrograde), R (retrograde), I (retrograde). Notice how various forms of the row are unfolded simultaneously, beginning on different beats of the bar and interlocking (see below). This all helps to create a complex rhythmic structure, a characteristic of Webern's compositional style.

In his *Symphony Op. 21* (1928), and all the works that followed, the twelve-tone technique was used with unprecedented strictness and the concept was extended to include, not just pitch, but also timbre and rhythm. In Webern's words,

> So what has in fact been achieved by this [twelve-note] method of composition?… What territory, what doors have been opened with this secret key? To be very general, it's a matter of creating a means to express the greatest possible unity in music.[118]

Serialism with other pitch-class collections

Before he arrived at his twelve-tone system, Schoenberg compositions included series containing a number of pitch classes greater or lesser than

---

118   Letter from Anton Webern to Alban Berg cited in *Die Reihe 2: Anton Webern*. (London: Universal Edition, 1960): 42.

12. In the *Five Piano Pieces Op. 23*, for example, No. 2, uses a series of nine different pitch classes and No. 3 is based on a 14-note series. Similarly, before Stravinsky fully adopted 12-note serialism in *Threni* (1957–8) he used series with fewer than 12 pitch classes; *In memoriam Dylan Thomas* (1954), for example, uses a series of only five pitch classes. There are also examples of series with more than 12 pitch classes which include Berio's *Nones for orchestra* (1954) which is based on a 13-note series made up of two overlapping heptachords, the second being the retrograde inversion of the first.[119]

Rhythmic serialism

As Paul Griffiths points out 'interpretations of rhythmic serialism are problematic. There is no equivalence class to correspond with the pitch class ... there is no analogue for inversion'.[120] An early example of the use of ordered patterns of durations can be found in the third movement of Berg's *Lyric Suite* (1926) where he creates a rhythmic series made up of 12 durations, each of one, two or three units. The series is used in exact retrogrades, and is varied by adding rests and 'transposed' by multiplying all the values by the same integer. In 1940 Webern composed his *Variations Op. 30* for orchestra which uses versions of two rhythmic motifs presented in the opening bars and derived from the note row. These are in effect sets of durations.

The American composer Milton Babbitt (1916-2011), a trained mathematician, demonstrated and formalized many aspects of 12-tone compositional technique in several important essays where he introduced algebra and number theory to model 12-note rows and operations. In 'Some Aspects of Twelve-Tone Composition' (1955), 'Twelve-Tone Invariants as Compositional Determinants' (1960), and 'Set Structure as a Compositional Determinant' (1961) he introduced terms derived from mathematics such as 'source set', 'aggregate,' 'secondary set', and 'derived set.' These terms were used in the classification of different types of pitch class set and helped to describe the different procedures used by such sets. He coined the term 'combinatorial' to describe 12-tone sets that yield aggregate and secondary

---

119   Paul Griffiths in 'Serialism' in *Grove Music*
120   Ibid.

set formations. This nomenclature has since become widely adopted as the basis for theoretical work notably in music set theory.[121]

In 'Twelve-Tone Rhythmic Structure and the Electronic Medium' (1962) Babbitt demonstrated a variety of methods for interpreting the structures of pitch class sets in the rhythmic domain.[122] This included an analogy between the octave (in pitch structure) and the bar (in rhythmic and metrical structure) by dividing the bar into 12 equal units each of which can be articulated by individual points of attack. In this way pitch class sets can be mapped onto 'time-point sets' where a set of integers can be interpreted both as a pitch class set and as a time-point set, defined as the duration which separates the attack from the beginning of the bar. So, for example, 0, 11, 6, 7, 5, 1, 10, 2, 9, 3, 4, 8 can be interpreted as a pitch class set where the numbers are generated by counting up in semitones from the first note (designated as 0) (see below).[123]

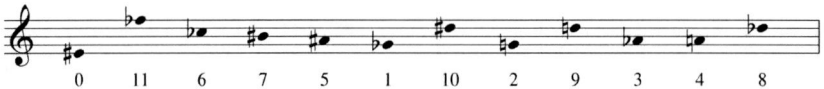

or as a time-point set a particular point of attack is a measure of its position within the bar. In the example below the metrical unit is a demi-semiquaver, a 12th of the whole bar. Here the 12 available points of attack within a bar are ordered according to the numerical set given above. Time-point 0 occurs on the first demi-semiquaver of the bar, time-point 1 on the next, and so on (see below).

---

121 Set theory in music originated with Milton Babbitt and was then formulated in 1973 by the American music theorist Allan Forte. This led to more rigorous theoretical formulations by John Rahn, Robert Morris and David Lewin who applied mathematical group theory to music.

122 "Twelve-Tone Rhythmic Structure and the Electronic Medium," *PNM*, i/1 (1962), 49–79; repr. in *Perspectives on Contemporary Music Theory*, ed. B. Boretz and E.T. Cone (New York, 1972), 148–79.

123 Elaine Barkin, revised by Martin Brody and Judith Crispin. 'Milton Babbitt' in *Grove Music*

Babbitt used this method in his *Second String Quartet* (1954). The time-point series is manipulated to produce different versions of the rows: inversion by complementation of the time-point numbers to 12; transposition by the addition of a constant value to each time-point number; and retrograde by using the time-point set backwards.[124]

Total serialism

In the early 1950s, several composers including Boulez, Stockhausen, Maderna and Nono extended the procedures of serialism to the other aspects of the music beyond pitch, such as rhythm, dynamics, tempo, timbre and note attack. This method has become known as total serialism or integral serialism. These composers were much associated with the Darmstadt School, a loose grouping of composers associated with the International Summer Courses for New Music in Darmstadt, West Germany.

An early example of total serialism can be found in Babbitt's *Three Compositions for Piano* (1947). Here points of articulation are determined by a set along with dynamics and pitch set classes. In 1949, Messiaen composed his piano piece *Mode de valeurs et d'intensités* (Mode of Durations and Intensities) which was based on scales, not only of pitch but also of duration, attack and dynamics. Two years later Boulez based his piece *Structures 1a* (1951) entirely on the note row used by Messiaen in *Mode de valeurs et d'intensités*. From this he created two number matrices which represented all 48 versions of the row. An integer was assigned to each pitch class, so for example Eb = 1, D = 2 and so on. From these matrices he derived another system to determine the durations of notes where the integers were read as numbers of demi-semiquavers (sixteenth notes). In addition, each statement of the row was given a particular dynamic

---

124   Griffiths, 'Serialism', *Grove Music*.

and mode of attack.[125] These matrices could be described as a pair of magic squares (see Chapter 14 for more detail).

Another leading figure in the serialist avant garde was Karlheinz Stockhausen (1928-2007), himself a teacher at Darmstadt. In his works from 1953 onwards, serial organization permeates every level of the formal process. His works *Kreuzspiel* (1959) and the *Schlagtrio*, are examples of 'total serialism' where the basic series is permutated and applied to durations, dynamics and articulation as well as pitch. In his *Elektronische Studien* (1954) he applied similar rules to the organization of pitch, rhythm and timbre. His work *Gruppen* (1957) for three orchestras (combining 109 players) and three conductors explores the possibilities of different simultaneous tempos using sets of tempi.

Some mathematical considerations

Serialism draws heavily on mathematical principles as we have seen above: it is algorithmic in its use of a strict set of procedures designed to be applied systematically; it uses symmetrical transformations in the construction of different rows (vertical and horizontal reflection, translation and 180^0 rotation) and it uses combinatorics in its formulation of harmonies.

Babbitt's theoretical writings about 12-note music eventually led to the formulation and development of music set theory which has some parallels in mathematical set theory and group theory. In music a set is a group of pitch classes, usually a 12-note set, it may also be a set of other musical elements such as durations or dynamics. Music set theory assigns integers to different pitch classes, categorises musical objects and analyses their relationships through operations such as transpositions and inversions.

Because the series can use transpositions of the 12 notes of the chromatic scale, as can each of the inversion, retrograde and retrograde inversions, the original series can exist in 48 different forms. However it is not always the case that a note row will generate 48 different forms. There are some rows which will generate the same row under certain operations, particularly if

---

125   Jonathan Cross. 'Composing with numbers' in John Fauvel, Raymond Flood and Robin Wilson. *Music and Mathematics*. (Oxford: Oxford University Press, 2003): 137 and Paul Griffiths in 'Serialism' in *Grove Music*.

SERIALISM AND THE 12-NOTE SCALE

the original row demonstrates some kind of symmetry. For example, if we were to take a descending chromatic scale beginning on C as the note row then the Prime order would be as follows.

The Inversion would be

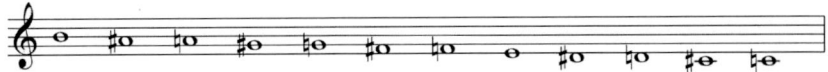

and the Retrograde Inversion would be

which is, of course, the same as the original row. In other words it is invariant. In mathematics, an invariant is a property of a mathematical object which remains unchanged after operations or transformations are applied to the objects.

To find the total possible number of note rows, we use the mathematical symbol $n!$ which is referred to as n factorial. It is the product of all positive integers less than or equal to n.

$n! = n \times (n-1) \times (n-2) \times (n-3) \times 3 \times 2 \times 1$

There are 12! possible permutations of the row which is calculated thus

$12! = 12 \times 11 \times 10 \times 9 \times 8 \times 7 \times 6 \times 5 \times 4 \times 3 \times 2 \times 1 = 479{,}001{,}600$

Another, more tenuous, connection to mathematics has been made to Einstein's 1915 Theory of General Relativity. In his book *Music by the Numbers*, Eli Maor argues that a comparison can be made between Schoenberg's serialism and Einstein's theory of relativity where all systems of reference are equal to each other, the democracy of the twelve notes and their lack of hierarchical relationships meant that 'Henceforth only the position of each note relative to its immediate predecessor would matter; you might call it relativistic music'. Maor quotes the words of the composer Pierre Boulez 'With it [the twelve-tone system], music moved out of the world of Newton and into the world of Einstein'[126] Maor's argument, however, is lacking in detail. Although it is true to say that at the beginning of the twentieth century, Schoenberg's new system created a profound revolution in music just as Einstein's Theory of Relativity shook the foundations of science, there is little or no evidence to suggest that Schoenberg's twelve-tone system was influenced by the work of Einstein. When speaking about any potential link, Schoenberg pronounced that 'There may be a relationship in the two fields of endeavour but I have no idea what it is. I write music as music without any reference other than to express anything but music'.[127] Einstein in turn was baffled by Schoenberg's music which he described as 'crazy'.[128]

Some musical considerations

When Schoenberg invented his twelve-note system he abandoned the tonal system which had been used in music for the previous 300 years. In comparison with the hierarchies of the tonal system, serialism took a democratic approach where all 12 notes of the chromatic scale were equal and no note was bound to the home key. Tonality emphasised the importance of the tonic and dominant and every note had a specific relationship to the tonic. Put simply, in the words of the composer Christopher Fox, 'The overriding characteristic of the series is that it is non-hierarchical – everything is as

---

[126] Eli Maor. *Music by the Numbers. From Pythagoras to Schoenberg.* (Princeton: Princeton University Press, 2018): 125.
[127] https://www.schoenberg.at/index.php/de/1933-r-p-arnold-schoenberg-receives-the-american-press
[128] Andrew May. *The Science of Sci-Fi music.* (London: Springer, 2020): 88.

important as everything else ...'[129] The algorithmic nature of serialism with its set of mathematical rules led some to see the method as the compositional equivalent of painting by numbers. As Jonathan Cross puts it 'Accusations of lack of artistry, lack of creative imagination, and even lack of musicality have been hurled by critics and music-lovers alike at very many twentieth-century composers not least at the Viennese composer, Arnold Schoenberg'.[130]

The new system of serialism raised several questions, not least whether it could be perceived within the music by the listener or whether instead it was incoherent with a limited capacity to communicate the composer's thoughts. The musicologist Fred Lehrdahl maintains that 'if the serial construction is so important – and yet it is not an explicit part of the listeners' experience, the listeners' experience must be impoverished'.[131] In his book on aesthetics, *Music, the Arts, and Ideas*, the philosopher Leonard B Meyer argues that listeners are conditioned to the perception of tonal music making it more difficult to perceive serial pieces, a situation compounded by the fact that composers often used quite different serial procedures in different pieces of music, and that a satisfactory perception of serialism in one work would not necessarily help the listener in others.[132] In tonal music the hierarchical relationships between pitches in the diatonic scale help to establish and define the listener's expectations. The counter arguments from serial composers usually adopt the position that serial procedures are not intended to be perceived by the listener or that although they are not perceived consciously, the music nevertheless gives an effect of coherence which the listener cannot explain.[133]

Many works using serial techniques were premiered at the Darmstadt International Summer Courses for New Music and were subject to much debate.[17] Such discussions tended to foreground the technical analysis of the music rather than the expressive purposes to which it was applied. Perhaps the final word should go to Christopher Fox who, in his essay 'Darmstadt

---

129   Christopher Fox. 'Music after Zero Hour' *Contemporary Music Review*, Vol. 26, No. 1, 2007: 16.
130   Cross, 'Composing with numbers', 131.
131   Fred Lehrdahl 'Cognitive constraints on compositional systems'. *Contemporary Music Review*, Vol. 26, No. 1, 1992: 97-121, cited in Christopher Fox. 'Darmstadt and the Institutionalisation of Modernism' *Contemporary Music Review*, Vol. 26, No. 1, 2007: 120.
132   L.B. Meyer: *Music, the Arts, and Ideas* (Chicago and London, 1967)
133   Griffiths, 'Serialism', *Grove Music.*

and the Institutionalisation of Modernism', argues that 'generally the aesthetic purpose of Darmstadt serialism is not that the series should occupy the musical foreground; rather, it is that the serial principle is the method whereby musical transformations can be achieved.'[134]

---

[134] Christopher Fox, 'Darmstadt and the Institutionalisation of Modernism', *Contemporary Music Review*, Vol. 26, 2007: 120.

Forms and Structure

9 Canons and fugues

THIS CHAPTER FOCUSES on two musical forms, the canon and the fugue, where geometric transformations and imitation are central to their composition. The word canon is used to refer to both a musical form and a compositional technique where an initial melody is imitated at a specified time interval by one or more parts. A section of a piece is described as canonic if the imitation prevails throughout the section, if the imitation is exact and continues through the whole piece, it is called a canon. As a strict form canon makes use of different types of geometric transformation: reflection, translation, scale and, less frequently, rotation. Canons fall into several discrete categories which are outlined in this chapter. These are distinguished in different ways: by the number of voices used; imitation at different distances; imitation at different upper or lower intervals; and by the geometric transformations used. The fugue, a more complicated form, follows a detailed set of rules; the composition of fugues has often been regarded as one of the most highly-skilled compositional techniques.

One of the earliest examples of the canon as a musical form is 'Sumer is Icumen In' which dates from the mid-thirteenth century. Four voices sing the same melody one after the other, accompanied by two lower voices (the *pedes* meaning 'foot') which themselves alternate and overlap. A culmination of 14th-century canonic technique was reached in the works of Guillaime de Machaut (c1300-1377), his rondeau 'Ma fin est mon commencement' is the earliest known piece based on retrograde procedures (see pages 63-4). The canon had its heyday during the late fifteenth and early sixteenth centuries with the works of composers such as Guillaume Dufay, Johannes Ockeghem and Josquin des Prez. During this period, mastery of canonic technique was equated with proficiency in composition; practical treatises of the 16th century often included compendia of canonic devices. Johannes Ockeghem (c1410-1497) almost certainly invented the prolation canon where each melodic line uses the same music but played at different speeds and is one of the most difficult types of canon to execute.[135]

Canon as a learned form of counterpoint lost much of its popularity during the Enlightenment: it was seen more as an outdated academic exercise which placed ingenuity ahead of musical value and freedom of expression. J S Bach (1685-1750), however, used canon throughout his career notably in the *Musical Offering*, the *Goldberg Variations*, the canonic variations of *Vom Himmel hoch* and the *Art of Fugue*. In these works the form hit a new peak and, chiefly through Bach's influence, the canon once again became an important musical device.

The use of canonic principles, although less popular, carried on and examples can be found in the works of Haydn, Mozart, Beethoven, Brahms and Mahler.[136] The twentieth century saw a renewed interest in canonic principles: its use of geometric transformations was central to both serialism and minimalism. There are many examples of canons and canonic writing in the music of Schoenberg, Stravinsky and Anton Webern.

Rounds and catches

A straightforward form of canon is the 'catch' or 'round' where each of the voices enters one after the other with the same melody creating a polyphonic texture.[137] Because all the voices sing the same tune, rounds are relatively easy to sing; well-known examples are the children's songs 'Row, row, row your boat' and 'Frère Jacques'. A single-line melody is constructed so that a round forms its own harmony when sung at the unison, consequently they are frequently constructed around only one or two chords to make the compositional process easier. During the seventeenth century, rounds,

---

135 John McDonough and Andrzej Herczynski. *Chaos, Solitons and Fractals, Science Direct 170* (2023).

136 A well-known example of a canon can be found in the third movement of Gustav Mahler's *Symphony No. 1* (1888) which is based on a minor version of 'Frère Jacques'

137 In some ways the terms 'round' and 'catch' are interchangeable but 'catch' is often used to refer to comic, sometimes bawdy, English rounds written between roughly 1580 and 1800.

often drinking songs with bawdy words, were largely regarded as light entertainment being sung in clubs and taverns – usually by men, frequently on the topics of drinking and sex, and often with lewd words. Henry Purcell (1659-1695) contributed many such bawdy songs such as 'Once, twice thrice'. In this context, they were usually referred to as catches.

The main types of canon

Canon in unison is one in which the imitating part(s) enters at the same pitch as the leading part. This is the most common form and is often found in folk music around the world, a well-known example being 'Shalom Chaverim'. Canon at the octave is one in which the imitating part(s) enter an octave apart from the leading part. Canon at the fifth is one in which the imitating part(s) enter a fifth apart from the leading part. Entries at any other interval are similarly explained.

The following two examples are taken from the first volume of *Tabulatura nova* (1624) by Samuel Scheidt (1587-1684). In both, the two canonic parts form contrapuntal lines upon a *cantus firmus* taken from the Magnificat.[138] The first is an example of canon in unison where the imitating part follows the leader a quarter of a bar later at the same pitch (see below).

---

138 *Cantus firmus* is a Latin term referring to a pre-existing melody used as the basis of a new polyphonic composition. It is found in Medieval and Renaissance music.

The second example is of canon at the fifth where the imitating part follows the leader a quarter of a bar later a fifth lower (see below).

The thirty harpsichord variations of the *Goldberg Variations* by J S Bach (1685-1750) are grouped in threes where each trio of variations culminates in a canon. The canons themselves progress sequentially according to intervals. The first canon is at the unison, the second canon at the second, the third canon at the third and so on through to variations 25–27, which culminate in a canon at the ninth.

In **canon by inversion** (sometimes referred to as *Al rovescio*) the imitating part plays the melody in inversion: an upward interval becomes a downward one and vice versa. This use of inversion can be seen in the opening bars of Canon No. 2 in *Fünf Canons, Op. 16* (1924) by Anton Webern (1883-1945). The five pieces are composed as strict canons and the texts themselves could be regarded as 'canonical', given that they are taken from Latin liturgical texts. The work is scored for soprano, clarinet and bass clarinet. Canon No. 2, *Dormi Jesu*, is for soprano and clarinet. Notice how the inverted intervals are precise. The clarinet opens with a leap of an augmented 5th (nine semitones) from Bb up to F# whereas the soprano opens a bar later with a descending minor 6th (nine semitones), E down to G#. The next two clarinet notes rise up a minor 3rd, A to C, whereas the singer follows with a falling minor 3rd F down to D.

CANONS AND FUGUES

Double canon uses two melodies which are given out at the same time by two parts and are imitated by two other parts: in other words, two two-part canons proceed simultaneously. The Trio of Wolfgang Amadeus Mozart's *Serenade No. 12 in C minor* (1728) is a double canon using two melodies in inversion for two oboes and two bassoons (see below). It is marked 'Al rovescio'; Oboe II leads with Oboe I entering two bars later in inversion. Bassoon 1 leads the second canon with Bassoon II entering two bars later also in inversion.

Symphony Op. 21 (1928) by Anton Webern makes much use of mirrors and palindromes through a series of double canons.

Retrograde canon is a type in which the imitating part presents the melody backwards. It is also known as canon cancrizans or crab canon (even though crabs move sideways rather than backwards). Unlike most other canons, the entries are not staggered. Instead both parts start at the same time. Crab canons are relatively uncommon. One of the most famous crab canons is included in J S Bach's *Musical Offering* (1747). This is a collection of pieces based on what is known as the Royal Theme, so called because it was presented to Bach by Frederick the Great, himself a composer and flautist, as a subject for an on-the-spot improvisation. 139 Here is the Royal Theme.

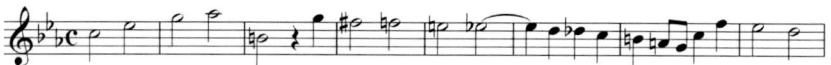

The *Musical Offering* includes 10 canons of different types. These were notated as puzzle canons in the original printed edition, and the full parts were not transcribed. A puzzle or riddle canon is one in which the canon is notated in an enigmatic way where the composer gives only the leading voice along with cryptic instructions for its resolution. It is then up to the performer to solve the intellectual exercise in order to discover the correct time and interval distance for the voice(s).[140]

Three of the canons in the *Musical Offering* have no title or instructions as to when the imitations should be played by the follower. Instead they have the Latin inscription *Quaerendo invenietis* (Seek and ye shall find) with clues provided within the music. So, for example, in No. 1, Canon *a 2 cancrizans*, the title tells us that the canon is for two voices and it should be played backwards. Furthermore at the end of the main melodic line, the clef and key signature were originally written facing backwards. The Royal Theme is presented in the first five bars of the upper part (see below). The lower part is an exact retrograde of the upper part and the upper part is an exact retrograde

---

[139] Webern used this royal theme in his 1935 orchestral arrangement: *Ricercare Fuga (Ricercata) a 6 voci* from J S Bach: *Musical Offering*).

[140] Two of Bach's former students, Johann Philipp Kirnberger and Johann Friedrich Agricola are credited with solving these in the *Musical Offering* as cited in http://www.early-music.com/js-bach-musical-offering/ and Gareth E Roberts. *From Music to Mathematics.*(Baltimore: John Hopkins University Press, 2016): 178.

of the lower part. The point of symmetry, a vertical reflection, is between bars 9 and 10. This canon as well as displaying symmetry has another interesting mathematical aspect: it can be visualised on a Möbius strip. A Möbius strip is a 2-dimensional strip where one continuous side is formed by joining the ends of a rectangle after twisting one end through 180°. The canon should be written as one long line of music on a strip of paper and then cut in half at the end of bar 9. It should then be glued together. It could then be played by two instruments travelling in opposite directions around the strip. The twist is the point at which the two parts interchange.

Mirror canon usually refers to a canon in which the combined principles of inversion and retrograde are used in the imitating part. In other words, an inverted entry moves in contrary motion – in the opposite direction. Sometimes it is used to refer to canons in inversion. Canon 3 (a 2 *per Motum contrarium*) in J S Bach's *Musical Offering* is a mirror canon at the fifth. Here the Royal Theme is used as an accompaniment and is not treated canonically. It can be found in the upper voice, but using diminution where the original note values are halved (and consequently played twice as fast). The title tells us that the follower sings the leader's theme in contrary motion. It is also played backwards (see below).

Canon by augmentation has the imitating parts in longer notes than the leading part. The notes are usually twice as long.[141] The following example is the taken from the opening bars of the first movement of the Brahms motet *Schaffe in mir, Gott, ein rein Herz, Op. 29 No. 2*, a setting of Psalm 51. Here the bass II part imitates the soprano part, this time at the same pitch but in augmentation. The note values are twice as long. This means that the bass part takes twice as long, consequently the soprano line is repeated. The example below shows the entire canon at the octave in augmentation between the Soprano and Bass II. To make this clearer the other voices have been omitted.

---

141   Canon by augmentation is sometimes known as a sloth canon.

CANONS AND FUGUES

Canon by diminution has the imitating parts in shorter notes than the one that they are imitating. The notes are usually half as long. In his *Miscellanea Musica*, C P E Bach (1714-1788) composed several canons, partly for teaching purposes. These include 'Diminution canon for two voices in C major'. Examples of canon by diminution are rare. This is because the voice with the shorter note values soon overtakes the 'slower' one with its longer note values. C P E Bach avoided this in his 'Diminution canon' by beginning the piece with straightforward imitation at the lower fifth and then from bar 5 imitating the leader (two octaves lower) but with half the note values - effectively at twice the speed.

It should be noted that in the above examples the transformational devices used are often unrecognisable to the listener unless they have analysed the score first. Although the main melodic themes can act as a unifying factor, holding the music together, the transformations are often easier to see than to hear.

Prolation canons

A prolation canon combines two or more identical musical lines at different rates; each voice sings or plays the same music, but at different speeds. Voices may either enter successively or simultaneously. The concept is simple but the compositional technique is difficult, hence prolation canons are quite rare. The earliest master of the prolation canon is Johannes Ockeghem. Each movement of his *Missa Prolationum*, dating from the second half of the fifteenth century, uses a different variant of this form where there are different gaps between the entries and different relative speeds of the voices. 'Kyrie Eleison I' is a double prolation canon, where two separate pairs of voices, soprano/alto and tenor/bass, take up a different motif. The ratio of tempos between the soprano and the alto is 3:2. Each of the first six note values of the soprano part is multiplied by 3/2 in the alto part. After the opening passage shown below, the music continues as a regular canon.

Other examples of prolation canons include J S Bach's *Canon a 4 per Augmentationem et Diminutionem*, the final movement of *14 Canons, BWV 1087*, which is built on a repeating bass line taken from his *Goldberg Variations*. The Estonian composer Arvo Pärt (b 1935) uses a prolation canon in his vocal work *Cantus in Memory of Benjamin Britten* (1977) which was used in the 2004 film *Fahrenheit 9/11*. Here a series of falling A minor scales is heard across five voices with each group entering an octave lower and at half the speed. Another relatively recent example can be heard in the first

CANONS AND FUGUES

movement of Shostakovitch's *Symphony No. 15*. It has been argued that prolation canons are examples of fractals in music (see pages 199-200).

Rhythmic canons

The final type of canon to be explored is the rhythmic canon, one that is relatively rare although used by both Alban Berg and Olivier Messiaen (see page 28). A rhythmic canon is one which is based around rhythm alone. It is again based on the principle of strict imitation, but here it is an initial rhythm that is imitated at a specified time interval by one or more parts. Canons are found throughout the opera *Lulu* (1929-1935) by the Austrian composer Alban Berg (1885-1935). In Act I, scene 2, the death of the Painter is accompanied by a five-part rhythmic canon played on unpitched percussion - drums, a tam-tam and a gong.

A more specialised form of the rhythmic canon is the **rhythmic tiling canon.** This is a type where the canon is crafted so that once all the players have begun to play or sing, there will be exactly one player striking each beat. In other words the rhythms yield one and only one onset per pulse. A basic form of the rhythmic tiling canon can be found in the vocal genre, *katak* music, which is sometimes referred to as the Balinese monkey chant (see pages 46-7).

Fugues

Unlike the canon, where one theme continues from the beginning to the end, the fugue is a more complicated form which follows a detailed set of rules: two or more voices use the systematic imitation of a principal theme (the subject) an answer and (sometimes) a countersubject (a second theme that accompanies the subject), in simultaneously sounding melodic lines (counterpoint).[142] The answer follows the subject in the second voice. It is a statement of the main subject but in a different key, usually the dominant. Statements of the material incorporate contrapuntal devices that alter the subject in some way. These devices are based on symmetry and include those of scale (augmentation and diminution) and horizontal reflection (inversion).

The term 'fugue' has been in continuous use since the 14th century. At first the word held a variety of meanings with imitation being the defining characteristic. However, from the mid-seventeenth century, a theoretical model began to evolve and in 1725, this model was largely set by the Austrian composer and theorist Joseph Fux (1660-1741) in *Gradus ad Parnassum*, a theoretical treatise on composition whose middle sections focus on species counterpoint and fugue. *Gradus ad Parnassum* served as a textbook for several generations of composers and the rules set out were followed by many, Haydn, Mozart and Beethoven amongst them. Central to Fux's treatise are the four rules for voice-leading which are applied to species counterpoint

---

[142] The fugue opens with the subject, the main theme of the fugue. The answer follows the subject in the second voice. It is a statement of the main subject but in a different key, usually the dominant. Some fugues also have a countersubject, a second theme that accompanies the subject. The word episode is used to delineate a passage where no voice states the subject in its entirety. The music in episodes is usually, but not always, developed from the subject or countersubject. Stretto is an overlapping effect where one voice states the subject and is closely followed by another voice before the first one has finished.

in two, three and four voices before sections on imitation and fugue. The method of instruction is through a dialogue between teacher and pupil and is based on exercises using a given *cantus firmus* for which a counterpoint is to be constructed. Several rules are set up in the first exercise which include:

- all intervals must be consonant
- parallel motion of perfect intervals is forbidden
- perfect intervals must not be approached by similar motion
- disjunct motion by skip must be used sparingly.

This strict set of procedures has much in common with a mathematical algorithm where a set of precisely described instructions or routine procedures are designed to be applied systematically through to a conclusion in a number of steps.

Gradus ad Parnassum was held in high esteem by J S Bach whose keyboard work *The Well-Tempered Clavier*, a set of preludes and fugues in all 24 major and minor keys was completed in 1742. This collection of fugues is commonly viewed as the zenith of the form (see page 77). By the 1750s the fugue began to be seen as outdated and it no longer enjoyed a central role in contemporary compositions. However, the study of fugue and counterpoint was still an important part of a composer's training and fugal imitation was often found in compositions. Haydn wrote fugues as finales to several of his works, as did Mozart, and Beethoven who adopted a free approach to fugues, notably in the finale to the *Hammerklavier Sonata* Op. 106 (see pages 68-9) and the string quartet the *Grosse Fuge Op. 133*. Tonality was embedded in the strict rules of the structure of fugues therefore twentieth-century developments in atonality did not lend themselves to the form. Between the 1920s and 1940s however, Neo-classicism revived some of the elements of eighteenth-century musical precepts translated into a modern idiom.[143] Later on both Shostakovitch and Hindemith composed collections of fugues inspired by J S Bach's *The Well-Tempered Clavier*: Shostakovich's *24 Preludes and Fugues* (1950–51) and *Ludus Tonalis* (1943) by Paul Hindemith (1895-1963). *Ludus Tonalis*, subtitled 'Studies in Counterpoint, Tonal Organization and Piano

---

143 Examples of fugues written in this style include the second movement of Stravinsky's *Symphony of Psalms* (1930) and Bartók's *Music for Strings, Percussion and Celesta* (1936).

Playing', includes twelve three-part fugues.[144]

It should be noted that the formulaic/symmetrical rules of the fugue are sometimes modified to fit the irregular/asymmetrical nature of the major/minor scale. So, for example, in diatonic music, although strictly speaking the answer in a fugue is a statement of the main subject in the dominant (a real answer), the intervals are sometimes adjusted based on the key signature. The melodic contour remains the same, but the transposition is not exact (a tonal answer). So for example in J S Bach's Fugue No. 16 in G minor (from Book I of the *Well-Tempered Clavier*), the subject opens with a rising semitone from D to Eb. If the answer were an exact transposition of the subject, then it would open with A to Bb, however, it opens with a rising minor 3rd – G to Bb, a tonal answer.

As time went on artistic licence increasingly overrode the formulaic approach to the point where in the fugues of Hindemith and Shostakovitch, twentieth-century contemporary musical idioms, (harmonic and rhythm techniques, for instance) are integrated into fugal procedures in ways that are impossible to reduce to formulas.

Fugues, computers and Artificial Intelligence

Composers of fugues followed a set of steps and procedures and as well as adhering to the rules of counterpoint, they also had to understand how to handle the entity of thematic, contrapuntal, and harmonic elements so that even the most complex counterpoint had a firm harmonic basis. In

---

144 Hindemith, living in the United States, was inspired to compose *Ludus Tonalis* following a then much derided broadcast of Shostakovitch's *Leningrad Symphony*. Hindemith condemned the trend toward "despicable rubbish" in orchestral music and hoped to "remind those who have not succumbed what music and composition really are" cited in Alex Ross. *The Rest is Noise*. (London: Fourth Estate, 2008): 299.

conceiving of the original subject, they needed to bear in mind the answer and the countersubject to ensure that they were a satisfactory harmonic and contrapuntal combination; few could disagree that the design of a good fugue subject is a significant part of the process of writing a fugue. It could be argued that the multi-faceted reasoning employed is similar to that used in solving a mathematical problem. As Joel E Cohen writes of the kinship between mathematics and music 'The processes of creation are similar; that is, in both the most beautiful combination is selected from an infinitude of possibilities and its logical potentials are developed consistently'. He goes on to write 'The end products of mathematics and music depend for their meaning upon the successive relationships of their elements and upon the order imposed by the creator'.[145] To this could be added that, ideally, the end product should be convincing and musical. Given that the set of procedures which need to be followed in order to compose a fugue could be described as an algorithm, perhaps a computer programme could be designed to fulfil this function. As the computer scientist Andrés Garay Acevedo writes of Fux's *Gradus ad Parnassum*, 'such a well-studied process starts to suit the idea of computer assisted composition.'[146] This fact was recognised by the American electronic music composer Laurie Spiegel (b. 1945). In 1981 she delivered a conference paper entitled 'Manipulation of musical patterns' where she argued that a 'working knowledge of all the processes of transformation which can be aesthetically applied' to musical patterns should be important considerations in computer music system design adding that there also needs to be a 'practised awareness of how such materials and operations … relate to and influence each other's' potentials'. She goes on to list relevant materials and operations which include, transposition, retrograde, inversion and scaling.[147] In 1986 Spiegel went on to design her algorithmic composition software *Music Mouse* which she labelled as an Intelligent Instrument with reference to the programme's built-in knowledge of chord and scale

---

145 Joel E Cohen. 'Some Relationships between Music and Mathematics'. *Music Educators Journal*, Vol. 48, No. 1, 1961: 108-109.
146 Andrés Garay Acevedo. 'Fugue Composition with Counterpoint Melody Generation Using Genetic Algorithms'. *Computer Music Modeling and Retrieval*, Volume 3310, 2005.
147 Laurie Spiegel. 'Manipulation of musical patterns'. In *Proceedings of the Symposium o Small comuters and the Arts*: 19-22. Philadelphia, PA: IEEE, 1981.

conventions, and stylistic constraints. She composed several works using *Music Mouse* including *Three Sonic Spaces* (1991).

One of the first to attempt to create computer-generated fugues was the American musicologist and composer, David Cope, who published *The Well Programmed Clavier* a set of keyboard pieces which he had generated through a computer programme 'Experiments in Musical Intelligence' devised to produce new works in the styles of various composers. The works are discussed in his books *Experiments in Musical Intelligence* (1996) and *The Algorithmic Composer* (2000).[148]

In 2001, an experiment was conducted at Cornell University in New York. The aim of the artificial intelligence project 'Fugue Generation with Genetic Algorithms' was to establish whether the project team could create fugues 'from scratch'.[149] The subject was generated first by the programme and then the answer and countersubjects were generated, following 'certain rules and guidelines'. The first part was 'accomplished through the use of a genetic algorithm' using 'random subjects which were slowly improved 'into something decent'. A 'fitness function' was used to evaluate the suitability of the different features of the subject. This looked at, for example, similarity of pitch where each note was discouraged from being 'different from its predecessor', similarity of note length where notes of similar length were encouraged to avoid 'switching around arbitrarily', and key, where notes were awarded for 'being in the key of C' which is followed by the rather naïve explanation that 'This goes a long way toward making the subject sound better. It removes the majority of sharps and flats from the subject, making it much nicer to listen to.' This set of criteria betrays a lack of musical knowledge in its assumptions. Testing the final product on a team of listeners, the research team came to the conclusion that although the system was 'able to successfully generate subjects, and from there create the beginning of a fugue' it was unable to generate complete fugues, due to the complexity involved. This is not surprising given the naïve assumptions of the fitness function. They found that 'while many of the pieces generated by our system have been rated highly by our test listeners, they are still not competition for a human composer'.

---

148   David Cope. *Experiments in Musical Intelligence* (1996) and *The Algorithmic Composer* (2000) published by A R Editions, MIT Press.
149   Eric Milkie and Joel Chestnutt, S 473 Artificial Intelligence Project, Fugue Generation with Genetic Algorithms, Cornell University.

In his paper 'Fugue Composition with Counterpoint Melody Generation Using Genetic Algorithms' (2005), Andrés Garay Acevedo presented the results of the implementation and evaluation of a genetic algorithm which was used to help in the task of automatic counterpoint generation. A fugue subject was used as an input for the system and then a genetic algorithm was used in order to find a suitable counterpoint melody that could be arranged in a basic fugue structure with an answer and two counter-subject melodies arranged over time for three voices. As such, the process was more sophisticated than that used by Cornell University; Acevedo recognised that 'if an algorithm is to be used, then it must incorporate higher-level concepts of musical arrangement and coherence' in order to have 'some sort of aesthetic value.' The algorithm was tested with two different input melodies, and evaluated for fitness: the results were deemed to be satisfactory.

In 2014, a further piece of research was undertaken by Yu Yue Yue Yang and Andrew Horner which sought to improve on David Cope's results and those of Cornell University. 'Automated Fugue Generation' worked on the premise that 'A fugue is a musical composition of multiple voices built on a subject (recurring theme) that imitates itself frequently throughout the piece. The objective was to design and build a system that generated three-voice fugues, emulating the style of J. S. Bach. The subject was to be two bars long and then the position of the new entries was determined bearing in mind the voice, bar, key and 'tonal centre progression'. The characteristics of Bach's fugues were taken into account and the results were evaluated in terms of the frequency of repetition, the dominance of stepwise motion, the range, the link between segments and the fitness of the chord and the pitch structure. The evaluation found that their results 'made musical sense in general, occasionally with unnatural transition and were significantly better than the Cornell results but 'pale' compared to David Cope's pieces. They concluded that they had built a system that could generate polyphonic music similar to fugues, but that it had limitations and the results sounded more like pop music than authentic Baroque music.

It would appear that although the composition of fugues is often referred to as one of the most mathematical and formulaic procedures, it cannot be reduced to these two features; understanding the mathematical structure does not tell us anything about the effect on the audience. Although the algorithm is a partner in the creative process it could be argued that it is no more than that.

10 Proportion: Golden Section and the Fibonacci series

GOLDEN SECTION AND the associated Fibonacci series give rise to satisfying natural proportions. This chapter explores their use in music, looking in particular at the music of Mozart, Satie, Bartók, Debussy, and composers associated with the Darmstadt School, questioning whether such ratios are used consciously by composers or otherwise. The final section outlines the theory of proportional parallelism in the music of J S Bach. It asserts that the composer consciously revised his works so that total number of bars was a multiple of 10, 100 and sometimes 1000 resulting in perfect proportions such as, 1:1 or 1:2.

The term Golden Section (GS) refers to the unequal division of a line into two parts such that the ratio of the smaller part to the larger is the same as that of the larger to the original whole. This ratio is approximately 1:1618. It was first documented by the Ancient Greek mathematician Euclid in the *Elements* (c 300 BC) where it was found that this 'division in extreme and mean ratio' appeared frequently in geometry.[150]

---

150 The *Elements* is a mathematical treatise, one of the most influential works in the history of mathematics, most notably geometry and for over 2000 years has had a huge influence on scientific thinking. The work is attributed to the ancient Greek mathematician Euclid and is a compilation of mathematical research from the previous two centuries including Pythagoras, Archytas and Eudoxus.

Golden Section

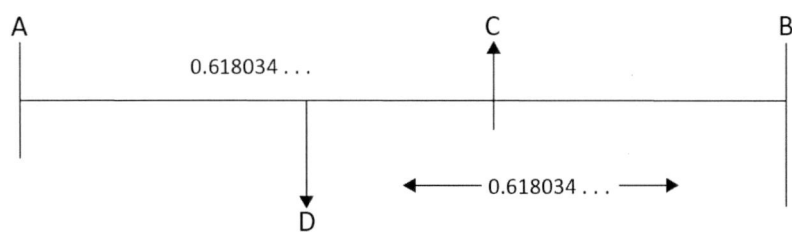

At this time the concept was known simply as the 'section' but during the period of the Renaissance it was taken up by artists, sculptors and architects as a 'divine proportion'; a link was made between the golden ratio and abstract ideas, such as aesthetic beauty and perfection. The educator and composer John Paynter wrote

'The asymmetrical relationship of one-third to two-thirds in measurements of duration or space has immense significance in the history of the world's poetry, literature, visual arts, architecture and music… It is found the world over, in music of every kind, old and new. It is a proportion that is especially satisfying when we observe it in nature - in the shapes and patterning of seashells and fir cones, for example and, perhaps for this reason, it has been consciously emulated in painting and sculpture…. It is discernible in numerous ancient manmade structures and in the 'magic' shapes of the pentagon and five-pointed star….'[151]

Mathematically GS is expressed in the Fibonacci series, a summation series in which each number is the sum of the two which precede it.[152] The ratio between the successive terms (0, 1, 1, 2, 3, 5, 8 13, 21, 34, 55 and so on) is an expression of Euclid's golden ratio.

1/1	2/1	3/2	5/3	8/5	13/8	21/13	34/21	55/34
1.000	2.000	1.500	1.333	1.600	1.625	1.615	1.619	1.617

---

151 John Paynter 'Music in the school curriculum: why bother?' *British Journal of Music Education*. 2002 19:3, 215-226.
152 The Fibonacci series is named after Lionardo Fibonacci the thirteenth- century Italian mathematician who first presented the sequence in his manuscript *Liber abbaci* (1202).

As can be seen, the ratios gradually approach the value known as the golden ratio –

1: 1618033988749894. This is designated by the Greek letter *phi* – Φ, an irrational number.[153] Since the nineteenth century, the number

$$\Phi = 1/2(1 + \sqrt{5}) = 1.6180339887 \ldots.$$

has been called the golden ratio, golden section or golden number. A golden rectangle is a rectangle with sides in this ratio.

The golden ratio can also be applied to durations. As Paynter wrote '… the highly satisfying proportion is also perceptible in defined periods of time, such as musical works, which frequently take off in new and unexpected directions around 0.6 or 0.7 of the overall duration'. It is true to say that the proportions of one third to two thirds are frequently found in music, not least in sonata form (see below). In pop and rock verse and chorus songs, for example, this is the approximate point where the middle eight, a contrasting section, is most frequently to be found.[154] A clear example of GS in pop music can be found in Lady Gaga's 2016 song 'Perfect Illusion' where there is a dramatic key change at exactly this point; the song is 179 seconds long and the key change happens at 111 seconds (179 x 0.618 = 110.622). Paynter argued that GS can also be found in the 12-bar blues but warns that 'It would be unwise to make too much of this, but it is interesting to note how often a composer's intuitive sense of proportion in time structures coincides with the Golden Section divisions'.[155] Many classical pieces feature a dramatic arc somewhere after the midway of the piece, so inevitably this climax will happen close to GS proportions according to the number of bars or the time which has elapsed. Although GS can be viewed and measured in, for example, the façade of a building, Paynter points out that this is more difficult with music; we have to hear the music through. As he wrote, 'Of all mankind's attempts to model perfection, music is, perhaps,

---

153   An irrational number is a real number which cannot be expressed as an integer or as a quotient of two integers. Irrational numbers have infinite, non-repeating decimals.

154   The middle eight (sometimes referred to as the bridge) is a contrasting section (not necessarily eight bars long) where new material is introduced with, for example, a different arrangement of instruments, and/or different chords.

155   John Paynter. *Sound & Structure* (Cambridge: Cambridge University Press, 1992): 215.

the most subtle. Its meaning is manifest not in objects viewed or touched but in events that can only be experienced in the time it takes to make each one audible'.[156] Consequently it can be difficult to gain any accurate purchase on structural plans in music through listening alone and the use of GS can be audibly imperceptible.

In Mozart's time, sonata form was conceived in three parts: the exposition in which the musical themes are introduced; the development and recapitulation sections where the themes are developed and then revisited. In 1995 John Putz set out to determine whether Mozart had composed the movements of his piano sonatas according to GS. In order to establish this he examined the lengths of two sections: the exposition and the combined length of the development and recapitulation across 16 of Mozart's piano sonatas. Putz found that Mozart was interested in mathematics but that although he 'may have known of the golden section and used it' there is 'considerable deviation from it [which] suggests otherwise'. He came to the conclusion that 'Perhaps the golden section does, indeed, represent the most pleasing proportion, and perhaps Mozart, through his consummate sense of form, gravitated to it as the, perfect balance between extremes.[157]

In some ways this is a chicken and egg situation: Putz points to the argument put forward by the music critic and academic Eduard Hanslick in his 1854 treatise on aesthetics, *The Beautiful in Music (Vom Musikalisch-Schönen)*

> ... we should be wrong were we to construe ... that man framed his musical system according to calculations purposely made, the system having arisen through the unconscious application of pre-existent conceptions of quantity and proportion, through subtle processes of measuring and counting; but the laws by which the latter are governed were demonstrated only subsequently by science.[158]

Musical analysis by means of GS proportions has aroused much

---

156   John Paynter, Bernarr Rainbow, *Music Education in Crisis*, Woodbridge, Suffolk: Boydell Press, 2013): 50.
157   John F. Putz. 'The Golden Section and the Piano Sonatas of Mozart'. October 1995 *Mathematics Magazine*
158   Eduard Hanslick, *The Beautiful in Music*, translated by Gustav Cohen (London: Novello, 1891): 151.

controversy. In her study of GS in the music of Erik Satie (1866-1925), Courtney Adams argued that because the concept itself involves approximation, 'lack of precision provides easy fuel for argument' and consequently 'GS analysis has engendered some scepticism.' As Adams wrote, in compositional analysis it is important to minimize the extent of acceptable deviation from the exact GS ratio because 'GS proportions are perilously close to one-third and two-thirds, fundamental divisions in music.' A useful margin of error is 1 per cent or less. 'Typically, analysts find 2 per cent a reasonable margin, although occasionally a writer will allow a deviation as high as 10 per cent, which I find wholly unacceptable.'[159]

In order to establish the degree of deviation across Mozart's piano sonatas, a similar table was constructed based on Putz's own table but focusing only on first movements (see Table 1).[160] Here the first column identifies the piece by the Köchel cataloguing system, 'a' represents the number of bars in the exposition,[161] and 'b' represents the combined length of the development and recapitulation (without including any codas). The column 'c' shows the number of bars that would have been used if the movement had adhered strictly to the proportions of GS and the final column shows the percentage difference from the actual number of bars in the Mozart sonata.

---

159   Courtney S. Adams. 'Erik Satie and Golden Section Analysis'. *Music & Letters* , May, 1996, Vol. 77, No. 2: 242-252, Oxford University Press: 243-244.
160   The first movement of K. 331 in A has been omitted because it is not in sonata form, rather it is a set of variations.
161   Although the expositions of Mozart's piano sonatas are normally repeated in performance, Putz gives the number of bars of the exposition without repeats.

Table 1 Golden Section proportions in the first movement of Mozart's piano sonatas

Köchel number	a - No of bars in exposition	b - No of bars in development + recapitulation	a + b	c - b according to Golden Section	% difference
K. 279 in C	38	62	100	61.8	< 1%
K. 280 in F	56	88	144	90.0	> 2%
K. 281 in Bb	40	69	109	67.4	> 2%
K. 282 in Eb	15	18	33	20.4	< 2%
K. 283 in G	53	67	120	74.2	> 1%
K. 284 in D	51	76	127	78.5	> 3%
K. 309 in C	58	97	155	95.8	> 1%
K. 310 in A minor	49	84	133	82.2	> 2%
K. 311 in D	39	73	112	69.2	> 7%
K. 330 in C	58	92	150	92.7	< 1%
K. 332 in F	93	136	229	141.5	> 3%
K. 333 in Bb	63	102	165	102.0	Exact
K. 457 in C minor	74	93	167	103.2	> 9%
K. 533 in F	102	137	239	147.7	> 7%
K. 545 in C	28	45	73	45.1	< 1%
K. 570 in Bb	70	130	200	123.6	> 5%
K. 576 in D	58	160	218	134.7	> 5%

In terms of adherence to GS proportions, five of the piano sonata movements stand out – K. 333 is exact according to GS proportions, and K. 279, K. 283, K. 309, K. 330 and K. 545 all have less than 1% difference. As was mentioned earlier, Adams considered a difference smaller than 2% to be a reasonable margin. This would mean that K. 282 would also fit into this category giving a total of 6/17 movements - (35%). On the other hand some movements, K. 311, K. 570, and K. 576, for example, show what Putz describes as 'considerable deviation' leading us to the same conclusion as Putz, that is that Mozart lent towards the 'pleasing proportion' of GS and gravitated towards it intuitively.

Before we move onto the survey of in the music of Erik Satie, it is revealing to examine a piece of music which follows GS proportions exactly and was written only 34 years after Mozart completed his final piano sonata. In her

PROPORTION: GOLDEN SECTION AND THE FIBONACCI SERIES

analysis of Schubert's lied 'Du bist die ruh' (You are my calm) (1823), the music theorist Pozzi Escot discovered that, discounting the first seven bars of solo piano introduction, the song falls into two distinct parts. It has a total of 75 bars (82 - 7), Part I (bars 8- 53) is 46 bars long and Part II (bars 54-82) is 29 bars long. This means that Part II starts at exactly at the point of Golden Section.[162] Furthermore, at this point the music is marked by a dramatic increase in tension.

$75 \times 0.618 = 46.35$

'Du bist die ruh' is a setting of a love poem by Friedrich Rückert. The first part tells of calm repose, the opening bars (below) have a feeling of stillness reflected in the simple harmony and quiet dynamic. The vocal line opens with the following four bars repeated.

When the point of GS is reached there is a dramatic change as the mood is transformed from one of calm repose to deep yearning. There is a tremendous tonal shift as the harmony modulates from Eb to Cb and we hear the first crescendo as the vocal line rises to the highest note in the song. This is followed by a dramatic silence.

---

[162] Pozzi Escot. *The Poetics of Simple Mathematics in Music*. (Cambridge: Publication Contact International, 1999).

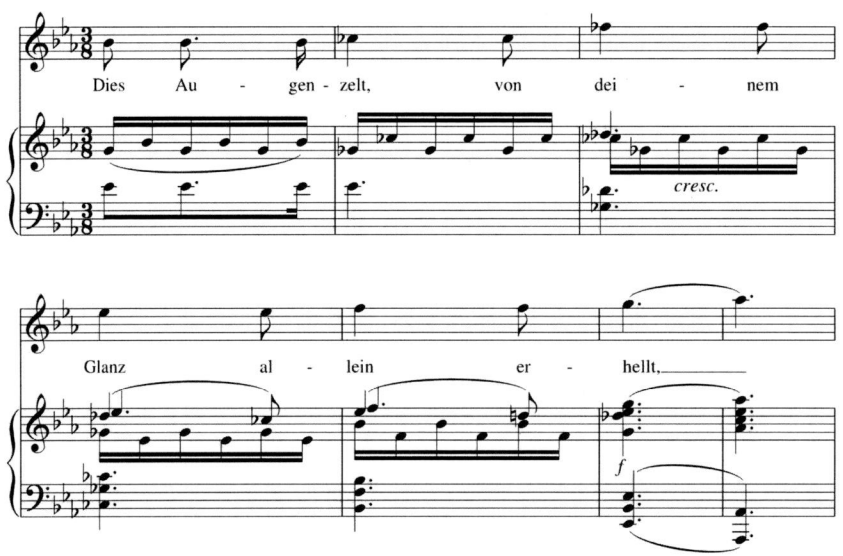

Erik Satie and Golden Section

Returning to the GS analyses of Adams, in her survey of this mathematical device in the music of Erik Satie, Adams found four multi-movement sets and six individual movements using GS proportions 'that are exact or within a deviation of one per cent.'[163] The works belong to both the early (1887-92) and late (1914-19) periods of Satie's output. She set out to find an explanation as to these two clusters, aiming to establish whether the appearance of GS was the result of 'conscious use, coincidence or, as some would argue, instinctive application.' In summary, she found that although it was possible that Satie had learnt about the principle from Debussy in late 1891 and had experimented with it, there was no convincing answer with regard to the early pieces, and that the use of GS in these was largely either instinctive or coincidental. This was reinforced by the 'absence of any calculations in the sketchbooks over this long period' However, she found that in the later period 'there is ample evidence of his close association with a number of people who were demonstrably aware of GS' and that the GS proportion appears regularly in Satie's music between 1914 and 1919, including the

---

163   The sets are the *Trois Gymnopedies, Les Trois Valses, Avant-dernieres pensees* and the first three *Nocturnes*. The individual movements are *Le Fils I, Sonneries I* and *III* and *Trois melodies*.

'overall movement proportions of most of his three-movement piano works' but also the internal form of each of the three songs in his song cycle *Trois Mélodies* of 1916. She found that the usage here was 'both too consistent and too precise to attribute to chance or instinct.'[164] The three songs of *Trois Mélodies* are 'La Statue de bronze', 'Daphénéo' and 'Le Chapelier'. 'Daphénéo' is used here as an example (see below). The song opens with both the vocal line and the piano accompaniment formed largely of quavers.

'Daphénéo' is 39 bars long so we would expect the GS division to occur shortly after bar 24 and for there to be a new turn in the music. As Adams points out, 'the long GS (after bar 24) marks the end of two bars which include the lowest note in the piece; moreover it introduces a sudden semiquaver motion that leads to a new register at the reprise.' So a case could be made here for the use of GS.[165]

---

164 Adams. 'Erik Satie and Golden Section', 250-251.
165 Adams, 'Erik Satie and Golden Section', 248.

Erik Satie 'Daphénéo' bars 17 - 28

Béla Bartók, Claude Debussy and Golden Section

Other claims for the use of GS in music, notably by Bartók and Debussy, have aroused more controversy. In his book *Béla Bartók: An Analysis of His Music* (1971), the Hungarian music analyst Ernő Lendvai argued that the composer used formal principles based on GS and the Fibonacci series, in, for example, his *Sonata for Two Pianos and Percussion* and *Music for Strings, Percussion and Celesta* which were both composed in 1937.[166] Lendvai studied the latter piece in detail and cited, amongst other examples, the use of Fibonacci numbers as structural devices in the first movement. Unfortunately he made a few errors and fudged some of his calculations. The music analyst Roy Howat discredited the work and he countered these claims in his own detailed analysis of the work which exposed some of the inaccuracies. He found for example that 'numbers of bars begun are sometimes confused with bars completed'. Howat argued that the use of proportional systems was most likely to have been subconscious given that there was 'no definite

---

166 Ernő Lendvai. *Béla Bartók: An Analysis of His Music*. (London: Kahn and Averill, 1971).

proof of conscious application'.[167] He did however make a case for the use of Fibonacci numbers in the slow third movement of Bartók's *Music for Strings, Percussion and Celesta* (music to familiar to those who have seen the film *The Shining* where it is used to create an eerie atmosphere). The Fibonacci series is quite clear to see in the xylophone solo of the opening bars where the rhythmic pattern uses 1–2–3–5–8–5–3–2–1.

Howat found further examples of the GS and Fibonacci series in this movement by dividing the movement up into crotchet beats, rather than bars as Lendvai had done, revealing clear structural examples.[168]

The question remains as to whether Bartók was making conscious use of these mathematical proportions. The musicologist Paul Griffiths is very dismissive writing that the 'appearance of the Fibonacci series in a rhythmic pattern at the start of the slow Movement of Bartók's *Music for Strings, Percussion and Celesta* (1–2–3–5–8–5–3–2–1) is suggestive, but no more'.[169] Lendvai acknowledged that Bartók said very little about his compositional techniques stating 'Let my music speak for itself; I lay no claim to any explanation of my works'.[170] As Laszlo Somfai wrote, in his research into Bartók's extant sketches and autograph, he did not find 'a single calculation of the proportion of a composition - with Fibonacci or other numbers'.[171] Howat wrote that Bartók was secretive and reluctant to divulge the 'use of highly

---

167 Roy Howat. 'Bartók, Lendvai and the Principles of Proportional Analysis' *Music Analysis*. Vol. 2, No. 1 (March 1983): 69-95.
168 Howat, 'Bartok and Proportional Analysis': 80-82.
169 Paul Griffiths, 'Numbers in music' in *Grove Music*.
170 Mario Livio. *The Golden Ratio: The Story of Phi, the World's Most Astonishing Number*. (New York: Broadway Books, 2002): 190.
171 Laszlo Somfai. *Béla Bartok: Composition, Concepts and Autograph Scores*. (Berkeley: University of California Press, 1996).

abstract constructions in what many critics already regarded as over-cerebral music' but he goes on to point out that 'More positive manuscript evidence of proportional calculations exist in Bartók's transcriptions of folk music' citing as evidence Manuscript 80FSS1 in the New York Bartók Archive, a sketchbook devoted largely to Bartók's first drafts of Turkish folk songs. These include a metrical sequence of numbers which is easily identifiable as the Lucas summation series (1, 3, 4, 7, 11, 18 ...) where, in the same way as the Fibonacci sequence, each term is the sum of the two previous terms, and the ratios of successive terms approach the Golden ratio.[172] Howat argued that this demonstrates that the song's 'metrical organization is analysed wholly in terms sequence numbers'.[173]

In 1983, Howat went on to make a detailed case for GS as a structural device in Debussy's music in his book *Debussy in Proportion: A Musical Analysis* where he set out to demonstrate Debussy's use of 'intricate proportional systems', in particular the Golden Section .[174] His study included detailed analyses of the piano pieces *Reflets dans l'eau* (1905), *L'isle joyeuse* (1904), and the symphonic poem *La mer* (1908), and demonstrated how the pieces are built around GS and the Fibonacci series. In *Reflets dans l'eau*, the first of three pieces in Debussy's first volume of *Images*, as part of the detailed analysis Howat found that the principal climax at bars 56-61 tallied with the overall point of GS i.e. after 58 bars out of a total of 94. He also discovered that Fibonacci numbers are often found at 'strategic places' such as in the 55 bars of introduction to the final section, 'Dialogue du vent et de la mer', of *La Mer* (where the bar groups follow the Fibonacci numbers 3, 5, 8, 13, 34 and 55) and the 34 bars of 'build-up to the climactic coda' of *L'isle joyeuse* (bars 186-219). Howat considered the question of whether Debussy's proportional patterns were 'designed consciously' or 'intuited unconsciously' but came to no definite conclusion he did however acknowledge that Debussy very probably knew about GS and Fibonacci through a series of articles in which the mathematician Charles Henry discussed such structural principles in

---

172   Lucas numbers are named after the French mathematician François Édouard Lucas (1842-91) who launched the *American Journal of Mathematics* in 1878 with a long paper dealing with the Fibonacci sequence along with the sequence starting 1, 3 which he named after himself.
173   Howat, 'Bartok and Proportional Analysis', 85.
174   Roy Howat. *Debussy in Proportion: A Musical Analysis* (Cambridge: Cambridge University Press, 1983).

the Symbolist journals which Debussy 'read avidly'.[175] Howat later added a caveat 'How consciously this came about is unproven, and the subject can still be contentious; its main interest lies in linking different aspects of the structure into a naturally balanced dramatic flow'.[176]

In the 1940s, the Russian/American teacher and composer Joseph Schillinger (1895-1943) devised his own system of composition based on mathematical principles.[177] His thinking behind this was that a mathematical approach would be more natural because nature was intrinsically mathematical. In his words, 'Music imitates nature, and particularly the forms of motion in the universe, i.e. the growth and evolution of natural forms. The forms of organic growth appeal to us as a form of beauty when expressed through an art medium'.[178] In his books *The Schillinger System of Musical Composition* (1941) and *The Mathematical Basis of the Arts* (1948) he suggested creating pitch structures based on the Fibonacci sequence.[179] His idea is based on counting semitones where each semitone represents one unit. So, for example, starting on C and moving up one semitone would mean that the second note would be Db. Schillinger's system alternated between ascending and descending intervals. In this way the Fibonacci series 1, 1, 2, 3, 5… starting on C would create the following sequence of notes.

C up one semitone **Db**, down two semitones **B**, up three semitones **D**, down five semitones **A,** as below.

---

175   Roy Howat. *The Art of French Piano Music: Debussy, Ravel, Fauré, Chabrier*. (London: Yale University Press, 2009).
176   François Lesure and Roy Howat, 'Debussy' in *Grove Music*.
177   After Joseph Schillinger had emigrated to the USA he taught his mathematical methods to a large number of pupils, many of these were popular musicians and included George Gershwin, Glen Miller and Quincy Jones amongst their number. Another pupil, Lawrence Berk, became the founder of the Berklee College of Music where Schillinger's methods were taught in its early days. Schillinger's ideas included various mathematical ways in which to produce melodies, rhythms and chords and, although they were littered with miscalculations and misunderstandings of mathematical concepts, for many years they were in high demand.
178   Joseph Schillinger: *The Schillinger System of Musical Composition* (1941).
179   Joseph Schillinger: *The Schillinger System of Musical Composition* (1941) and *The Mathematical Basis of the Arts* (1948).

Darmstadt International Summer Courses for New Music in the 1950s and 1960s

In 1854, Eduard Hanslick had argued in *The Beautiful in Music* that 'No mathematical calculation ever enters into a composition, be it the best or the worst. Creations of inventive genius are not arithmetical sums'.[180] One hundred years later, however, there were several composers associated with the centre of new music in Darmstadt who made conscious and open use of GS and the Fibonacci series. Central to the Darmstadt International Summer Courses for New Music were premieres of new works and the teaching of composition.[181] It soon became what Alex Ross describes as the 'principal showcase for the avant garde'.[182] In his 1957 lecture on the development of serial technique the Italian composer Luigi Nono (1924-1990) coined the term 'Darmstadt School' for a group of composers that included Bruno Maderna, Karlheinz Stockhausen, Pierre Boulez and Nono himself.

Stockhausen (1928-2007) went on to make extensive use of the Fibonacci series in his music of the 1960s and, according to the American music theorist Jonathan Kramer, used it 'prominently and systematically'. Kramer argues that in Stockhausen's music the Fibonacci series contributes 'more significantly to the total form than it does in the [music of] Bartók'; the Fibonacci series is used proportionally in many ways, some simple and some complicated'. In *Klavierstuck IX* (1961), for example, majority of bars have Fibonacci-related time signatures and in the coda, each bar contains either 1, 2, 3, 5, 8, 13, or 21 attack points. A larger scale use of Fibonacci proportions can also be found in *Adieu* (1966) for wind quintet where the durations of all the bars 'except the five which contain tonal references and the four with unmeasured silences' are given by Fibonacci numbers from 1 to 144. Kramer wrote that the 'properties of the series are readily heard because each

---

180 Hanslick, *The Beautiful in Music*, 92.
181 Darmstadt International Summer Courses for New Music (*Ferienkurse für neue Musik*) were initiated in 1946 by Wolfgang Steinecke.
182 Alex Ross. *The Rest is Noise*. (London: Fourth Estate, 2008): 391.

duration contains a largely static ... unfolding of a sonority' which changes when the music moves to the next bar.

In Nono's cantata *Il Canto Sospeso* (1956) he utilised the Fibonacci series in a different way. Rather than generating formal proportions Nono determined individual note lengths by means of the series. In the second movement, for example, the durations of notes are generated by the Fibonacci numbers 1 2 3 5 8 13.[183] The Danish composer Per Nørgård also experimented with the properties of the Fibonacci series in some of his music. In the programme note for his orchestral piece *Iris* (1968) he compares his use of the Fibonacci series to the way it can be found in nature:

> The basic idea is ... a network of lines where each one represents a rather simple melody or rhythm. The whole thing is not unlike the flowers of the daisy, where you see 21 spiralling lines moving in one direction and 34 spiralling lines in the other, in other words the proportion of The Golden Mean (as expressed in the Fibonacci series.[184]

The Austrian composer and writer Ernst Krenek (1900-1991), was a regular attendee at Darmstadt. In his 1964 piece *Fibonacci Mobile* Op. 187 for string quartet and piano duet, he uses the Fibonacci series in the construction of the proportions.

Although the ideas of the radical Greek composer Iannis Xenakis (1925 – 2001) were often at odds with the serialism of the Darmstadt School, his orchestral piece *Metastaseis* (1954) was the subject of a lecture given there in 1962 by György Ligeti (1923-2006). Following his arrival in Paris in 1947, Xenakis had worked as an architect and engineer for 12 years with Le Corbusier where proportion was central to his work (see also pages 187-8). This was to have a strong influence on the composition of *Metastaseis*. In the words of Xenakis, "In my composition *Metastasis* ... the role of architecture is direct and fundamental by virtue of the Modular. The Modular was applied in the very essence of the musical development"[185] Here he is referring to a system devised by Le Corbusier, an architectural approach

---

183   Jonathan Kramer. 'The Fibonacci Series in Twentieth-Century Music'. *Journal of Music Theory*, Spring, 1973, Vol. 17, No. 1 : 110- 148.
184   Per Nørgård, programme note for his orchestral piece *Iris*, 1988.
185   Sharon Kanach. *Iannis Xenakis. Music and Architecture*. (New York: Pendragon Press, 2008).

to form and proportion and used by Xenakis to shape pitch envelopes and time structures in *Metastaseis*. *Metastaseis* is built in four sections. The first section begins on a sustained single note G played very quietly by all 46 strings gradually sliding outwards by means of slow glissandi as the dynamic intensity increases, arriving at a massive note cluster for full orchestra with each instrument sustaining its own note. This large cluster is treated as one sonic unit where note lengths are derived from the Fibonacci/Modulor series by means of dynamic and timbral changes.[186]

Proportional parallelism in the music of J S Bach

As we have seen, GS is closely linked to proportion therefore readers may also be interested in the theory of proportional parallelism in the music of J S Bach that has been put forward by the musicologist Ruth Tatlow. This asserts that 'all Bach's revised fair copies and published collections have three characteristics in common: the total number of bars are a multiple of ten, one hundred, and sometimes one thousand; there are perfect proportions such as, 1:1 or 1:2 on at least three different levels; and there is an embedded signature.' Tatlow discovered that the 'total number of bars in the six Brandenburg Concertos is exactly 2220, Concertos 4, and 5 having an exact total of 1110 bars, and Concertos number 1, 2, 3, and 6 also with 1110 bars, creating a parallel 1: 1 (1110: 1110 bars) in 1: 2 (4: 2 concertos)'. Bach created these parallel proportions when he revised his works and collections in preparation for publication by adding a 'few bars to movements and movements to collections'.[187] According to Tatlow, proportional parallelism offers an explanation for these revisions, hitherto unexplained and with no apparent musical objective; she argues that Bach was motivated to make these changes because of his Lutheran beliefs in the theory and practice of music that leant heavily on universal harmony.[188].

---

186   James Harley, *Xenakis. His Life in Music*. (London: Routledge, 2004): 10.
187   Daniel R Melamed.'Parallel proportions in J S Bach's music'. Published online by Cambridge University Press: 05 February 2021
188   Ruth Tatlow. *Bach's Numbers: Compositional Proportion and Significance*. (Cambridge: Cambridge University Press, 2015).

Tatlow's theory challenges a long-held and influential theory of the German Bach scholar and theologian Friedrich Smend (1893-1980) which argues that J. S. Bach's works contain hidden symbolic references based on the German 'natural-order' number alphabet (A= 1 ... Z=24).[189] Smend's work spawned many further studies of Bach's presumed extensive use of number symbolism which was seen as in keeping with his 'mystical' musical outlook. The response to Tatlow's work has been mixed, with some scholars being critical, notably Daniel Melamed.[190] Alan Shepherd explored Tatlow's theory further in *Let's Calculate Bach* (2021) which sets out to apply theories of probability and statistical analysis to numbers in music.[191]

Golden Section and the associated Fibonacci series give rise to satisfying natural proportions. Many examples of their use can be found in music, sometimes these adhere strictly to the exact ratios and at other times they are approximations. The question remains as to whether they are used by composers consciously or subconsciously. A study of first movement sonata form across Mozart's piano sonatas reveals that, although more than a third of them fall within what might be considered to be a reasonable GS margin, it is more likely that Mozart lent towards the pleasing proportions intuitively through his innate sense of form. Cases have been made for various pieces using GS by Satie, Bartók and Debussy, but these have been inconclusive in the absence of documentary evidence to prove that they were based on mathematical calculations. This is not the case with several composers associated with the centre of new music in Darmstadt during the 1950s and 1960s; Stockhausen, Nono, Krenek and Nørgård, for example, all both consciously and openly integrated the use of the Fibonacci series into their compositional techniques.

---

189   Friedrich Smend. *Luther und Bach*. (Germany: Verlag Haus und Schule, 1947).
190   Daniel R. Melamed, "'Parallel Proportions' in J. S. Bach's Music," Eighteenth-Century Music 18, no. 1 (2021): 99–121. 4 See Melamed, "'Parallel Proportions,'" 100–103.
191   Alan Shepherd. *Let's Calculate Bach: Applying Information Theory and Statistics to Numbers in Music* (Cham, Switzerland: Springer, 2021).

11 Randomness and chance

Random numbers in mathematics

GENERALLY SPEAKING, RANDOMNESS means having no specific pattern, purpose or principle of organization. Random sequences of events have no order and single random events are unpredictable. Chance is the unknown and unpredictable element that causes an event to have one outcome rather than another. Nowadays random numbers are computer generated. They are widely used in both sample selection and in allocating treatments to units in designed experiments. Randomized control trials are used on two groups – a study group and a control group. In medical trials, for example, scientists test the study group (those who receive a new treatment) and a control group (those who are given an existing treatment or a placebo). Trials could be biased if it is known which group the patient belongs to so random selection is used to avoid this bias.

Just as random selection is used to avoid bias in scientific experiments by taking control away from the project leader, so too in music the use of chance operations means that total control is taken away from the composer. The terms indeterminacy, chance music and aleatoric music are often used interchangeably to describe this random element. Music using chance processes falls into three main groups: the use of random procedures to produce a fixed score; indeterminate notation, including graphic notation and texts to be interpreted by the performer(s); and scores where the indeterminate element arises from choices made by the players about elements of the performance.

This chapter explores the different ways in which composers have used randomised elements in their music from the use of rolls of dice by eighteenth-century composers to the computerised chance operation of Iannis Xenakis who coined the term 'stochastic music'. The leading composer of aleatoric music was undoubtedly John Cage who used chance procedures in almost all the music he created after 1951.

The use of dice in eighteenth-century novelty music

Dice (singular: die) were one of the earliest means of generating random numbers and examples can be traced back to 24,000 BC. During the eighteenth century a fashion developed where dice were used to introduce an element of chance into musical compositions. This genre was known as *Musikalisches Würfelspiel* (musical dice game). It was a system for randomly generating compositions from pre-composed bars of music. The games consisted of a number of pre-composed bars along with a method for selecting their precise sequence usually the throwing of a number of dice. Random numbers were used to order the melodic fragments thus generating a new piece. One of the first such games was published by the German composer and music theorist Johann Kirnberger (1721-1783) in 1757. *Der allezeit fertige Polonoisen und Menuettencomponist* (The at all times prepared composer of polonaises and minuets.) comprises a 'score' and a sequence of possible bars for both of the musical forms. The sequence of bars is determined by the throwing of either one or two dice.

Some pieces were attributed to well-known eighteenth-century composers such as C P E Bach, Mozart and Haydn. One such piece attributed to Mozart, but not authenticated, is *Anleitung zum Componieren von Walzern so viele man will vermittelst zweier Würfel, ohne etwas von der Musik oder Composition zu verstehen* (Instructions for the composition of as many waltzes as one desires with two dice, without understanding anything about music or composition) (1792). Rolls of the dice are used to select bars of music to be used in sequence and then played as a complete waltz. Each number rolled corresponded with a bar number given in a table. There are 176 numbers given in two tables (one table for the first eight bars of the waltz, and the second table for bars 9 to 16 of the composition). Each of the numbers from 1 to 176 corresponds with a bar of music. To select the first bar of the waltz, two dice are thrown and then the corresponding bar is chosen from the first column, for the second bar two more dice are thrown and the appropriate bar is selected from the second column and so on. Given that there are 11 different options for each of the 14 bars along with two options for one of the bars (bar 8) and only one option for the final bar (bar 16).[192] This means that there are 2×11^{14} possible variations on the waltz – 759, 499, 667, 166, 482 trillion. Here is the first table and the first 47 bars of the music.

Mozart dice game

	A	B	C	D	E	F	G	H
2	96	22	141	41	105	122	11	30
3	32	6	128	63	146	46	134	81
4	69	95	158	13	153	55	110	24
5	40	17	113	85	161	2	159	100
6	148	74	163	45	80	97	36	107
7	104	157	27	167	154	68	118	91
8	152	60	171	53	99	133	21	127
9	119	84	114	50	140	86	169	94
10	98	142	42	156	75	129	62	123
11	3	87	165	61	135	47	147	33
12	54	130	10	103	28	37	106	5

---

192   Giovanni Albini. 'Combinatorics, probability and choice in music composition'. Bridges 2018 Conference:

The appeal of the games was that they appeared to make it possible for anyone to be able to compose a piece of music. In fact composers used their knowledge of compositional procedures, harmony and formal design, coupled with a basic understanding of mathematics to design the games in such a way that whatever options were arrived at 'by chance', the resultant composition would sound convincing. Many bars are identical (bars 8 and 13, for example), many have the same notes in the left hand (3, 6, 32, 40, 41 and 42, for example) and the number of chords implied in the harmony is limited. So, for example, bars 3, 6, 7 and 8 are all based on the tonic chord of C major (C

E G), whereas bars 2, 4 and 5 are all based on the dominant chord - bar 2 is based on G (G B D) and bars 4 and 5 have an added 7th (G B D F#). This means that the table of bar numbers can be manipulated so that the devised piece makes harmonic sense. An example of this is Column H; this gives the selection for the eighth bar of the piece. According to the number of the dice thrown the bar selected will be either 30, 81, 24, 100 or 107, and so on. In fact each of these bars is based on a dominant chord with either an F natural or an F#. This implies an imperfect cadence which, in this Classical style of music would be expected half way through the 16 bar melody at the end of an eight bar phrase. Similarly, all the possible options for bar 16 (14, 73, 89, 170 and so on) are identical, meaning that whatever dice are thrown, the piece ends on a tonic chord as would be expected and sounds finished.

These compositions involving chance were novelties. Until the twentieth century, Western classical music had traditionally been a field in which chance had little or no role to play. As John Paynter writes, 'Musical action involves feeling, responding, thinking and making' and until the early years of the twentieth century, mainstream composers took this to mean that they should 'have overall control of their musical ideas in order to express the consciousness of their being'.[193] When chance music, often known as aleatoric music, emerged in the mid-twentieth century it challenged the traditional idea of a composition being a closed entity fixed by its composer; elements of chance which were undetermined by the composer were introduced into the process of composition and/or in performance. As such it explored what Paynter describes as 'ways of creating music which, if possible, would be divorced from the will and the taste of the composer – the very opposite of the traditional expressing and communicating objective'. Composing rather than 'being a matter of putting together all the details of a carefully calculated and evaluated structure' instead 'set up opportunities for "sound events" to happen.'[194]

> All sounds and any sounds could come in and find a place in the music; and the accidental structures they created could be as delightful in their own way as the random sounds of nature – which we can enjoy without their having been 'Composed'. [195]

---

193 John Paynter. *Sound and Structure*. (Cambridge: Cambridge University Press, 1992): 166.
194 Ibid
195 Ibid

Chance in twentieth-century music – Charles Ives, Henry Cowell, Morton Feldman and John Cage

The American composer Charles Ives (1874–1954) allowed a greater degree of freedom for performers in some of his pieces through the experimental use of alternatives, free passages and obscure notations inviting the performer's interpretation. A friend of Ives, the American composer Henry Cowell (1897-1965) continued this line of experimentation in aleatoric music. His *Mosaic Quartet* (*String Quartet No. 3*, 1934) is an experiment in musical form; a collection of five short movements in five different tempos where the order of the movements, and the number of times each is played, is left up to the performers. The piece also calls for some improvisation, another chance element. However it was Cowell's sometime pupil, John Cage (1912-1992), who, starting in the early 1950s, was to make the fullest exploration of chance operations. Cage's exploration of chance processes was partly inspired by *Extensions 1* (1951) by Morton Feldman (1926-1987) where sounds are written as numbers on graph paper, the figures indicating only the number of notes to be played and the register in which they are to be performed. Cage admired Feldman's use of 'whatever sound comes along'[196] and in his 'Lecture on Something' (written in early 1951), he described Feldman's graph pieces as having 'changed the responsibility of the composer from making to accepting.'[197]

In 1951 Cage completed his *Music of Changes,* a piano piece whose title makes reference to the *I Ching,* the Chinese oracle text sometimes known as *The Book of Changes.* The *I Ching* is concerned with divination – predicting the future through a systematic process, in this case using random processes to produce and interpret a series of symbols. The *I Ching* represents the binary poles of reality as Yin and Yang (negative/positive, night/day, winter/summer…) these are often discussed as female and male in the text of the *I Ching.* In the *I Ching* images are selected at random from a set of 64 by means of tossing yarrow sticks or coins. The *I Ching* is structured around an idea which is essentially combinatorial, that is it uses principles which stem from

---

196   Barry Russell and Julia Winterson. *Everything we do is Music. Cross curricular Experiments Based on the Music of John Cage.* (London: Edition Peters, 2016).
197   John Cage. 'Lecture on Something' in *Silence. Lectures and Writings by John Cage.* (Middletown, Conn.: Wesleyan University Press, 1961): 129.

combinatorics, the mathematical study of the enumeration, combination and permutation of sets of elements and the mathematical characteristics of their properties. A broken line represents Yin, and an unbroken line represents Yang. These lines are combined in sets of three to produce the eight basic trigrams, which are in turn combined to give 64 hexagrams. Each hexagram describes a different state of mind and is accompanied by an explanatory text. The text discusses each of the six lines as separate entities as well as explaining the meaning of the hexagram as a whole. Once the hexagram is cast, the *I Ching* is consulted for insight into its meaning. Cage made extensive use of the *I Ching* in the composition of *Music of Changes* using chance operations to create charts for tempi, dynamics, sounds and silences, and durations.

He went on to use chance operations in many other compositions and designed several different chance-controlled systems. In the *Music for Piano* series (1952–6) he translated the imperfections on paper into musical notes by the application of staff lines and clefs. *Atlas Eclipticalis* (1961-2) used templates drawn from maps of the constellations. *Concert for Piano and Orchestra* has no score, but rather consists of 63 highly detailed parts. It was composed using chance operations as well as the use of the imperfections found in the paper upon which the music was written. The notation of each part uses a system wherein space is relative to time. The amount of time is determined by the musician and then altered during performance, by the conductor, whose arms simulate the movement of the hands of a clock. The pianist may play the material in whole or in part, choosing any notations, elements, or parts, and playing them in any order.

In *HPSCHD* (1969) Cage used a computer to generate random musical material for a multi-media event that involved harpsichords and computer-generated sounds. The first performance lasted five hours and included slide projections. Three large posters were created featuring images chosen by chance operations, copies were sold at different prices arrived at by using the *I Ching*. The music comprises 20-minute solos for 1-7 amplified harpsichords and tapes for 1-51 monaural machines distributed unpredictably to make an indeterminate concert of any length having 2 - 58 separate channels with loudspeakers around the audience. The harpsichord solos used music by composers including Mozart (primarily the music of the aforementioned Mozart dice game), Beethoven, Chopin and Schoenberg.

In 1952 John Cage was one of a group of artists, musicians, poets, film makers and dancers to take part in what is said to be the first 'happening', a title which covers a range of multi-media performance activities where many things happen simultaneously with no narrative structure. Cage's first happening was at Black Mountain College. For that event, later called *Theatre Piece No. 1*, Cage gave all the participants time-brackets during which they were to dance, read poetry, show film and/or play music. The time brackets were used to specify the intervals during which sounds must start and stop. He then went on to use the concepts of both time brackets and happenings in many other works.

Cage was a prolific composer and most of his mature pieces included some element of chance. He stated that his goal was to be 'free of individual taste and memory'.[198] In some ways this is similar to the use of random selection to free bias in scientific experiments by taking control away from the project leader. The introduction of chance into a piece of music undermines the idea that creation requires a definite choice at every level on the part of the composer. With Cage this abandonment of control reached its extreme point 4' 33" (1952),or 'My silent piece,' as Cage called it, an empty structure in which the only sounds – those of the environment – are the most full of possibilities. As Cage once stated in his lecture 'Indeterminacy'

...the purpose of this purposelessness music would be achieved if people learned to listen; that when they listened they might discover that they preferred the sounds of everyday life to the ones they would presently here in the musical program; that was alright as far as I was concerned.[199]

Fluxus, Terry Riley and Cornelius Cardew

Cage's use of chance operations, particularly those used in multi-media performances, influenced many other composers. As Michael Nyman writes 'By the late sixties indeterminacy ... had made itself available to a larger

---

198   Cage. *Silence*, 59.
199   Cage. *Silence*, 267.

number of people with a wider range of abilities and experience'.[200] It was central to the work of the New York group Fluxus which formed in 1963 and went on to stage performances which were 'characterised by simplicity, experimentalism, chance, playfulness and humour'.[201] The indeterminate scores of Cage and his contemporary Christian Wolff often demanded technical and musical expertise, but with Fluxus this was no longer the emphasis, instead it encouraged unskilled players thereby, it could be argued, increasing the element of randomness. An advertisement for a concert in 1965 read as follows

> FLUXORCHESTRA PERFORMS 20 WORLD PREMIERS!
> Of avant-gagist music, ying yang music, Donald Duck music, anti-neobaroque music, pataphysical music, no music, La Monte Young conducting an orchestra of twenty unskilled instrumentalists.[202]

Fluxus counted amongst its members Dick Higgins, La Monte Young, Joseph Beuys, Yoko Ono and Terry Riley and eventually became an international movement with offshoots in Germany and elsewhere. In 1964 the American composer and performer Terry Riley (b 1935) went on to compose one of the most frequently played pieces where chance is central to its performance – *In C*.

The score of *In C* comprises 53 'repeating patterns' which should be played in consecutive order starting with 1 and ending with 53. All performers (any number playing any instrument) play from the same part apart from the 'pulse'. A steady quaver pulse is played on the top octave of a piano, marimba or vibraphone. 'Each performer decides for himself when to enter' and 'is free to move from figure to figure at his own rate'.[203] This element of choice makes the detail of each performance of *In C* unique. It could also be regarded as a precursor of the Minimalism movement.

In London Cornelius Cardew (1936-1981) formed the Scratch Orchestra which had a similar philosophy to that of Fluxus. All members were encouraged to participate on an equal footing regardless of skill or previous

---

200   Michael Nyman. *Experimental Music. Cage and Beyond*. (Cambridge: Cambridge University Press, 1999): 110
201   *Every Day is a Good Day. The Visual Art of John Cage*: 62.
202   *Village Voice*, 23 September 1965.
203   Score of Terry Riley *In C*.

experience. Formed in 1969, it brought together trained and untrained musicians from various backgrounds and was dedicated to free musical exploration. The band's repertoire included simple classics as well as Cardew's own compositions. Probably the most famous of his compositions is *Treatise* (1967) which has a totally graphic score (apart from the very occasional musical symbol). Cardew also worked as a graphic designer and the score – a melange of geometrical forms – raised graphic notation to the level of visual art as does the score for *Octet '61 for Jasper Johns* (1961). At the same time the score of *Treatise* provided the performer with little or no information as to how it was to be interpreted, consequently the ways that the sounds can be realized are endlessly diverse. As Cardew writes in the score 'Any rigidity of interpretation is automatically thwarted by the confluence of different personalities'. There are many recorded interpretations of *Treatise* and these are not confined to performances by experimental music groups. In 1999 the American rock band Sonic Youth included page 183 on their album *SYR4: Goodbye 20th Century*.

A key piece in the repertoire of the Scratch Orchestra was Cardew's *The Great Learning* (1971) based on the first chapter of the Confucian text with the same name. It was developed collectively by an experimental music group which Cardew ran at Morley College in South London. The piece consists of seven extensive movements - 'Paragraphs'- and is a blend of improvisation, formal composition and Maoist propaganda. In order to fulfil his intention that anyone could enjoy collective music-making, Cardew uses a variety of notations predominantly graphic notation and simple verbal descriptions of performance processes. 'Paragraph 7' is for voices alone, any number of trained or untrained singers. The text instructs the performers to start on a random note and with each breath to move to a new note sung by one of their neighbours.[204] This means that in performance, having started with a completely unpredictable chordal texture, the pitch content of the piece gradually narrows as notes are shared among the ensemble, until there's just a single note remaining. As a result every performance of Paragraph 7 is different in terms of its notes, its length and the overall sound. The outcome is random. As Cardew once pointed out, one of his standards was 'not to make a sound that's like something, but to make a sound that is just that …

---

204   Harris, Tony. *The Legacy of Cornelius Cardew*. (Farnham, Surrey: Ashgate, 2013): 66-67.

I want the feeling that everything you do is for the first time'.[205]

Iannis Xenakis and stochastic music

Although the above chance methods rely on random selection of one sort or another, none of them are as strictly mathematical as what became known as 'stochastic music'. Stochastic music was pioneered by the Greek composer Iannis Xenakis (1925 – 2001) who coined the term. In mathematics a stochastic process is one in which the steps are governed by rules of probability: a sequence of random objects often ordered in time and space. Xenakis used stochastic processes in his composition to determine musical parameters such as pitches, tempi, durations and timbres. Such numerical calculations were usually undertaken on computers. He wrote several articles and essays on stochastic processes, game-theory and computer programming in music. 1963 saw the publication of his seminal work on mathematics and music: *Formalized Music: Thought and Mathematics in Composition* (1971) in which he explains the thinking behind his techniques for composing music with stochastic mathematical functions.[206]

No discussion of the work of Xenakis, composer, architect and engineer, would be complete without mention of his extraordinary life. Of Greek parentage, he studied engineering in Athens and later, in Paris, composition with Olivier Messiaen. Messiaen advised him to take advantage of his architectural background 'You have the good fortune of being Greek, of being an architect and having studied special mathematics. Take advantage of these things. Do them in your music'. [207]Towards the end of World War II he fought for the Communist Greek resistance and in 1944 was severely injured in street fighting with British tanks. He was hit in the face by shrapnel receiving severe facial injuries and losing the sight in his left eye. When the new non-Communist government came to power in Greece, he was exiled to Paris under a death sentence which was not lifted until the end of the Greek junta in 1974. Following his arrival in Paris in 1947, he

---

205 Cited in Nyman, *Experimental Music*, 127.
206 Iannis Xenakis. *Formalized Music: Thought and Mathematics in Composition*. (New York: Pendragon Press, 1992).
207 Nouritza Matossian. *Xenakis*. (London: Kahn & Averill, 1986): 48.

worked for 12 years with the architect Le Corbusier. In 1958 Le Corbusier was commissioned to design the Philips Pavilion for the Brussels World Fair. He gave complete creative control of the project to Xenakis. As part of the World Fair, the Philips Pavilion staged a multimedia event in the Xenakis's steel and concrete structure which was based on parabolic curves. As visitors entered and exited the building they heard the music of Xenakis.[208] Once inside the auditorium *Poème électronique* by Edgar Varèse was projected from 350 speakers via 20 amplifier alongside ever-changing visuals creating a ground-breaking random simultaneity.

Xenakis's theories about stochastic synthesis were published in *Formalized Music, Thought and Mathematics in Composition*.[209] Here he advocated the use of stochastic processes to efficiently produce sonorities with 'numerous and complicated' transients arguing that the 'transient part of the sound is far more important than the permanent part in timbre recognition and in music in general'.[210] Stochastic processes are random and non-deterministic, that is, the next state of the environment is not fully determined by the previous one. Probability theory is used to determine what should happen next. In *Formalized Music*, Xenakis makes references to macroscopic (large scale) structures and the microscopic finer details of stochastic music. His music is often extremely elaborate in its detail, but that detail is usually at the service of the whole. This is well-illustrated in his orchestral piece *Pithoprakta* (1955-56) where Xenakis focuses on the overall block of sound, using probability theories to build different clouds of sound.[211] The finer detail, the individual notes and timbres are 'unpredictable' but are used to make up the combined mass of sound.[212]

Pithoprakta draws on probability theories including Gaussian distribution.[213] It is scored for string orchestra (with 46 individual parts), two trombones, xylophone, and wood block. The title translates as 'actions by means of probability'. The piece is based on the kinetic theory of gases

---

208   Xenakis' sound work *Interlude Sonore* which was subsequently titled *Concret PH*.
209   'New proposals in microsound structure' in Xenakis, *Formalized Music*, 242-254.
210   Xenakis, *Formalized Music*, 243-244.
211   Xenakis, *Formalized Music*, 12.
212   Gareth Roberts. *From Music to Mathematics {Exploring the connections}*. (Baltimore: John Hopkins University Press, 2016): 280.
213   Gaussian distribution (often known as normal distribution) is a very common continuous probability distribution and is the basis of a large proportion of statistical analysis.

where the temperature of a gas derives from the independent movement of its molecules. An analogy could be drawn between the movement of the molecules through space and that of the string instruments through their pitch ranges. At a macroscopic level, the work is made up of four sections which differ from each other in their use of textural and timbral characteristics, such as glissandi and pizzicato. As composer, Xenakis designed these large-scale features, but the individual components of sound such as which pitches and dynamics to use are generated by probability theories. Each sound-particle of the score is precisely defined through stochastic distribution functions at the same time as contributing to the overall sound impression. Xenakis created a graph representing a set of speeds of temperature and time; the pitches were drawn as the ordinates on the vertical scale and each of the instruments was represented by a jagged line representing a speed taken from the table of probabilities according to Gaussian distribution. The graph was then transcribed into traditional notation and the score was fixed. Continuous sounds are heard in the glissandi in the strings and trombones, for example, and discontinuous sounds include pizzicato plucking in the strings, tapping the strings with the opposite side of the bow, and the use of the wood block.[214]

In 1962, Xenakis composed his first string quartet *ST/4-1,080262*. The coded title translates as ST (stochastic composition), 4-1 (four instruments, first of its kind) created on *080262* (8 February 1962). The work's material was calculated by an IBM 7090 Computer. The computer was programmed with compositional parameters that determine the point in time that a sound sequence occurs, next its timbre (arco, pizzicato, glissando and so on), choice of instrument, pitch, direction of glissando, duration of notes, and dynamics. The string quartet also made use of pioneering extended techniques such as playing with the wood of the bow, bowing the body of the instrument and other new tapping and plucking techniques. In 1963-4 the composition of *Eonta* for piano, two trumpets and three trombones was also based on the theory of probabilities where some of the instrumental parts were calculated on the IBM 7090 computer at the Place Vendome in Paris.

Xenakis used the idea of random walks for the creation of *Mikka* (1972), a short work for solo violin. A random walk is a process in which a sequence

---

[214] Gareth Roberts lecture. 'Composing with Music. Iannis Xenakis and his Stochastic Music'. Gareth E. Roberts. Math/Music: Aesthetic Links, Montserrat Seminar, Spring 2012.

of discrete steps of fixed length is described in terms of the movement of a particle so in a one-dimensional random walk the state of the process is described as a position on a straight line. After starting at, say, 0 the first step takes the particle to either +1 or -1 with equal probability, after two steps it is +2, 0 or -2 and so on.[215] In *Mikka*, computer printouts of synthesized sounds are directly transformed into a continuous sequence of glissando curves for violin. The pitch is in continuous movement, with the left hand continuously sliding on the strings brushing past the microtones marked in the score. Plotted graphs of stochastic synthesis are also used in *N'Shima* (1975) and *Mikka S* (1975) where Xenakis read the horizontal axis of the graphs as time and mapped the vertical axis onto a grid of quarter-tone pitch values.

The music of *N'Shima* is based on the principle of Brownian motion, a continuous-time version of the random walk, displayed by minute particles of solid matter when suspended in a fluid or a gas resulting from their collision with the fast-moving molecules in the fluid. This translates in the music as short glissando figures sliding form one microtone to another. *N'Shima* is a Hebrew word meaning 'breath' or 'exhalation'. Scored for to mezzo sopranos and five instruments, the text of *N'Shima* text is taken from 'The Emperor's daughter and the King's son' a parable about two rival families whose children fall in love. Xenakis does not use whole words however; the vowels are used for tone colour and the consonants for articulation.

In the early 1980s, Xenakis's research, together with that of other colleagues specialising in electronics, software and signal processing, found a home at the *Centre d'Etudes de Mathématique et Automatique Musicales* in Paris along with the newly developed Unité Polyagogique Informatique du CEMAMu (UPIC) system completed in 1977. The UPIC system enabled composers to create sounds directly by 'moving an electromagnetic "pencil" across a sloping sensitised "drawing board"', and to hear the sounds they had created almost immediately. In the words of Richard Steinitz, the founder of the Huddersfield Contemporary Music Festival where the works of Xenakis were frequently performed, 'It thus united the visual and aural domains of Xenakis's career both as architect and composer'.[216]

---

215   A two-dimensional random walk is represented by a set of steps along a grid or lattice. Brownian motion is a continuous-time version of the random walk.
216   Richard Steinitz. *Explosions in November: The First 33 years of Huddersfield Contemporary Music Festival*. (Huddersfield: University of Huddersfield Press, 2011): 91.

Each of the composers above combined mathematical devices with musical considerations in their chance compositions. The eighteenth-century dice composers manipulated and controlled the harmonic and melodic possibilities to ensure that whatever pieces arose 'by chance' would be musically convincing. In contrast, the aleatoric compositions of the twentieth century deliberately avoided musical control. Ives and Cowell experimented with episodes of chance and one of Cage's aims was to be 'free of individual taste and memory'. By the late sixties Cage's use of indeterminacy influenced many other composers amongst these Terry Riley whose piece *In C* could be regarded as a precursor of the Minimalism movement. However, the strictest mathematical approach was taken by Xenakis who coined the term stochastic music in which the compositional steps are governed by rules of probability.

12 Fractals and chaos theory

FRACTALS BELONG TO a class of curves or complex geometric shapes in which each part has the same statistical character as the whole, that is, it is made up of smaller scale copies of itself. Their properties are found in many irregularly shaped objects and non-uniform phenomena in nature such as coastlines and mountain ranges. The word fractal is derived from the Latin word *fractus* meaning broken.

Can fractals be found in music? This chapter examines the evidence. It opens by looking at fractals in mathematical terms describing the characteristics and properties of the von Koch curve and the Cantor set and outlining the early work of Benoit Mandelbrot in this field. Over the years various attempts have been made to identify fractal patterns in music, and several ideas have been proposed including the use of nested sequences and self-similarity. These include the prolation canons dating from the fifteenth century by composers such as Ockeghem and des Prez. More recently the Hungarian composer György Ligeti showed a great interest in both fractals and chaos theory, inspired by the computer-generated illustrations of Heinz-Otto Peitgen and Peter Richter. Several compositions of Ligeti are examined and analysed in terms of their fractals characteristics. The American composer Charles Wuorinen was also fascinated by fractal geometry and he used some of its mathematical properties in the construction of his music. In recent years several composers have taken advantage of the capabilities of computers to generate fractal inspired pieces, amongst these the Norwegian composer Rolf Wallin. Robert Sherlaw Johnson was one of the first to explore this field and he provides an illuminating critique of his method. Nowadays there are increasingly sophisticated software packages specifically designed to created fractal music. The chapter concludes with a brief discussion of the original question 'Can fractals be found in music?'

What is a fractal?

Fractals commonly have 'fractional dimension' a concept which was first introduced by the mathematician Felix Hausdorff in 1918 and a measure of their complexity. Although fractional dimension, and other key concepts associated with fractals, had been known about for some time, it was not until the French-American polymath Benoit Mandelbrot (1924-2010) coined the term 'fractal' in his 1975 book on the subject that more interest was shown in the field.[217] Later Mandelbrot's seminal 1982 book, *The Fractal Geometry of Nature* catalogued the ubiquity of geometric patterns found in nature and is widely credited for bringing fractals to popular attention. He highlighted the need for fractal mathematics and pointed out that they could be useful in applied mathematics for modelling a variety of phenomena from physical objects to the behaviour of the stock markets. Since the 1980s virtually every scientific field has been explored from a fractal viewpoint and fractal geometry has become a major area of mathematics. Fractals are useful in modelling structures in which similar patterns recur at progressively smaller scales, as well as describing partly random or chaotic phenomena such as crystal growth and galaxy formation.

The von Koch curve

The properties of fractals can be illustrated in the von Koch curve (see Figure 1). An intricate and complicated object, the main von Koch curve contains many tiny von Koch curves which are made up of smaller scale copies of itself. This property is known as self-similarity. A self-similar object is one whose component parts resemble the whole. Details or patterns are reiterated at progressively smaller scales so that in effect, it remains invariant under

---

217 Benoit Mandelbrot. *Les Objets Fractals: Forme, Hasard et Dimension*(1975) later translated in 1977 as *Fractals: Form, Chance and Dimensio*. London: W H Freeman and Co,1975).

FRACTALS AND CHAOS THEORY

changes of scale, that is, it has scaling symmetry. In classical mathematics curves are usually described in terms of tangents but the von Koch curve does not have a well-defined slope or direction at any one point, hence it is too irregular to be described in traditional mathematical language. Mathematicians disagree on a precise definition, but a fractal is typically described as exhibiting self-similarity,

The von Koch curve

The curve is constructed by repeatedly replacing the middle third of each line segment with the other two sides of an equilateral triangle. Because the same step is repeated over and over again this is known as a recursive construction. When three von Koch curves are fitted together they form a snowflake curve (see below).

The von Koch snowflake

The main tool of fractal geometry is fractional dimension. The von Koch curve has dimension

$\log 4/\log 3 = 1.262$.[218]

The Cantor set

In 1883 the German mathematician George Cantor (1845-1918) introduced what he referred to as the middle third Cantor set. This was obtained by repeatedly removing the middle thirds of intervals which results in a basic self-similar fractal made up of two scaled ½ copies of itself (see Figure 3).

The middle third Cantor set

---

218   Kenneth Falconer. *Fractal Geometry. Mathematical foundations and Applications.* (Chichester: Wiley, 2003): xix.

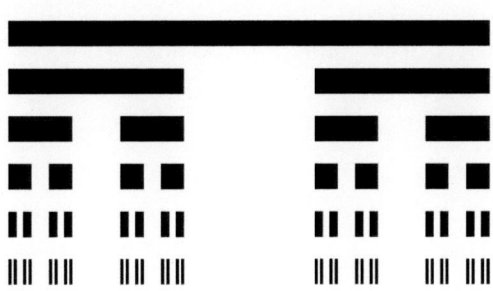

Each stage of the construction is obtained by removing the middle third of the previous stage. Take the closed interval [0, 1]. First delete the open interval that forms the middle third [1/3, 2/3] then delete [1/9, 2/9], then delete [7/9, 8/9] and so on.

In 1918 Felix Hausdorff showed that the middle third Cantor set had dimension of log2/log3=0.631.

In summary the main features of fractals (F) as given by Kenneth Falconer in his classic text *Fractal Geometry. Mathematical Foundations and Applications* are:

- F has a fine structure i.e. detail on arbitrarily small scales
- F is too irregular to be described in traditional geometrical language
- Often F has some form of self-similarity, perhaps approximate or statistical, made up of small scale copies of itself in some way
- In most cases F has a simple recursive construction.[219]

Early attempts to find fractals in music

Although there is no widely accepted consensus as to what constitutes a fractal pattern in music, a variety of statistical tools have been proposed over the years. The earliest contributions came from the American physicists Richard F. Voss and John Clarke in the 1970s who analysed the spectral density of audio power (effectively loudness) in a range of recordings from news radio, to Scott Joplin rags and Bach's Brandenburg Concerto No. 1.

---

219 Falconer, *Fractal Geometry*, xxv.

Through this they identified what they referred to as scaling behaviours (the word fractal had not yet been coined) in the fluctuations of volume as well as some pop music melodies.[220] They observed that both pitch and volume fluctuations showed $1/f$ distribution, a type of distribution often associated with the hierarchical structure of fractals.[221]

Twenty years later, Henderson-Sellers and Cooper proposed a definition of musical self-similarity based on note lengths analogous to the Cantor set. They specified how the faster passages are to be related to the slower ones arriving at a definition of a musical fractal based on the development of a melodic line; different time scales appear sequentially, in a single line of music, so that the entire passage is built from copies of the original idea written in shorter notes. Each faster copy is transposed in such a way that it begins with a note from the previous order so that every new order retains the memory of all previous orders, creating a self-similar structure. The melody is thus constructed through layers of nested sequences in a single line of music, which becomes faster and faster at each order, but retains the outline of the slower version in the leading notes of each scaled copy.[222] This algorithm is clearly quite mechanical and prescriptive; it cannot be sustained musically over any length of time and examples found in music depend on creative adaptations. Such an example can be found in the opening bars of 'Uranus, the Magician' from Holst's *The Planets* (1917). Here the opening statement is made by trumpets and trombones in dotted semibreves, this is followed by a second statement by tubas, but this time the note values are halved. The note values are halved again for the last statement by the timpani. As can be seen in this final statement the pitch order of the notes is no longer followed strictly.

---

220   Voss RF, Clarke J. 1/f noise in music and speech. Nature 1975;258:317–8 and Voss R F, Clarke J.. J Acoust Soc Am 1978; 63(1). 258-163.

221   In terms of noise $1/f$ noise (or fractal noise) is a signal with a frequency spectrum such that the power per frequency interval is inversely proportional to the frequency of the signal.

222   Henderson-Sellers B, Cooper D. 'Has classical music a fractal nature?: a reanalysis. Comput Hum 1994, 27(4): 277–84.

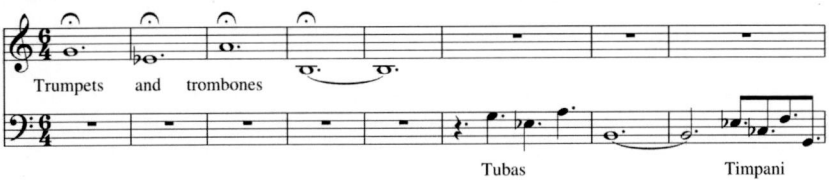

The American musician and mathematician Harlan Brothers has been exploring fractals in music for some years and has written extensively on the topic. He has pointed out that identifying fractals in music is more problematic than seeing them in an image. 'Unlike a picture, which is all laid out so that you can instantly see the structure, music is fundamentally a serial phenomenon… With music, the whole piece takes shape in your mind. This makes it more challenging to identify the self-similarity'.[223] It may be difficult to perceive fractals in music without looking at the score or listening to the piece repeatedly.

In 2007 Brothers published a study of the fractal structure of Bach's *Cello Suite No. 3* where he found that, at various points, patterns of long and short notes within bars reappeared as patterns of long and short phrases at larger scales. He referred to this as 'structural scaling' noting that this self-similarity bore a striking resemblance to the Cantor set. According to Brothers, Mandelbrot had suspected that music contained fractal patterns but that he didn't have time to investigate further. Subsequently Brothers contributed a chapter to *Benoit Mandelbrot: A Life in Many Dimensions* in which he lists the seven types of statistical self-similarity that he had found in music: duration scaling, the distribution of note lengths; melodic interval scaling, the distribution of changes in pitch; melodic moment scaling, the distribution of the changes in melodic intervals; harmonic interval scaling; structural scaling; and motivic scaling. Motivic scaling involves the simultaneous rendition of the same motif or theme at various tempos resulting in an intricate interplay of the theme with its faster or slower versions. An example of this musical self-similarity is the prolation canon (see pages 150-1) where each voice in the canon sings or plays the same music, but at different speeds with voices entering either successively or simultaneously.

---

223   Harland Brothers. 'Structural scaling in Bach's Cello Suite No. 3'. *Fractals*. 15, 2007: 90.

The prolation canon

The fifteenth-century Franco-Flemish composer Johannes Ockeghem was the master of the prolation canon and possibly its inventor.[224] His *Missa prolationum* (c. 1450) presents a series of prolation canons each offering a different variant of the form and whose interval of imitation moves from the unison progressively through to the octave. Many of his compositions are grounded in some rational, often ingenious, conception, some also serving a didactic as well as musical purpose. 'Kyrie Eleison I' is a double prolation canon, where in the opening bars, two separate pairs of voices, soprano and bass, alto and tenor use two different motifs. The four parts begin together, each of the four voices follow the entire six-bar theme exactly once. For each pair, the ratio of tempos is 3:2. This is clearest to see in the alto and tenor parts where the alto uses four minims and a crotchet (all divisible by 2), whereas the tenor part uses four dotted minims and a dotted crotchet (all divisible by 3). After this passage, the music continues as a regular canon (see page 150).

Prolation canons continued to be composed in the twentieth century in, for example, Arvo Pärt's vocal work *Cantus in Memoriam Benjamin Britten* (1977) and the first movement of Shostakovitch's *Symphony No. 15 (1971)*. *Cantus in Memoriam Benjamin Britten*, scored for string orchestra and bell, is a prolation canon in five voices, with a ratio of speeds of 16: 8: 4: 2: 1 (violin I, violin II, viola, cello, and bass). The theme is based on the descending octave of an A minor scale, developed sequentially with one note added at each repetition. Thus, the theme proceeds as A-A-G-A-G-F-A-G-F-E-A thus creating what could be described as an ever-elongating fractal sequence. In the same way as Ockeghem and des Prez, the composers were using this compositional device consciously, albeit being unaware of the concept of fractals. Once the concept of fractals became well-known, a number of composers used fractal mathematics as part of the compositional process. Amongst these are the Hungarian György Ligeti, the Norwegian composer Rolf Wallin and the American Charles Wuorinen.

---

224   John McDonough and Andrzej Herczynski. *Chaos, Solitons and Fractals* (Science Direct 170, 2023).

The use of fractals by György Ligeti

György Ligeti had a keen interest in fractals: he was well-informed and knowledgeable, and he took some of the ideas he had learnt and applied these to his compositions. In a 1990 interview, Ligeti commented on the influence of mathematics and fractals in his compositional process.[225] He said, '... in my music, there are mathematical considerations of fractal geometry. Its kind of growth and its processes of pattern transformation have occupied me for a great deal'.

In 1985 Ligeti first met the German mathematician Heinz-Otto Peitgen (b 1945). Peitgen was a pioneer of fractal geometry who had helped to introduce fractals to the broader public, partly through the publication of his lavishly illustrated book of computer-generated images *The Beauty of Fractals*[226]. Their friendship lasted until Ligeti's death in 2006. In Peitgen's words 'He introduced me to new music and to him I opened the door to the study of fractals, fractal geometry and other fields of mathematics ... However dissimilar Ligeti's origin and life as a musician was from my scientific background, we both saw that what we did was, in some way, remarkably connected and interwoven'.[227]

It is important to note that Ligeti did not apply fractal geometry to his music with systematic mathematical rigour; rather he took some of the principles and formulated compositional procedures based loosely upon them. He once said that only two of his compositions were 'deliberately based on ideas from contemporary mathematics, the first piano etude 'Désordre' (1985) which is self-similar - an iterated structure based consciously on the Koch snowflake' - and the fourth movement of the *Piano Concerto* - 'a fractal piece'.[228]

---

225   Stephen Satory. 'Colloquy: An interview with Gyorgy Ligeti'. *Canadian University Music Review*. 1990.
226   Heinz-Otto Peitgen & Peter Richter. *The beauty of fractals* (Berlin & New York, 1986).
227   Heinz Otto Peitgen. 'Continuum, Chaos and Metronomes – A Fractal Friendship' in Louise Duchesneau and Wolfgang Marx. *György Ligeti. Of Foreign Lands and Strange Sounds.* (Martlesham, Suffolk: Boydell Press (2011).
228   Ligeti in conversation with Heinz-Otto Peitgen and Richard Steinitz, Huddersfield Contemporary Music Festival (November 1993) cited in Richard Steinitz. 'The Dynamics of Disorder'. *The Musical Times*, Vol. 137, No. 1839 (May, 1996): 8.

Ligeti – 'L'escalier du diable (The Devil's Staircase)'

These two pieces will be looked at later in more detail, but first some mention should be made of another piano etude - 'L'escalier du diable' (The Devil's Staircase)' (1995-2001), the thirteenth etude which makes direct reference to a construction based on the Cantor set. The devil's staircase, sometimes referred to as the infinite staircase or the Cantor function, has unequal ascending steps constructed by using, for example the recursive 1/3 to 2/3 proportions of the most common middle-thirds Cantor set (see below).

The Devil's staircase

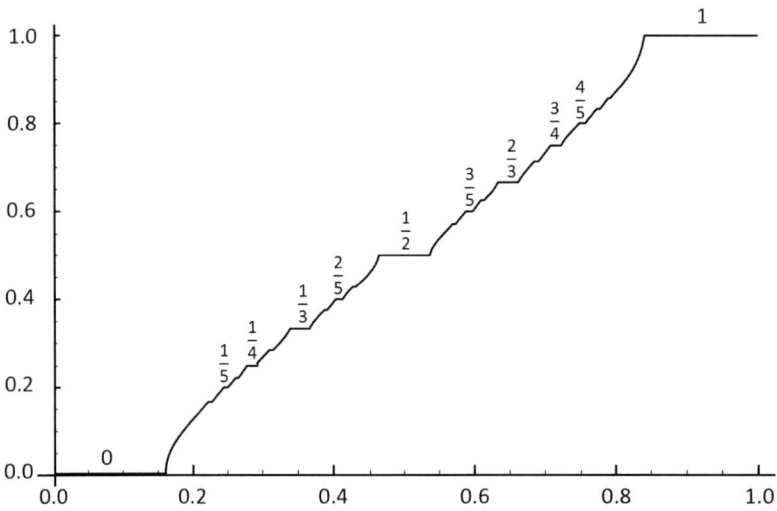

'L'escalier du diable' is a flamboyant virtuosic piece, *presto* with polyrhythms and rising chromatic scales getting progressively higher. Richard Steinitz describes it thus:

> The rotating repetitions of the principal motif climb up an endless staircase, flight upon flight, octave by octave. Meanwhile, the pattern restarts in low register, as if emerging from dark subterranean dungeons. Like the synthetic spiral - the computer-generated illusion

- it seems to rise ad infinitum, yet remains enigmatically the same. Its patterns can be represented numerologically, but are intended first and foremost to generate polyrhythmic energy. Here we have Ligeti at his most melodramatic, in music overwhelmingly powerful and thrilling.[229]

Although it has recursive qualities, it does not follow the strict mathematical formula prescribed by the devil's staircase. As Steinitz writes, 'Ligeti constructs his musical staircase using his own numerical system', and although 'Its patterns can be represented numerologically' they 'are intended first and foremost to generate polyrhythmic energy'.[230]

Ligeti – 'Désordre'

'Désordre' is the first of Ligeti's piano etudes and, as was mentioned above, Ligeti described it as having an 'iterated structure based consciously on the Koch snowflake'. The piece is marked *molto vivace*, very fast, and could be described as a study in rapid polyrhythms moving up and down the keyboard. The right hand plays only white keys and the left hand is restricted to the black keys in a pentatonic mode. Although both the right hand and left hand have eight quavers to the bar, the barlines and accents are placed differently. Hence the material of the two hands unfolds simultaneously but independently. As Steinitz puts it, 'At first glance their musical material looks alike. However, it is their dissimilarity which is crucial.' Later in the piece the same phrase structure is resized, the melodic material is similar but the phrase lengths are shorter and the accents appear more frequently.

In the words of Steinitz, 'Repeating an operation over and over again, on ever smaller scales culminates almost inescapably in a self-similar structure, a classic example being the 'Koch curve''. How do these musical procedures measure up against Falconer's fractal characteristics that were listed earlier? The music has elements of a 'fine structure' with small scale detail and it exhibits some form of 'self-similarity'. However, although it could be argued

---

229   Richard Steinitz.'Maths and Chaos'. *The Musical Times, Vol. 137, No. 1837 (March, 1996)*: 19.
230   Ibid.

that it has a 'recursive construction', this is not created in an orderly fashion in the way that a von Koch curve would be by repeating the same steps and more specifically replacing middle thirds.

Ligeti – The Piano Concerto

Ligeti was particularly influenced and inspired by computer fractal images particularly those in *The Beauty of Fractals*. Indeed he was so fond of one of the images of a Julia set that Peitgen dedicated it to him naming it the Ligeti fractal, and Peitgen's '29 Arms at Seahorse Valley', a mathematical image of the Mandelbrot set, was an inspiration for the *Piano Concerto*.[231] Although Ligeti understood the mathematical calculations behind fractals, these were not directly involved in his compositional methods. When describing the fourth movement of his *Piano Concerto*, he wrote

> The whole structure of the piece is self-similar and the impression we get is that of a giant interconnected web ... This vast self-similar maelstrom can be traced back - indirectly – to musical ideas which had been unleashed by beautiful fractal imaged of the Julia and Mandelbrot sets ... Not that I use iterative calculations when I composed this piece ... rather, it originated out of an intuitive synthetic correspondence on a poetic level.[232]

Steinitz describes the movement thus,

> Indeed, we do find in this movement a particular musical gesture repeated endlessly at different magnifications... The movement is literally flooded with iterations of a three-note fragment, its extensions, contractions and derivatives - all progressively superimposed in varying tempos, with varying articulation, coloration and magnitude. The musical design builds up like a complex graphic image scanned,

---

[231] Richard Steinitz. *György Ligeti. Music of the Imagination.* (London: Faber and Faber, 2003).
[232] Gyorgi Ligeti 'Zu meinem Klavierknonzert (1988)' in Gesammelte Schriften, Vol. 2 :299, translated by Louise Duchesneau cited in *György Ligeti. Of Foreign Lands and Strange Sounds*. Boydell Press (2011): 103.

pixel by pixel, on a computer screen. By the end of the movement we've arrived at an elaborate, multi-dimensional fantasy of self-replicated whirls, riotous colour and polymetric energy, an exuberant vortex of order and chaos, symmetry and freedom, like the magnificent fractal images of Mandelbrot and Peitgen.[233]

We are reminded of the problems in identifying fractals in music where, as Brothers pointed out, 'Unlike a picture, which is all laid out so that you can instantly see the structure … With music, the whole piece takes shape in your mind'.[234] If, as Hans Lauwerier writes in the introduction to *Fractals. Images of Chaos*, 'A fractal is a geometric figure in which an identical motif repeats itself on an ever-diminishing scale' then this movement of the *Piano Concerto* movement cannot be described as fractal.235 It would not be true to say that it unfolds progressively over time moving systematically from large statements of the three-note fragment to ever smaller more intricate patterns although some aspects of this are evident, the ever-decreasing values are not systematic. The movement opens with loud statements of the three-note motif interspersed with bars of silences. Over the course of the movement the music does become more complex but reaching a climax about three quarters of the way through, rather than the end, before petering out to a pianissimo conclusion. Perhaps the fractal images are more evident in the dynamics and orchestration where the finer detail is represented by the high notes of the glockenspiel and piccolo, and towards the end of the movement the piano makes increasing use of the higher register, moving upwards, higher and higher to the very top of the keyboard register.

Tom Johnson and Naryana's Cows

Much of the music of the American composer Tom Johnson (b. 1939) follows mathematical principles and logical procedures such as permutations,

---

233   Richard Steinitz. 'Weeping and Wailing'. *The Musical Times*, Vol. 137, No. 1842 (Aug, 1996): 17-22.
234   Brothers. 'Structural scaling', 90.
235   Hans Lauwerier. *Fractals. Images of Chaos*. (London: Penguin. 1991): xix.

combinations, tiling, block design and fractals.[236] He too was inspired by Benoit Mandelbrot's book *Fractals* (1977) with its 'pictures of the Koch curve, the Minkowsky sausage, the Sierpinski sponge, the Peano island and the Cantor triadic bar'. For Johnson they were 'essentially maps showing the route that I was about to follow'.[237]

When interviewed by New Music USA in 2003, Johnson was asked 'What role has theory played in your compositions and how important is it for people to know the theory behind the music in order to appreciate it?' He replied by saying 'Theory is when you know everything about it but it won't work. Practice is when it works but you don't know why' adding that good composers not only compose but also think a lot about how they compose. This was the thinking behind what he describes as his 'purely technical' book, *Self-Similar Melodies* [238](1996), a didactic study with specially composed examples based on this characteristic of fractals.[239]

Many of his pieces use a variety of techniques in self-similarity, although as he pointed out in his IRCAM lecture of 2006, 'true self-similar structure is relatively rare.' In the lecture he defines these pieces as 'music that somehow contains itself within itself and does so on at least three different levels of time. The use of self-similarity is quite evident to the listener his piece, *Narayana's Cows*. It was 'derived from a 14th-century Indian problem in which a mother cow gives birth to a female calf at the beginning of each year and each calf becomes a mother and does the same thing beginning in her fourth year. By the 10th year, the herd numbers 60 mothers and daughters… repeating one process over and over always results in some kind of self-similarity' The following illustration shows the 60-note Narayan sequence that has evolved by the 10th year. The first line of numbers below represents the 60 cows of the herd in its 10th year. The second line singles out the 19 mothers, that is, the quarter-notes, of the 10th year, and this happens to be the notes of the 19

---

236   For more information about Johnson's use of tiling procedures see - Tom Johnson. 'Tiling in my music'. https://web.northeastern.edu/seigen/MusicDIR/Tiling_in_my_music_Johnson.pdf
237   Tom Johnson. 'Self-Similar Structures in my Music: an Inventory lecture' presented in the MaMuX seminar, IRCAM, Paris, Oct. 14, 2006 in context with a lecture on self-similarity by mathematician Emmanuel Amiot
238   Tom Johnson. *Self-Similar Melodies*. (Two Eighteen Pr, 1996)
239   https://newmusicusa.org/nmbx/What-role-has-theory-played-in-your-compositions-and-how-important-is-it-for-people-to-know-the-theory-behind-the-music-in-order-to-appreciate-it-Tom-Johnson/ April 2003

cows of the 7th year, and the mothers of the 7th year are equivalent to the six mothers and daughters of the 4th year, shown on the last line.

```
1 2 2 2 2 3 2 3 3 3 2 3 3 3 3 4 2 3 3 3 3 4 3 4 4 2 3 3 3 3 4 3 4 4 3 4 4 4 2 3 3 3 3 4 3 4 4 3 4 4 4 3 4 4 4 5
1     2 2 2   2   3 2   3 3   2   3 3   3   2   3 3   3     3   4
1           2       2       2           2   3
```

In Johnson's musical work *Narayana's Cows* there are two layers: one verbal and the other musical. In the verbal layer, the speaker transposes Narayan's numbers into words: 'The first year there is only the original cow and her first calf. The second year there is the original cow and two calves. The third year there is the original cow and three calves. The fourth year the oldest calf becomes a mother, and we begin a third generation of Narayana's cows.' And so on until the seventeenth year is reached. The second layer is made up of musical sounds where the pitch correlates with the cows' generation, and the rhythm correlates with the difference between a cow (long note) and a calf (short note). Clearly unfolding to the listener, together they evolve into an accumulative and complex melody.

Chaos theory

In the words of Peitgen, 'Ligeti was just as fascinated by the discovery of deterministic chaos as he was by Benoit Mandelbrot's fractal geometry'. Chaos theory (the science of dynamical systems) focuses on the behaviour occurring in a system under iteration and is the study of apparently random or unpredictable behaviour in systems governed by deterministic laws. Fractals form part of the visual identity of chaos. In recent decades a diversity of systems has been studied that behave unpredictably, despite the fact that the forces involved are governed by well-understood physical laws. The common element is sensitive dependence to initial conditions and to the way in which they are set in motion. The connection between chaos and fractals is the strange attractor. In the field of dynamical systems an attractor is a set of states towards which a system tends to evolve from a wide variety of starting conditions. A strange attractor is a complicated set with a fractal structure. One effect of chaos is commonly known as the Butterfly Effect, where a small change in initial conditions can lead to a large change in the behaviour of a system. The term comes from the meteorologist Edward Lorenz who accidentally discovered the effect in 1961 while trying to model the weather. In one run-through he entered 0.506 into his data instead of 0.506127 and was surprised to see that the original results were vastly altered by such a small change in one variable; where there was originally sun, there was now rain, a windy day became a calm day and so on. The Butterfly Effect therefore describes how a small change in one state of a deterministic system can bring about large differences in a later state with the potential to render long-term predictions impossible.

According to Steinitz 'Ligeti realised that the new theories which sought to explain the precarious balance between order and disorder, pattern and chaos, and the apparent origin of both conditions in measurable deterministic situations, had intriguing parallels with the way he composed.'[240] In a later article he writes 'That he [Ligeti] now views this interaction from the vantage-point of current mathematical thinking is indicated by his naming the first study after a crucial issue in the science of dynamical systems (more commonly known as chaos theory), the concept of 'disorder'.'[241] 'Désordre', writes Steinitz 'demonstrates how tiny discrepancies quickly breed confusion. Albeit in microcosm and in a finite context, Ligeti illustrates a fundamental idea of chaos - that small differences in initial conditions rapidly lead to dramatic outcomes.' In his 2012 lecture on 'Chaos and Fractals in Music' the mathematician Gareth Roberts explained how this is achieved:

> Each hand opens with identical 8-beat rhythmic patterns (3 + 5). In the fourth measure, the right hand drops a beat, playing a 7-beat pattern rather than an 8-beat one, but continues the 8-beat pattern for the next three measures. This small change starts to cause a big shift, audible for the listener due to the shifting accents in each hand. In the eighth measure, the right hand drops another beat, playing 7 instead of 8. Now, the left hand is two beats ahead instead of one. Again, the right hand only drops a beat in this one measure. The "iterative"

---

240   Steinitz, 'Maths and Chaos', 15.
241   Steinitz. 'Dynamics of Disorder', 8.

process of dropping a single beat continues, as the right hand drops a beat approximately every four measures so that the two hands become completely out of synch, and the butterfly effect is realized.[242]

Closer analysis of 'Désordre' shows that this system is not rigorous, however, so it is not obeying the deterministic laws of chaos theory. In the same lecture, Roberts argues that the American composer Steve Reich employs a similar Butterfly Effect device where 'small changes in rhythmic structure (e.g. slight phase shifts) lead to big changes in the music' in, for example, *Clapping Music* (see pages 32-4). In *Clapping Music* (for two players) it could be argued that Reich applies deterministic laws in the way that the phase shifts he uses are applied systematically. In phase shifting constantly repeated patterns are subjected to gradual changes, one part repeats constantly and another gradually shifts out of phase with it, a compositional device that can be seen in terms of a mathematical translation. In *Clapping Music* the phase shifting is systematically applied quaver by quaver, with Player 2 shifting further out of phase with Player 1, effect is one of huge rhythmic diversity until eventually the parts come together again. It is interesting to note that *Clapping Music* was composed in 1972 so it pre-dates the period when chaos theory was widely known.

The use of fractals and chaos theory in the music of Rolf Wallin

The Norwegian composer Rolf Wallin (b. 1957) combines computer-generated systems and fractals with his intuitive approach to composition. He is dismissive of what he refers to as Ligeti's 'supposedly 'fractal' music'. In a lecture given in 1989 he said

> ... when one investigates Ligeti's supposedly 'fractal' music, for instance his piano etudes from 1985, one finds that his music could very well be achieved without having heard of the existence of chaos theory or

---

242   Gareth Roberts. 'Chaos and Fractals in Music'. Maths and Music: Aesthetic Links, Montserrat, April 16, 2012.

having seen the Peitgen-Richter pictures. The techniques he uses are derived exclusively from traditional compositional practice, and the music is neither more nor less fractal than African drum rhythms or a Bartok string quartet.[243]

Wallin outlined a more mathematical approach to composing with fractals in a lecture at the Nordic Symposium for Computer Assisted Composition, Stockholm in 1989. Wallin describing several ways to apply fractal mathematics and chaos theory to music using different mathematical formulas. As he points out there are 'countless ways of applying fractals to music'. His rationale for the use of computers and chaos theory is that he can give the computer a 'task where the direction is clearly defined, but where the details are unpredictable, and therefore generating a balance between global order and local disorder'. As he says, 'this has kicked me out of some of the tracks I have been stuck in'.

Stonewave (1990), one of his most popular and frequently performed percussion pieces, is made purely from fractal mathematics and in his programme note to *Stonewave* he writes that 'These formulas, used in the fast growing field of "Chaos theory", are relatively simple, but they generate fascinating and surprisingly "organic" patterns when shown graphically on a computer screen, or played as music.' He adds that 'One should think that such a mathematical approach would lead to sterile and 'theoretical' music. The sound world of *Stonewave*, however, is not one you would associate with math books. The steady, insistent pulse, and the use of sequences put squarely up against each other or divided by long rests suggest an invisible ritual.'

The use of fractals in the music of Charles Wuorinen

Much of the catalogue of the American composer Charles Wuorinen (1938-2020) was constructed using idea taken from fractals; the generation of infinite and chaotic structures through the iteration of finite elements. He was fascinated by fractal geometry, in particular the work of Benoit Mandelbrot

---

243   Rolf Wallin. Lecture given at the Nordic Symposium for computer Assisted Composition, Stockholm, 1989.

whose ideas seemed to confirm his own ideas about musical structure and form. Mandelbrot had an interest in Wuorinen's music and, just as Ligeti struck up a long friendship with the mathematician Peitgen, so too did Wuorinen when he got know Mandelbrot. In his essay, 'Music and Fractals', Wuorinen identified the ways in which fractals arose in his music – acoustically, rhythmically, structurally and in terms of pitch generation. Acoustically, the signal has a $1/f$ distribution (as identified by Voss and Clarke). Rhythmically, his music has a self-similar, hierarchical division of time, and pitch generation is similar across different levels. In terms of structure, a single harmonic progression can be used to determine a single phrase, part of a section, or a whole section.[244] In this way Wuorinen developed a logical structure made up of scaled units on which he built his compositions. As he writes, these fractal techniques act as a preparation for composing adding that 'Having made such preparation, then I have found it possible to compose with a kind of intuitive freedom which still assures macrostructural coherence'.

Computer generated fractal music

There have been many instances of computer generated compositions based on fractals as well as computer programmes and software specifically designed to create these. Robert Sherlaw Johnson (1932-2000) was one of the first composers to explore computer generated fractal music. He speculated that 'if meaningful visual patterns can be created by fractal generation, then it should also be possible to create aural ones'. In 'Composing with fractals' he describes the process whereby he takes various iterative formulas to generate musical patterns leading to completed compositions. Echoing the words of Harlan Brothers, he points out that one of the difficulties in composing in this way is that although in visual patterns it is the 'accumulation of values that gives rise to a sensible pattern' in the case of music, 'the whole is not perceived simultaneously and only localised patterns can make sense'. He ends by posing the question 'Can the computer be said to have composed anything?' concluding that in his compositional process although the

---

244 Michael Frame and Amelia Urry. *Fractal Works. Grown, Built and Imagined.* (Yale University Press, 2016): 104.

computer, using various formulas, generates a stream of variables, 'it is only when the stream of variables is harnessed in a particular way that musical ... sense is derived from it otherwise it remains a chaotic sequence'.[245]

So, can fractals be found in music? To recap, in simple terms, a fractal is a geometric figure featuring self-similarity where an identical motif repeats itself on an ever-diminishing scale. So it could be argued that a great deal of music has a fractal element to it in terms of repeated motifs and rhythms used at different pitches or durations, augmentation (scaling up) and diminution (scaling down) being long-established compositional techniques. As we have seen, Wallin criticised what he refers to as Ligeti's 'supposedly 'fractal' music' on the grounds that the techniques that Ligeti uses can be found in traditional compositional practice.[246] Fractals are rarely used systematically, mathematically they are often incomplete or their appearance is only fleeting. Much has been written by musicians about chaos in music, but when aligning compositions with chaos theory, confusion often arises between the everyday definition of chaos as a state of utter disorder or a total lack of organization rather than the scientific definition whereby dynamical systems display unpredictable behaviour at the same time as obeying deterministic laws.

Nested sequences, for example, are necessarily fragmentary because they cannot be sustained across a whole piece. The algorithms used to produce nested sequences could be described as musically mechanical and prescriptive hence they need to be adapted with some creative licence. Of the examples given in this chapter, the prolation canon, the oldest form, seems to be the most consistent with fractal characteristics in its use of motivic scaling and self-similarity. There is a certain irony in this of course: prolation canons were at their most popular over 500 years ago, long before the concept of fractals had been discovered.

---

245   Robert Sherlaw Johnson 'Composing with fractals' in *Music and Mathematics. From Pythagoras to Fractals*. (Oxford: Oxford University Press, 2003).
246   Rolf Wallin. Lecture given at the Nordic Symposium for computer Assisted Composition, Stockholm, 1989.

13 Musical cryptography

THERE WAS MUCH talk when Pink Floyd's album *The Wall* concealed a secret message, a message which could only be heard when the record was played backwards. This was achieved through back masking, a technique where the reversed recorded sound rendered the unintelligible noise when played forward as clear speech. This was in 1979, but concealing secret messages in music is not a new idea. Various cryptographic techniques have been used in music, based on mathematical rather than technological premises, and going back about 500 years.[247] Although in everyday language there is little distinction made between coding and cryptography, in mathematical terms coding theory refers to the reliable transmission of data and to the detection of and correction of errors in its transmission whereas cryptography is the branch of mathematics which is the practice of writing in code or cipher aiming to conceal information. The original message is called the plaintext and the enciphered message is called the cryptogram. The process of converting the plaintext to ciphertext is called encryption, with decryption denoting the reverse process. A code is a way of hiding meaning by changing whole words or phrases by giving them some different significance, often substituting one word for another, whereas a cipher uses an algorithm which usually replaces a letter or other single character with another to convert the plaintext, a message, for example, into another text known as the ciphertext.

This chapter examines various uses of cryptography in music from an early example by the Renaissance composer Josquin des Prez to Olivier Messiaen's

---

[247] Track eight of *The Wall*, '*Empty Spaces*', conceals a hidden message which cannot be understood when the record is played normally. However if the record is played backwards a secret message can be heard which includes the words 'Congratulations. You have just discovered the secret message.'

use of a coded musical language in the twentieth century. It explores the use of monograms as cryptograms by composers including Schumann and Shostakovitch. At the same time it looks at some of the limitations of cryptograms in music, questioning whether musical encryption can produce a convincing piece of music and work as a successful encryption, emphasising the relative simplicity of musical encryptions in comparison with those used in mathematics. The chapter concludes with an examination of one of the most famous pieces of music embodying a secret message – Edward Elgar's *Enigma Variations*.

One of the first instances of a musical cryptogram can be found in *Missa Hercules Dux Ferrariae* a setting of the mass dedicated to the Duke of Ferrara by the Renaissance composer Josquin des Prez (c. 1450 – 1521). Josquin takes the Latin name of the dedicatee 'Hercules Dux Ferrariae' and matches the vowel sounds to the vowel sounds of the solmization system. Solmization was devised by the eleventh-century monk Guido of Arezzo. He created a sight-singing system where a set of syllables is matched to the degrees of the scale - ut, re, mi, fa, sol, la (a system very similar to the one used today - do, re, mi, fa, sol, la, te, do). Josquin coupled the musical pitch of the solmization syllable with the vowel of text he wanted to represent. Thus 'Hercules Dux Ferrariae' translates as:

Her	cu	les	Dux	Fer	ra	ri	ae
re	ut	re	ut	re	fa	mi	re

The encryption becomes the pitches D-C-D-C-D-F-E-D in Josquin's *Missa Hercules Dux Ferrariae*. These pitches are used as the *cantus firmus*, the basis of Josquin's polyphonic mass. They can be heard in the opening bars of Kyrie I in the superius part, the top vocal line, and then moving to the tenor line in bar 9 (see below).

MUSICAL CRYPTOGRAPHY

This cryptographic system which was later named 'Soggetto cavato' by the music theorist Gioseffo Zarlino in 1558. 'Soggetto cavato dalle vocali di queste parole' in full, translates as a subject 'carved out of the vowels from these words.' The *Missa Hercules dux Ferrariae* is the most famous example of a soggetto cavato and is also the first.[248]

Musical symbols, usually pitches, have been often used to create ciphers by matching up single notes with individual letters of the alphabet. Early examples can be found in the work of the sixteenth century scientist

---

248   Lewis Lockwood, '*Soggetto cavato*', in Grove Music.

and polymath Giovanni Battista della Porta (1535–1615). During the Renaissance, at a time when political intrigue and war coincided with new scientific developments, there was a lot of interest in secret communication. Della Porta's seminal work on cryptography, *De Furtivis Literam Notis* (On the Secret Symbols of Letters, 1563) is primarily about codes and ciphers. One of his best-known ciphers uses a system where 11 different pitches are allotted letters of the alphabet.[249]

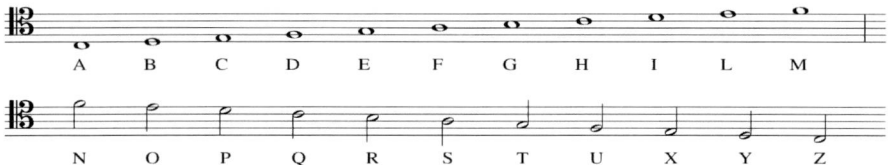

This system formed the basis of many subsequent systems across the years that followed. The musicologist Eric Sams, who has written extensively on cryptography in music, writes that it 'recurs in readily recognizable adaptations throughout the 16th and 17th centuries'. He goes on to list some of the different ways in which it evolved: the combination of crotchets and minims suggested by the British author Philip Thicknesse in 1772; the use of a cipher wheel where the notes and corresponding letters are written on two wheels, one fixed and one movable in the late eighteenth and early nineteenth centuries; the random allocation of musical notes to cipher letters; and the representation of one letter by a two-note group. As Sams writes, all of these methods were in the pursuit of a 'policy of analogy with real music'.[250]

John Wilkins (1614–1672) was the first to write a major book on secret communication in English -*Mercury, or the Secret and Swift Messenger. Shewing how a Man may with Privacy and Speed May Communicate his Thoughts to a Friend at any distance.* Chapter XVIII 'Concerning a Language that may consist only of Tunes and Musical Notes, without any articulate Sound' includes a cipher where musical notes are matched up with letters of the alphabet, no clef is given (see below).

---

249   Eric Sams. 'Musical cryptography' in *Grove Music*.
250   Sams, Cryptography, *Grove Music*.

MUSICAL CRYPTOGRAPHY

A b c d E f g h I l m n O p r s V t w x Y z

Wilkins writes 'Where the five Vowels are represented by the Minnums on each of the five lines, being most of them placed according to their right order and consequence, only the letters K and Q are left out because they may be otherwise expressed… By this you may easily discern how two Musicians may discourse with one another, by playing upon their Instruments of Musick, as well as by talking with their Instruments of Speech.'[251]

It is easy to see the limitations of this seventeenth-century cipher - there are only two note values and seven letter names- A B C D E F G. Philip Thicknesse (1719 – 1792) criticises the above example in his 1772 book *A Treatise on the Art of Deciphering, and of Writing in Cypher: With an Harmonic Alphabet.*[252] He argues that Wilkins system will 'instantly appear to anyone, the least conversant with music; that being without harmony or time, it must have no meaning or that some hidden meaning is *therefore disguised*'. He then puts forward his own method, an 'alphabet of musical notes' so that 'even a master of music shall not suspect it to convey any meaning'. 'I am persuaded an alphabet of musical notes may be so contrived, that the notes shall not only convey the harmony, but the very words of the song'. Thicknesse's proposed system is more sophisticated and uses a treble clef, minims and crotchets as well as a key signature to add authenticity (see below).[253]

---

[251] John Wilkins. *Mercury, or the Secret and Swift Messenger. Shewing how a Man may with Privacy and Speed May Communicate his Thoughts to a Friend at any distance.* (London: printed for Richard Baldwin, 1694): 75-76.

[252] Philip Thicknesse: *A Treatise of the Art of Decyphering, and of Writing in Cypher* (London: W. Brown, 1772).

[253] H. Neville Davies. 'The History of a Cipher, 1602-1772.' *Music & Letters.* October, 1967, Vol. 48, No. 4, Oxford University Press: 325-329

t a e i o u s l n r y x q k w b f c d m p h g z

The musicologist David Loberg Code questions whether musical encryption can be both a convincing piece of music and a successful encryption, coming to the conclusion that 'Musical encryption can rarely be both because the attributes needed for convincing musicality and strong encryption are not mutually conducive.' He finds that the music of those composers whose 'primary goal' was to 'create music that embedded extra-musical content by means of musico-alphabetic correspondences' used systems which 'were usually so superficial they should not really be considered encryption; whereas the systems used by the latter were so mechanical that most would not consider the results to be music.'[254] As Thicknesse observes, if music notation is to be used successfully to conceal information then it needs to look like a convincing piece of music.[255]

This lack of authenticity led to the downfall of a gambling group in 1940s New York. At the time, gambling was illegal and ingenious methods were devised to get around the law. One of the forms of gambling was a numbers game where bets were taken based on the U.S. Treasury Balance or baseball scores, for example. Those who recorded the numbers were known as policy collectors.

Back in 1940, a Brooklyn detective kept a policy collector under observation for the greater part of the day…he made the arrest but to his surprise, the pad on which the prisoner had been recording the bets did not contain the usual notations. It appeared to be the score of a musical composition…The detective was positive that the music represented some code…'For one thing, the whole piece was written on a range of ten notes. There seemed to be no variation in the value of the notes… So, I took it home and tried it out on a friend's piano. When I played it, I was sure that its atonalities were not music, either traditional or modern. So, I set to work to decipher it as a code…Not only were different musical notes used but their

---

254   David Loberg Code. 'Can musical encryption be both? A survey of music-based ciphers', *Cryptologia*, May 2022: 318-364
255   Davies, 'The History of a Cipher', 327.

positions on the scale changed their values...Each measure, indicated by the straight line, constitutes a separate wager'.[256]

Monograms as cryptograms

Known examples of musical ciphers being used for espionage are rare. However there are many pieces of music where composers have used ciphers to create motifs or themes which are there to be interpreted rather than as codes to be decrypted. A common device has been to use a motif comprising notes whose letter-names spell words. These are often based on the composers own name or one of their friends. The problem in translating letter names into musical notes is the limiting nature of having only seven named pitches. The question arises as how to cipher the remainder of the alphabet. In German music however Bb is known as B and B natural is named H, hence the B-A-C-H motif which was used by J S Bach in several of his compositions, and then by many other later composers. Sams writes that 'Beethoven, Schumann, Liszt, Rimsky-Korsakov, Busoni and several others' used the BACH motif. This sequence of notes is not uncommon, so many of its appearances in Bach's work may be a coincidence.[257]

Further note names can be derived from their sound, for example E-flat, 'Es' in German, can be used to represent 'S' and other names can be arrived at by using the sol-fa system. A combination of the above offers the following possibilities of notes for the letters A, B (Ger. Bb), C, D, E, F, G, H (Ger. B), L (la), M (mi), R (re), S (Ger. Eb, 'Es') and T (te). Some composers took advantage of these extra letter names or used musical notes for more than one letter whilst others simply ignored any letters in their name which did not represent a musical note or made up their own systems.

---

256   Anon. 'Codes are Fragile', *The Journal of Criminal Law. Criminology, and Police Science*. Spring 3100, 23 (New York, 1952), 10–13.
257   Sams, 'Cryptography', *Grove Music*.

A	B	C	D	E	F	G	H	L	M	R	S	T
A	B or Ger. Bb	C	D	E	F	G	Ger. B	la	mi	re	Ger. Eb	te

One well-known example of a thematic motif based on a person's name can be heard in Schumann's *Variations on the name "Abegg"* which are dedicated to the (possibly fictional) Pauline, Comtesse d'Abegg. In this instance the cryptogram is not used to conceal Abegg's name, rather it is used as a compositional technique.

Schumann (1810-1856) uses the notes A – Bb – E - G - G as the basis of his opening theme, quoting the notes directly in the opening bars over a dominant seventh chord and then using them to build a sequence. As the piece goes on, less attention is focused on the ABEGG motif and more attention is given to the developmental possibilities of its first two notes A – Bb.

The German composer Johannes Brahms (1833 – 1897), however, included a cryptogram in his 1868 *String Sextet No. 2 in G major* which quite possibly conveyed a secret thought. In the summer of 1858, he had fallen in love with Agathe von Siebold. They planned to get married, but Brahms broke off the engagement in order to focus on his musical career. Brahms never married and although Von Siebold later married someone else, Brahms continued to long for her. The notes A-G-A-(T) H-E can be found as the music rises to a heart-wrenching climax in the first movement (bars 162 - 168). In a letter to his friend Josef Gänsbacher, Brahms wrote 'by this work, I have freed myself of my last love.'[258]

In 1909 six composers were commissioned to celebrate the life of the composer Joseph Haydn by the *Revue musicale mensuelle de la Société Internationale de Musique.* Haydn had died 100 years earlier and the composers – Maurice Ravel, Claude Debussy, Paul Dukas, Vincent d'Indy, Charles-Marie Widor and Reynaldo Hahn – were invited to compose a piece based on Haydn's name. Each of the composers used the same cipher system.

In Ravel's short piano piece of only 54 bars, *Menuet sur le nom d'Haydn*, H was given its German equivalent, B natural and was built on the following motif.

Similarly, in 1976, the cellist Mstislav Rostropovich commissioned 12 prominent composers to write a piece based on a musical cipher, this time for

---

258 Jacquelyn E C Sholes. *Allusion as Narrative Premise in Brahms's Instrumental Music.* (Indiana: Indiana University Press, 2018): 33.

the 70th birthday of the Swiss conductor Paul Sacher. Rostropovich invited each of the composers Conrad Beck, Luciano Berio, Pierre Boulez, Benjamin Britten, Henri Dutilleux, Wolfgang Fortner, Alberto Ginastera, Cristobal Halffter, Hans Werner Henze, Heinz Holliger, Klaus Huber, and Witold Lutoslawski to write a variation. In *12 Hommages à Paul Sacher* each of the solo cello pieces is based on this cryptogram of Sacher's name.

E-flat (Es), A, C, B-natural (H), E and D (Re) which spell out eSACHERe

The variations are technically demanding and were composed in a variety of styles, some use traditional notation, others use extended cello techniques. Some of the pieces 'cleverly disguise' the hexachord whilst in others the pitches are used in a 'clearly recognisable manner'.[259]

The Russian composer Dmitri Shostakovitch (1906 – 1975) used his monogram D-S-C-H throughout most of his career. The notes transliterate to D Sch(ostakovitch) a musical encryption of his name. The monogram can found in several of his works including Symphonies No. 1 and 10, String Quartets No. 5 and 8, Violin Concerto No. 1 and Cello Concerto No. 1.

The signature motif permeates his *String Quartet No. 8* in C minor, Op. 110 (1960). Rather than disguising a secret message it contributed to what Shostakovitch described, in a letter to his friend Isaak Glikman, as the string quartet's 'superlative unity of form'.[260] It is an anguished work written after a

---

259   Ryane Dunnagan. An examination of compositional style and cello technique in *12 Hommages à Paul Sacher*. Unpublished PhD thesis. 2017.
260   Michael Mishra. *A Shostakovich Companion*. (London, Bloomsbury, 2008): 230.

visit to Dresden where he witnessed the devastation which had been caused by World War II bombing. In some ways it could be described as an autobiographical work, as well as the signature motif being woven seamlessly into nearly every page, the work is full of quotations from earlier works. The piece is dedicated 'To the memory of the composer of this quartet'. His use of the four-note motif is ingenious and imaginative. The piece opens with the personal motto heard in the cello part initially and then moving up through the strings in imitative counterpoint (see below). The parts are all in a low tessitura contributing to the sombre mood.

© Copyright by Boosey & Hawkes Music Publishers Ltd. Reproduced by permission of Boosey & Hawkes Music Publishers Ltd.

Later on in the first movement (bar 79) the DSCH motif is heard in all the parts but this time the texture is homophonic (chordal) rather than contrapuntal. The resultant chords are G major, Eb minor and F major moving on to the harshly dissonant tone cluster of G, Ab, B. This time the theme is in augmentation using notes of twice the value (see below)

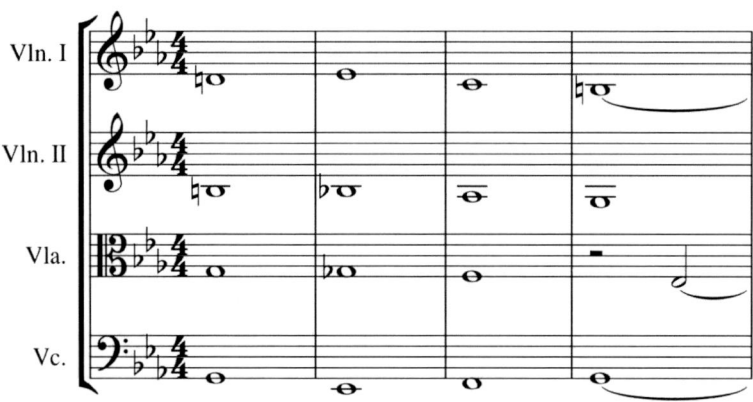

Rather than enciphering single words or names, the twentieth century French composer Olivier Messiaen (1908 - 1992) enciphers whole phrases and uses both codes and ciphers in his music. He devised what he referred to as a *'langage communicable'*. In the preface to the score of his 1969 organ work *Méditations sur le Mystère de la Sainte Trinité*, Messiaen outlines some of the compositional techniques he has used in the encryption of the work. Each letter of the alphabet is assigned a musical note and this cipher is used to encode quotations from the thirteenth-century *Summa theologica* of St Thomas Aquinas (a compendium of the theological teachings of the Catholic church). He also uses symbolic leitmotifs which act as codes, referring to these as *formules musicales*. Messiaen's works are imbued with religious significance. The following two melodic leitmotifs are used to represent the verbs 'to be' and 'to have'. Messiaen explains in the preface to the score that 'To be' uses a descending movement, because all that is comes from God (the Being par excellence, He who Is)'.

'To have' is an ascending movement because we can always gain more by raising ourselves towards God'.

As Andrew Shenton points out, in sharing the cipher, Messiaen has removed any 'problem for the *performer* discerning the 'hidden' message', but this still leaves the more complex problem of 'comprehension for the listener'.[261] This brings us back to Code's earlier question as to whether musical encryption can function successfully as both music and code. Part of his criticism is that the 'musico-alphabetic correspondences' frequently used by composers are often superficial to the extent that they should not really be considered as encryption.[262] It is certainly true to say that in comparison even the simplest systems of mathematical coding are usually much more complex and sophisticated: they can involve, for example, probability theory, frequency analysis or set theory; some use random number generators; and others utilise concepts based on number theory.

The mystery of Elgar's *Enigma Variations*

This chapter would not be complete without some reference to Edward Elgar's (1857 - 1934) famous orchestral piece *Enigma Variations* (1899) which has attracted, as the BBC radio presenter Tom Service once put it 'more musicological and pseudo-mathematical sleuthery than any other work of orchestral music before or since'.[263] There are two enigmas. The piece is made up of 14 variations on an original theme, each being a musical sketch of a friend of Elgar's. In all but one cases the dedicatees are named, but the penultimate variation is simply marked with three asterisks. The first much-discussed enigma (which does not involve a cryptogram) is the identity of this anonymous dedicatee. The second enigma takes the form of a sophisticated cryptogram created by a skilled cryptologist. As Sams writes of Elgar,

---

261   Andrew Shenton. *Olivier Messiaen's System of Signs: Notes Towards Understanding his Music.* (London: Routledge, 2008).
262   Ibid.
263   https://www.bbc.co.uk/music/articles/cb7ac9cf-207e-4244-8302-2436f2c2ba5a

He successfully solved a well-known challenge cipher, to which eminent experts later thought it worthwhile to publish their own solutions; he constructed a difficult if not impossible cryptogram; he made cipher entries in diaries and notebooks. One of his earliest works was an Allegretto for violin and piano on G–E–D–G–E, the name of a friend. It seems reasonable on the facts to conjecture that he used private ciphers in some of his compositions, and that suggestion has often been made in respect of the 'Enigma' Variations.[264]

Elgar suggested that the real theme of the Enigma Variations is not the theme that you can clearly hear, rather it is a familiar melody that can be played at the same time but never appears in full. In the programme note for the first performance Elgar is quoted as saying about the hidden theme that it is "so well-known that it is extraordinary that no one has spotted it".

> The Enigma I will not explain – its "dark saying" must be left unguessed, and I warn you that the connexion between the Variations and the Theme is often of the slightest texture; further, through and over the whole set another and larger theme "goes", but is not played . . . . So the principal Theme never appears… the chief character is never on the stage.[265]

In 1900 Elgar gave another clue in an interview he gave to the *Musical Times* where he said that the 'heading Enigma is justified by the fact that it is possible to add another phrase, which is quite familiar, above the original theme that he has written'.[266] So the key to the decryption would involve finding a well-known theme that would fit both harmonically and rhythmically in counterpoint with the original theme - no mean feat. Years of speculation followed with suggestions including God Save the Queen, Pergolesi's *Stabat Mater*, Rule Britannia and Auld Lang Syne as potential hidden melodies working in counterpoint with the stated theme, but none of these quite works. Furthermore, Elgar accepted none of the solutions proposed during

---

264 Sams, 'Cryptography', *Grove Music*.
265 Turner, Patrick (2007). *Elgar's 'Enigma' Variations – A Centenary Celebration*. (London: Thames Publishing, 2007): 49.
266 F G Edwards. 'Edward Elgar'. *The Musical Times*, May 1900, Vol. 41.

his lifetime. The question remains as to whether this matters when the piece can be enjoyed without any consideration of its inner puzzle. Indeed part of its attraction may lie in what the conductor Norman del Mar describes as 'the impenetrability of the riddle itself.'[267]

---

267 Norman Delmar.*Conducting Elgar*. (London: Clarendon Press, 1998).

14 Magic squares and Latin squares

A NUMBER OF composers have used magic squares to generate material for their compositions. The first section of this chapter explores the way that magic squares have been used by three composers; the English composer Peter Maxwell Davies, and the French composers Pierre Boulez and Phillipe Manoury. The chapter then goes on to explore the use of Latin squares in music, in particular the ancient palindromic 5 x 5 Latin square known as the Sator Square which Anton Webern is thought to have used in his *Concerto Op. 24*. Inspired by the work of Webern, the English composer John Tavener also employed the Sator square in his music. The ways that he built it into his compositional technique are explored in two of his compositions; the song cycle *To a Child Dancing in the Wind* and his piece for double choir and string trio - *Ikon of Light*. The Italian composer Bruno Maderna used both Latin squares and magic squares as part of the creative process, notably in his *Serenata No. 2* which is looked at in some detail in the final section.

Magic squares

A magic square is a square matrix where a different positive integer is written in each cell, each occurring only once. The 'magical' quality is that each horizontal, vertical and diagonal row adds up to the same number. Here is a 3 x 3 magic square using the consecutive numbers 1 to 9 (Table 1). Each row and column adds up to 15 and each of the two diagonals also adds up to 15.

Table 1 – Magic square of order 3

8	1	6
3	5	7
4	9	2

The constant number of the sum, in this case 15, is sometime referred to as the 'magical number' or the 'magic constant'.

The origins of magic squares are rooted in religious and esoteric contexts. One of the most famous magic squares is the Lo Shu 3 x 3 square (Table 1) which was known in China as early as 650 BCE. Legend has it that it was first seen on the back of a turtle emerging from the Lo river at a time of floods and the number pattern was seen as an omen. Every other 3 x 3 magic square can be derived from the Lo Shu by reflecting numbers of the square in the middle row or middle column and/or rotating numbers around the middle.

Magic squares have been a source of fascination for centuries and played a significant role in the development of numerology. Numerology attaches meaning and influence to numbers and number patterns. It is a belief in their divine, mystical power. Seven magic squares were dedicated to a planet or deity. The 3 x 3 square (Table 1) is known as the Square of Saturn. The 4 x 4 square is known as the Square of Jupiter where each row adds up to 34 (Table 2).

Table 2 – The Square of Jupiter

4	14	15	1
9	7	6	12
5	11	10	8
16	2	3	13

The others are:

Square of Mars 5 x 5
Square of Sol or the Sun 6 x 6
Square of Venus 7 x 7
Square of Mercury 8 x 8
Square of Luna or the Moon 9 x 9

Peter Maxwell Davies and magic squares

The British composer Peter Maxwell Davies (1934 - 2016) cultivated various styles of composition ranging from the monodrama *Eight Songs of a Mad King* (1969) which shocked audiences at its premiere, to a series of symphonies and occasional lighter pieces many of them inspired by Orkney (his place of residence) such as the ever-popular 'Farewell to Stromness'. His contribution to music education, particularly his part in the introduction of composing in schools, was significant. In 2004 he was made Master of the Queen's Music.

Davies used magic squares to generate material in several of his pieces. He was attracted partly by the internal rhythms of the squares and the way that they generated symmetric patterns, transpositions and inverted figures through both note values and pitch. His first piece based entirely on a magic square is *Ave Maris Stella* (1974). The composition is for six players and is based on a plainsong of the same name. Towards the end of the work, each aspect of the musical material is based on the 9 x 9 magic square - the Square of the Moon. The piece itself is in nine sections. He described the plainsong as being projected through the magic Square of the Moon and felt instinctively that the piece assumed some of the healing qualities associated with the square.

In his chamber piece *A mirror of whitening light* (1976-77) he uses the 8 x 8 Square of Mercury (Table 3).[268] The title makes reference to the alchemic process known as whitening when a base metal is transformed into gold. The Square of Mercury is associated with quicksilver and represents the perfect balance between the soul and the body. In Davies' words, the title

---

[268] In various lectures and writings Maxwell Davies mistakenly referred to his use of the Square of the Sun.

refers to the mirror of whitening light outside my own window...there the bay is in fact like a crucible of ever changing miraculous light. I took as a starting-point the plainsong *Veni Sancte Spiritus* which, if one knows it, one can hear quite plainly recurring throughout the work. I also took as a principle of design the magic square ... which I used as a kind of rhythmic and tonal grid-plan throughout the work.... the numbers 1 through 64 are arranged, on a square...they make very interesting patterns ... the fact that these are numbers is of no consequence whatever. One is dealing in fact with rhythmic lengths and with pitches. For the listener, this is not of prime importance but I must mention it in passing to reassure the listener that the structure, underneath even the wildest passages, is very rigidly controlled.[269]

Table 3 – The Square of Mercury

8	58	59	5	4	62	63	1
49	15	14	52	53	11	10	56
41	23	22	44	45	19	18	48
32	34	35	29	28	38	39	25
40	26	27	37	36	30	31	33
17	47	46	20	21	43	42	24
9	55	54	12	13	51	50	16
64	2	3	61	60	6	7	57

The number 8 governs the whole structure of *A mirror of whitening light*. Here are some of the techniques Davies uses.[270]

The plainsong *Veni sancta spiritus* was used to generate much of the pitch material.

---

269   MaxOpus (http://www.maxopus.com/works/mirror.htm)
270   Jonathan Cross. 'Composing with numbers: sets, rows and magic squares' in *Music and Mathematics. From Pythagoras to Fractals*. (Oxford: Oxford University Press, 2003).

ve - ni Sanc - te Spi_____ ri_____ re - ple tu - o - rum cor - de fi - de li - um

From the plainsong he derived this eight-note phrase G E F D F# A G# C.

Next he took the eight-note phrase and placed it down the furthermost left hand column (Column 1) and across the top row (Row 1).

Table 4

G	E	F	D	F#	A	G#	C
E							
F							
D							
F#							
A							
G#							
C							

Using the notes in Column 1 as the starting points, he then transposed the phrase seven times and inserted the transpositions into the 8 x 8 grid (Table 5).

Table 5

G^1	E^2	F^3	D^4	F#^{5}	A^6	G#^{7}	C^8
E^9	C#^{10}	D^{11}	B^{12}	D#^{13}	F#^{14}	F^{15}	A^{16}
F^{17}	D^{18}	Eb^{19}	C^{20}	E^{21}	G^{22}	G^{23}	Bb^{24}
D^{25}	B^{26}	C^{27}	A^{28}	C#^{29}	E^{30}	Eb^{31}	G^{32}
F#^{33}	D#^{34}	E^{35}	C#^{36}	F^{37}	G#^{38}	G^{39}	B^{40}
A^{41}	F#^{42}	G^{43}	E^{44}	Ab^{45}	B^{46}	Bb^{47}	D^{48}
G#^{49}	F^{50}	F#^{51}	D#^{52}	G^{53}	A#^{54}	A^{55}	C#^{56}
C^{57}	A^{58}	A#^{59}	G^{60}	B^{61}	D^{62}	C#^{63}	F^{64}

The next step was to map the notes onto the Square of Mercury matrix in the order that the numbers appear (Table 6).

Table 6

C^8	A^{58}	A#^{59}	F#^{5}	D^4	D^{62}	C#^{63}	G^1
G#^{49}	F^{15}	F#^{14}	D#^{52}	G^{53}	D^{11}	C#^{10}	C#^{56}
A^{41}	G^{23}	G^{22}	E^{44}	Ab^{45}(D)	Eb^{19}	D^{18}	D^{48}(Ab)
G^{32}	D#^{34}	E^{35}	C#^{29}	A^{28}(D)	G#^{38}	G^{39}	D^{25}(A)
B^{40}	B^{26}	C^{27}	F^{37}	C#^{36}	E^{30}	Eb^{31}	F#^{33}
F^{17}	Bb^{47}	B^{46}	C^{20}	E^{21}	G^{43}	F#^{42}	Bb^{24}
E^9	A^{55}	A#^{54}	B^{12}	D#^{13}	F#^{51}	F^{50}	A^{16}
F^{64}	E^2	F^3	B^{61}	G^{60}	A^6	G#^{7}	C^{57}

Notice that four of the numbers were altered by Davies at his discretion (and with no explanation); 45 and 48 have been interchanged, as have 25 and

MAGIC SQUARES AND LATIN SQUARES

28. These have been shown in brackets.[271] Having created the new matrix Maxwell Davies then took different routes through it to generate melodic lines, the 'very interesting patterns' he refers to: left to right across; right to left across; top to bottom; bottom to top; diagonals and spirals.[272] In this way the notes produced would be, for example,

left to right across C A A# F# D D C# G

top to bottom C G# A G B F E F

The first two instruments to play in *A mirror of whitening light* are the trumpet and the flute. Their pitches are taken from the top two lines of Table 6 (the first 13 notes). They use the following pitches

Trumpet C A A# F# D

At times throughout the piece Davies uses enharmonic equivalents so the trumpet part is notated as

---

271   Gareth Roberts. *From Music to Mathematics {Exploring the connections}*. (Baltimore: John Hopkins University Press, 2016): 263.
272   The manipulation of these rows and columns bears some similarity to the way that the note row is treated in Serialism (see Chapter 8).

C A Bb Gb D[273]

Flute D C# G G# F F# D# G
This is notated as D C# G Ab F Gb Eb G

In his analysis of *A mirror of whitening light*, the musicologist Peter Owens gives further examples of the ways in which Davies traced pathways through the magic square in order to generate pitches. The word '*Hauptstimmen*' is used to denote the principal parts.[274]

For each of the work's main subsections, beginning at rehearsal letters F, J, Q, W, Z, E1, H1 and two bars after J1, *Hauptstimmen* are created by tracing pathways through the matrix so that all cells are realised without repetition or omission. Bassoon and cor anglais, for example, share a presentation of the rows of the matrix - all read left to right - between F and J; violin 2 presents its columns - alternating ascending and descending readings - between J1 and Q1; other realisations trace zig-zags through the diagonals, or 'L' shapes, all, significantly, beginning and ending in different corner cells of the matrix, two of which contain the pitch class C.[275]

The Square of Mercury is also utilised at points to generate rhythms. The numbers in the Square of Mercury go from 1 to 64 (see Table 3). The range of note values is clearly impractical i.e. if number 1 was allocated a semiquaver

---

273   Notes that sound the same but are written (or 'spelt') differently are said to be enharmonic e.g. E# and F where E# is the enharmonic equivalent of F.

274   *Hauptstimme* is the name given by the serialist composers Schoenberg and Berg to a principal part in a complex texture, usually in serial or other rigorously non-tonal music.

275   Peter Owens .'Revelation and Fallacy: Observations on Compositional Technique in the Music of Peter Maxwell Davies'. *Music Analysis* , July - October, 1994, Vol. 13, No. 2/3: 161-202.

(sixteenth note), 2 a quaver (eighth note), 3 a dotted quaver (dotted eighth note) and so on, then the number 64 would be the equivalent of two breves. In order to overcome this potential problem, Davies used modular arithmetic to convert the numbers to those between 1 and 8. Modular arithmetic gives the remainder when dividing the magic square numbers by the eight. So, for example, 58/8 is 7 x 8 remainder 2 and 43/8 is 5 x 8 remainder 3. In mathematical notation this is shown as

$58 \equiv 2 \pmod{8}$ and $43 \equiv 3 \pmod{8}$

The value of a quaver is then allocated to each integer so that

1 = a quaver (eighth note)
2 = a crotchet (quarter note)
3 = a dotted quaver (dotted eighth note)
4 = a minim (half note)
5 = a minim tied to a quaver (half note tied to an eighth note)
6 = a dotted minim (dotted half note)
7 = a dotted minim tied to a quaver (dotted half note tied to an eighth note).

There is a slight flaw in this system in that 8, 16, 24, 32, ... 64 are all divisible by 8 so there is no remainder. So 8 takes the value of 8 quavers and becomes a semibreve. The resultant Square of Mercury can be seen in Table 7 which takes into account the alterations Davies made in his original transcription of the Square of Mercury (Table 6). It also assumes that a rest following a note counts towards it, a strategy that gave Davies more creative freedom.[276]

---

276   Roberts. *From Music to Mathematics*, 265.

Table 7

8	2	3	5	4	6	7	1
1	7	6	4	5	3	2	8(5)
1	7	6	4	5(8)	3	2	8
8	2	3	5	4(1)	6	7	1(4)
8	2	3	5	4	6	7	1
1	7	6	4	5	3	2	8
1	7	6	4	5	3	2	8
8	2	3	5	4	6	7	1

Cross (2003) questions whether any of this can be heard when listening to *A mirror of whitening light* noting Davies' comment that the 'sequences of pitches and rhythmic lengths ... [are] easily memorable once the "key" to the square has been found'. Although Cross observes that Davies might argue that the 'logic' given to the transformations may be 'subconsciously perceived' he goes on to state his own doubts as to this possibility.[277]

Pierre Boulez and magic squares – *Structures 1a*

In the early 1950s, several composers including Pierre Boulez (1925-2016) extended the compositional procedures of serialism to the other aspects of the music beyond pitch, a method which has become known as total serialism or integral serialism (see pages 133-4). Boulez based his piece *Structures 1a* (1951) entirely on a note row taken from Messiaen's piano piece *Mode de valeurs et d'intensités* (Mode of Durations and Intensities) (1950). From this he created two number matrices which represented all 48 versions of the row. These can be represented as a pair of magic squares (Table 8 and Table 9). In these squares, the number 1 always refers to Eb (pitch 1 of the original series) and to a demi-semiquaver (thirty-second note) - the first degree of the chromatic scale of durations. The number 2 always refers to D (pitch 2 of the

---

277   Cross, 'Composing with numbers', 140.

original series) and to a semiquaver (sixteenth note) - the second degree of the durational scale, and so on.

Table 8

1	2	3	4	5	6	7	8	9	10	11	12
2	8	4	5	6	11	1	9	12	3	7	10
3	4	1	2	8	9	10	5	6	7	12	11
4	5	2	8	9	12	3	6	11	1	10	7
5	6	8	9	12	10	4	11	7	2	3	1
6	11	9	12	10	3	5	7	1	8	4	2
7	1	10	10	3	5	11	2	8	12	6	9
8	9	5	4	5	7	2	12	10	4	1	3
9	12	6	11	7	1	8	10	3	5	2	4
10	3	7	1	2	8	12	5	5	11	9	6
11	7	12	10	3	4	6	1	2	9	5	8
12	10	11	7	1	2	9	3	4	6	8	5

Table 9

1	7	3	10	12	9	2	11	6	4	8	5
7	11	10	12	9	8	1	6	5	3	2	44
3	10	1	7	11	6	4	12	9	2	5	8
10	12	7	11	6	5	3	9	8	1	4	2
12	9	11	6	5	4	10	8	2	7	3	1
9	8	6	5	4	3	12	2	7	11	10	7
2	1	4	3	10	12	8	7	11	5	9	6
11	6	12	9	8	2	7	5	4	10	1	3
6	5	9	8	2	1	11	4	3	12	7	10
4	3	2	1	7	11	5	10	12	8	6	9
8	2	5	4	3	10	9	1	7	6	12	11
5	4	8	2	1	7	6	3	10	9	11	12

If the twelve columns in Table 8, reading from left to right across or down from top to bottom, represent the twelve possible transpositions of the original row, then the same columns read from right to left or bottom to top represent the twelve possible retrogrades. Similarly the columns of numbers in Table 9, (from left to right or top to bottom) represent the twelve inverted row forms, and (from right to left or bottom to top) the retrograde-inversions.

Phillipe Manoury - the Square of Jupiter in *Melencolia* (d'apres Dürer)

In medieval alchemy special qualities were assigned to each of the magic squares defining the relationship between the soul and the body. Each square was associated with a metal as well as its corresponding planet. The Square of Jupiter is associated with tin and represents the soul emerging from the body. The German artist Albrecht Dürer featured a 4 x 4 square (Table 10) with the magic number of 34 in his engraving *Melencolia I* of 1514. As can be seen, this is a variant on the Square of Jupiter.

Table 10

16	3	2	13
5	10	11	8
9	6	7	12
4	15	14	1

Notice how the date 1514 is embedded on the bottom row and the way in which the four squares at the centre and each of the four 2 x 2 square grids at each corner also add up to 34. The French composer Phillipe Manoury (b. 1952) used Dürer's engraving as part of the basis for his Third String Quartet *Melencolia (d'apres Dürer)* (2013). He used the tabulated data for generating collections of pitch classes – often tetrads (a set of four notes) – and sometimes used it for other purposes, such as creating rhythmic patterns.[278]

Latin squares

Another type of square grid (or matrix) is the Latin square: a square array of symbols arranged in rows and columns such that each row or column of the array contains each symbol precisely once. In mathematical terms this would be described as an $n \times n$ array of order n with entries from a set of n distinct symbols. So if $n = 4$ then a Latin square of order 4 using letters from the alphabet could be as seen below in Table 11. The word 'Latin' refers to the symbols which were taken from the Latin alphabet.

Table 11 – Latin square of order 4

A	B	C	D
B	A	D	C
C	D	A	B
D	C	B	A

Latin squares have proved to be useful in statistical experiments as well as to construct codes. They were discovered by the Swiss mathematician Leonhard Euler in 1779. Probably the most familiar use of a Latin square is in Sudoku (meaning 'single digit') where a skeleton, usually of order 9, is given containing a few numbers. The challenge is to fill in the blanks with the remaining numbers so that that each row or column of the array contains each number only once.

---

[278] Besada, J.L., Guichaoua, C. and Andreatta, M. (2022), From Dürer's Magic Square to Klumpenhouwer Tesseracts: On Melencolia (2013) by Philippe Manoury. *Music Analysis*, 41: 145-182.

Anton Webern and Latin squares

In his book *The Path to New Music* (1933), Anton Webern points out that there is a linguistic analogy between serialism and the ancient palindromic 5 x 5 Latin square known as the Sator Square (see Table 14) although he mistakenly refers to this as a magic square. The words translate loosely as 'Arepo[279] the sower holds the wheels for his work'.[280] The square can be read horizontally, vertically and backwards so it is easy to see the similarity with the manipulation of note rows in serialism – inversion, retrograde and retrograde inversion (see Chapter 8).

Table 14 – The Sator Square

S	A	T	O	R
A	R	E	P	O
T	E	N	E	T
O	P	E	R	A
R	O	T	A	S

David Cohen argues that the trichords found in the final 15 bars of Anton Webern's *Concerto Op. 24* (1934) are based on a Latin square. Although Webern's sketches give little indication of how he arrived at these trichords, Cohen argues that there seems little doubt that he was attempting to 'find a musical counterpart to the intricate structural relationship of the word square' given that the sketches of the work show several attempts to arrange the words of the palindrome under the trichords.[281]

---

279 The meaning of the word Arepo is unclear, there are several interpretation including the possibility that it was simply a residual word needed to complete the square.
280 Geoffrey Haydon. *John Tavener. Glimpses of Paradise*. (London: Victor Gollancz, 1995): 164.
281 David Cohen.'Anton Webern and the Magic Square'. *Perspectives of New Music*, Vol. 13, 1974: 213-215.

John Tavener and the Sator Square

The music of the English composer John Tavener (1944-2013) is imbued with religious symbolism; he was originally inspired by the Roman Catholic faith and later by Orthodox Christianity in works such as *The Protecting Veil*. Some years after Webern had encountered Latin squares, Tavener came across a copy of Hans Moldenhauer's chronicle of Webern's life and work wherein he found a diagram of the Sator Square.[282] The first piece in which Tavener used the Sator Square, or the 'Byzantine palindrome' as he referred to it, was in the song cycle *To a Child Dancing in the Wind* (1983). He took the square and worked out a system whereby he read it horizontally and assigned a number to each of the eight different letters.[283]

SATOR AREPO TENET OPERA ROTAS

The letters of SATOR were allocated the numbers 1 2 3 4 5, the new letters introduced in AREPO (E and P) become 6 and 7. The final letter is the N found in TENET, so the square becomes as shown below.

1	2	3	4	5
2	5	6	7	4
3	6	8	6	3
4	7	6	5	2
5	4	3	2	1

Tavener used a similar system the following year in his seven-movement work for double choir and string trio - *Ikon of Light*. The piece was largely inspired by the prayer *Invocation to the Holy Spirit* by St Symeon (949–1022). For the top line of his square Tavener chose a five-note phrase based on the Greek word *Elthe* (Come). The five notes are based on a descending pattern starting on the first note and moving down in step. To extend this range he drew up a second square where five notes ascend from the first note, the same

---

282 Hans Moldenhauer. *Anton Von Webern: A Chronicle of His Life and Work.* (London: Random House, 1979): 431.
283 Haydon, *John Tavener*, 164-165.

point. The first movement has five sections where the first section follows the pattern SATOR, ROTAS – SATOR, AREPO – SATOR, OPERA – and finally SATOR, TENET. This is not always obvious on listening because of Tavener's use of elaborations, extensions and microtonal decorations.[284] The second section for string trio is easier to follow on hearing; it follows the pattern SATOR, AREPO, TENET, OPERA, ROTAS with long silences between each phrase. Each of the other movements uses different manipulations of the Sator Square.[285]

Bruno Maderna and Latin squares – *Serenata No. 2*

The Italian composer and conductor Bruno Maderna (1920–73) used both magic squares and Latin squares (as well as other arrays) as part of the creative process in the construction of his music. Maderna was a central figure at the Darmstadt Summer School in the 1950s and his music was largely based on the principles of serialism (see Chapter 8). The arrays he designed were in response to what he perceived to be the shortcomings of serialism and the Second Viennese School (see page 125). In his words

> What I did not like about twelve-tone theory is the principle by which, once a series is given, it has to reappear in its entirety, continuously, vertically and horizontally, for the sake of consistency in the musical discourse. … Slowly but surely I proceeded to the study of serial [permutation, until I succeeded in developing more and more complex and rigorous systems of mutation.[286]

Serenata No. 2 (1954, revised 1957) is scored for eleven instruments. The first part of the work uses 11-note serial arrays rather than the usual 12 notes used in standard note rows (the note Bb is omitted). The second part of the *Serenata* is divided into four sections, each of them using a different set of nine pitch classes. The permutations of both the pitch classes and rhythmic material are determined by the two 9 x 9 squares below. Table 12 Is a Latin

---

284 Microtones are intervals that are smaller than a semitone.
285 For more details see Haydon, *John Tavener*, 172-173.
286 Cited in Christoph Neidhofer 'Bruno Maderna's Serial Arrays'. MTO a journal of the Society for Music Theory Vol. 13, No. 1, March 2007.

square based on the first nine letters of the alphabet. Maderna used this to determine the pitch-class permutations.

Table 12 – Latin square used by Maderna to determine pitch classes in *Serenata No. 2*

D	C	A	B	G	H	F	E	I
H	F	C	D	1	A	E	B	G
I	A	B	G	E	D	H	C	F
E	I	G	H	C	F	B	A	D
B	H	F	E	A	G	D	I	C
F	E	D	C	B	I	G	H	A
A	G	E	I	D	B	C	F	H
C	D	H	A	F	E	I	G	B
G	B	I	F	H	C	A	D	E

Table 13 is a magic square containing the values 1 to 81 once each. The values in each row, column, and diagonal add up to the same sum of 369. This magic square is used to generate the rhythmic structure of each of the four sections. The values of the durations were calculated using (semi-quavers) sixteenth notes; the numbers in the magic square were multiplied by 1/16 to calculate the overall duration so, for example, the number 8 corresponds to a minim (half note), the number 16 corresponds to a semibreve (whole note) and so on.[287]

Table 13 – Magic square used by Maderna to generate the rhythmic structure in *Serenata No. 2*

37	78	29	70	21	62	13	54	5
6	38	79	30	71	22	63	14	46
47	7	39	80	31	72	23	55	15
16	48	8	40	81	32	64	24	56
57	17	49	9	41	73	33	65	25

---

[287] For further details of how Maderna applied these techniques to *Serenata No. 2* and other works see Neidhofer 'Bruno Maderna's Serial Arrays'.

26	58	18	50	1	42	74	34	66
67	27	59	10	51	2	43	75	35
36	68	19	60	11	52	3	44	76
77	28	69	20	61	12	53	4	45

The following example shows how Maderna has assigned the nine pitch classes I to the letters A to I in bars 183 – 200.

A B C D E F G H I

Next these pitch classes were entered into the Latin square of Table 13 (rotated 90 degrees anti-clockwise) so that each row, column, and diagonal of the array contained each of the nine pitch classes exactly once (Table 14).

Table 14

I	G	F	D	C	A	H	B	E
F	B	C	A	I	H	F	G	D
F	E	H	B	D	G	C	I	A
H	A	D	F	G	I	B	E	C
G	I	E	C	A	B	D	F	H
B	D	G	H	E	C	I	A	F
A	C	B	G	F	D	E	H	I
C	F	A	I	H	E	G	D	B
D	H	I	E	B	F	A	C	G

I^{57}	G^{16}	F^{47}	D^{26}	C^{17}	A^{48}	H^7	B^{67}	E^{58}

The numbers indicate the path Maderna has chosen through Table 13.
Taking the first row across, this means that the pitches are

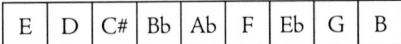

The durations are calculated by multiplying the numbers in Table 13 by 1/16.

So the music in bars 183 – 188 of *Serenata No. 2* is as follows.

This may appear to some as a rather clinical way of composing music, objective rather than subjective. Maderna argued that the use of objective procedures in his music, such as the manipulation of Latin squares and magic squares, had no expressive quality but once realized they led to the imaginative qualities of his compositions. As he wrote,

I have my own grammatical system. It arises from the principle of serialism and is sufficiently flexible. Above all it is sufficiently abstract to allow me complete freedom in realizing my musical imagination - which is not at all abstract – in a thousand ways.[288]

---

288 1965. 'La révolution dans la continuité.' *Preuves* 15/177: 28–29.

15 Change ringing

CHANGE RINGING IS the practice of ringing church bells in a methodical order prescribed by mathematical permutations. This chapter describes some of the mechanics behind bell ringing explaining how these put constraints on the playing of conventional melodies which use changing rhythms and repeated notes. These constraints led instead to the complicated mathematical manner of change ringing. This chapter explores some of the mathematical procedures involved in determining the order in which the bells are rung. During the seventeenth century Fabian Stedman, an English campanologist, wrote the definitive texts on change ringing – *Tintinnalogia* (1668) and *Campanalogia* (1677) - which encompassed several of the mathematical bases of group theory, a discipline that was not properly established until nearly a century later.

Change ringing began in England around the end of the sixteenth century and developed during the seventeenth century in terms of both complexity and popularity. Although the Reformation banned the liturgical ringing of bells, change ringing remained a secular hobby, but not on Sundays. In the second half of the nineteenth century, bell ringing was revived in the church and was again used to call people to worship and to herald important events and church festivals. Change ringing now continues to flourish across the United Kingdom and further afield, particularly in North America and Australia.

Normally there are six to twelve bells in a ring although there may be more or fewer, with 16 being the current maximum.[289] The record for the

---

[289] The record for the largest number of bells in a church tower is held by Christ Church Cathedral in Dublin which houses 19 bells in its tower.

largest number of bells in a church tower is held by Christ Church Cathedral in Dublin which houses 19 bells in its tower. The sequence of bells is usually tuned to a major key. The bells range in weight from around 200 lbs to several tons and are referred to by numbers. The highest bell, known as the treble, is usually numbered one and the lowest, the tenor, is assigned the highest number, with the other bells being numbered in sequence down the scale.

Bell ringers typically stand in a circle each managing one rope. Each of the bells is mounted on a large wheel that swings full circle with the bell sounding when the bell is pointing upwards. Bells can take up to two seconds before they can be sounded again and once a swinging bell is set in motion it is difficult for the bell ringers to vary the interval at which they will ring again. This means that it is difficult to play melodies in the conventional sense because of their repeated notes and changing rhythms. This mechanical constraint led to the creation of change ringing where all the bells are struck in a strict rhythm with an even spacing between one bell sounding and another. The bells are rung in a prescribed order where each bell is rung once moving on to the next prescribed arrangement, essentially a series of mathematical sequences known as changes. Before change ringing was developed a common way to sound a ring of bells was by playing rounds; a repeated sequence of bells descending from the highest to the lowest note. Change ringing now always starts and ends with this sequence.

Rules

To ring the changes means to ring a sequence of changes, whilst obeying three mathematical rules:

- The sequence starts and ends with a round (1 2 3, ... n).
- Except for the rounds, as the first and last changes, no change is repeated
- From one change to the next, any bell can move by no more than one position in its order of ringing.

A sequence that includes every possible permutation of bells (or change) is known as an extent. To find the total possible number of changes, the different sequences that can be obtained without repetition, we use the mathematical symbol *n!* which is referred to as *n* factorial. It is the product of all positive integers less than or equal to *n*.

$$n! = n \times (n-1) \times (n-2) \times (n-3) \times 3 \times 2 \times 1$$

So the number of possible permutations on three bells is factorial three

$3! = 3 \times 2 \times 1$, or six changes, six different sequences

123
213
231
321
312
132

and on four bells it is factorial four.

$4! = 4 \times 3 \times 2 \times 1$, or 24 changes;

1234	2314	3124
1243	2341	3142
1423	2431	3412
4123	4231	4312
4213	4321	4132
2413	3421	1432
2143	3241	1342
2134	3214	1324

There are *12!* possible permutations using twelve bells which is calculated thus

$12! = 12 \times 11 \times 10 \times 9 \times 8 \times 7 \times 6 \times 5 \times 4 \times 3 \times 2 \times 1 = 479,001,600$

The value of *n!* grows very quickly.

The table below (Table 1) indicates the numbers of changes in extents on different numbers of bells, and the approximate time needed to ring them. The names are those commonly used by bell ringers for the various sequences.

Table 1

n	Name	n!	Time required to ring them
3	Singles	6	12 seconds
4	Minimus	24	48 seconds
5	Doubles	120	4 minutes
6	Minor	720	24 minutes
7	Triples	5,040	2 hours 48 minutes
8	Major	40,320	22 hours 24 minutes
9	Caters	362,880	8 days 10 hours
10	Royal	3,628,800	84 days
11	Cliques	39,916,800	2 years 194 days
12	Maximus	479,001,600	30 years 138 days

On Wednesday 25th October 2017, twelve bell ringers at St Anne's Church, Alderney on the island of Guernsey, created a new world record when they rang for more than 16 hours – a total of 25,056 changes of Bristol Surprise Maximus. Because of the length of time taken to perform some of these extents, basically any using eight bells or more, it is usual to perform only part of a full extent. The word 'Peal' is used to refer to 5040 changes for seven bells or fewer and for at least 5000 changes for eight bells or more. Typically bell ringers will perform a quarter peal for weddings or other major festivals. This takes 40-45 minutes.

Plain Hunt

The simplest form of generating changing permutations in a continuous way is known as Plain Hunt, a fundamental building-block of many change ringing methods. The word 'hunt' refers to the path each bell makes among the other bells.

Each bell moves one position at each change, unless it reaches the first or last position, where it remains for two changes to enable a turn around. Table 2 below gives examples of Plain Hunt on three, four and six bells. Each row shows the order of striking after each change. In each of the sets of changes a line can be drawn along the path of any of the numbers resulting in a straight path from front to back and then from back to front, or vice versa. As can be seen from the table, Plain Hunt produces twice as many changes as there are bells.

Table 2 - Plain Hunt

Three bells	Four bells	Six bells
123	1234	123456
213	2143	214365
231	2413	241635
321	4231	426153
312	4321	462513
132	3412	645231
123	3142	654321
	1324	563412
	1234	536142
		351624
		315264
		132546
		123456

As can be seen in Table 2, with three bells, Plain Hunt produces all six possible changes (factorial three), but with four bells only eight of the 24 possible sequences of factorial four can be produced. This is because of the rule that from one change to the next, any bell can move by no more than one position in its order of ringing. An essential tradition of change ringing is to ring an extent, as many different changes as are possible without repetition, which means that Plain Hunt must be varied to achieve more of the possible changes.

One of the ways that this can be done is through Plain Bob which is based on the Plain Hunt but varied to produce more changes. On four bells Plain Hunt starts from rounds and returns to rounds in eight changes – this length from 1234 back to 1234 is called a lead (see Table 2). In Plain Bob Minimus for four bells, in order to prevent repetition at the end of the first lead the bells in third and fourth place (2 and 4) change places, so instead of ending with 1 2 3 4 the lead ends with 1 3 4 2 – this is called a 'dodge'. The second lead then opens with (1 3 4 2) (see Table 3).

Table 3 – Plain Bob Minimus

First lead	Second lead	Third lead
1234	1342	1423
2143	3124	4132
2413	3214	4312
4231	2341	3421
4321	2431	3241
3412	4213	2314
3142	4123	2134
1324	1432	1243
1342	1423	1234

A second lead is then produced by plain hunting until it reaches its end. Another dodge is made –
1 4 3 2 is changed to 1 4 2 3 which is used at the head of a third lead. The same dodge is used at the lead end to produce a round. In this way, all of the 24 possible changes on four bells – Plain Bob Minimus - have been made without repetition or omission. Table 4 demonstrates how a line can be drawn along the path of the numbers, a straight path from front to back and then from back to front, or vice versa (see below).

Table 4 Plain Hunting in Plain Bob Minimus

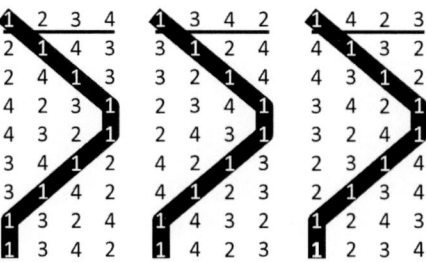

It is also possible to ring Plain Bob Doubles on five bells, and Plain Bob Minor on six bells and so on, each of them using dodges and having the same basic structure as Plain Bob Minimus.

During the seventeenth century Fabian Stedman (1640 – 1713) an English author and campanologist, wrote the definitive texts on change ringing, the first two publications on the subject, where he outlined the methods and rules on creating changes along with instructions on how to follow them. His book *Tintinnalogia – or the art of change ringing* (1668) was followed by *Campanalogia* (1677). Through his theoretical ideas and compositions he was implicitly drawing on several of the principles of group theory, a mathematical discipline that was not properly established until nearly a century later. These ideas akin to group theory include symmetry groups, permutation groups, cosets, and factorials and appeared many decades before the definition of an abstract group as a set with a binary operation satisfying certain axioms was established.[290][291]

The following diagram illustrates how the eight permutations in the first column of Plain Bob Minimus correspond to the eight symmetries of a square. It also illustrates how the transitions between the permutations correspond to flips of the square (see below).

Plain Bob Minimus. The eight symmetries of the square

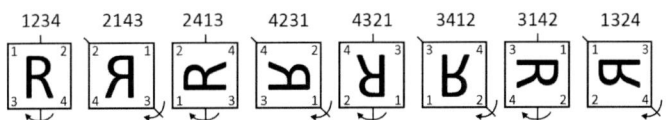

As a collection, the symmetries of the square form a mathematical structure known as the symmetry group of the square. This means that the separation of Plain Bob Minimus into three leads corresponds to the partition of the general symmetric group on four elements into the cosets (subgroups) of that group.[292]

---

290 A group is defined as a set with a binary operation if the following axioms are satisfied: closure, associativity, , identity and inverse.
291 To read more about Stedman's links with group theory see Arthur T. White. 'Fabian Stedman: The First Group Theorist?' *The American Mathematical Monthly*, Vol. 103, No. 9 (Nov., 1996): 771-778.
292 https://plus.maths.org/issue53/features/polsteross/2pdf/index.html/op.pdf Burkard Polster and Marty Ross. 'Ringing the changes'.

Change ringing is rooted in several different mathematical concepts. The number of possible permutations for a defined number of bells is calculated by using *n* factorials. The sequence of permutations, the changes, are generated by systematically following a set of rules which could be described as algorithmic in that precisely described instructions are designed to be applied systematically through to a conclusion in a number of steps. Furthermore, the art of change ringing draws on several of the principles of group theory.

Glossary of musical and mathematical terms

Glossary of musical terms

accent	Accented notes should be played with emphasis and a short attack.
additive rhythm	An additive rhythm is one which is formed by combining small metrical units. It moves from one note (x time units long) to another note (y time units long) where the sum of x plus y forms the metrical pattern such as 2 + 3 + 4 beats.
arpeggio	A type of broken chord in which the notes are played in order from the lowest to the highest or vice versa.
atonality	The absence of key or tonal centre.
augmentation	A rhythmic device where note values are made longer, often doubled.
bars and barlines	Music is divided up into bars (sometimes known as measures) that contain a specified number of beats. The bars are separated by barlines.
beat	The underlying pulse.
bpm	Beats per minute
cadence	Cadences are used to punctuate music, either bringing a melody to a point of repose before going on, or bringing it to a close. Cadences are found at the end of musical phrases and are usually harmonised by two chords.
canon	A canon is based on the principle of strict imitation, in which an initial melody is imitated at a specified time interval by one or more parts. . If the imitation is exact and continues through the whole piece, the piece is called a canon. A section of a piece is described as canonic if the imitation prevails throughout the section
cantata	An extended piece of music for voices and accompaniment.

cantus firmus	A Latin term referring to a pre-existing melody used as the basis of a new polyphonic composition. It is found mostly in Medieval and Renaissance music.
celesta	A small keyboard instrument with an ethereal bell-like sound.
chord	The simultaneous sounding of two or more notes to produce harmony.
chord progression or chord sequence	A repeated sequence of chords.
chorus	A setting of the refrain of the lyrics. The chorus usually returns several times, and, in popular music, is likely to be the catchiest part of the song.
chromatic	Chromatic notes are those outside the prevailing major or minor key.
chromatic harmony	Chromatic harmony uses notes from outside the prevailing key to colour the chords
chromatic scale	A scale made up of all the twelve notes in an octave and formed entirely of semitones.
circle of fifths (cycle of fifths)	The circle of 5ths is represented by a circular diagram demonstrating the relationship between different keys. It shows a series of chords whose roots are each a 5th higher than the previous chord e.g. C-G-D-A. From any starting note the pitch is raised repeatedly until the starting point is returned to.
coda	A concluding section.
colotomic structure	Where specific instruments (such as gongs) mark the beginnings and ends of rhythmic cycles.
combinatoriality	A technique found in twelve-note compositions whereby a collection of pitch classes can be combined with a transformation of itself to form an aggregate of all 12 pitch classes.
common time	This refers to the commonly-used time signature of 4/4 and is denoted by the sign C at the beginning of a piece.
contrapuntal	In counterpoint.
counterpoint	A texture where two or more melodic lines are combined.
crescendo	Getting louder.
cross rhythm	The effect produced when two conflicting rhythms are heard together using different metres.
decitala	A Hindu rhythm
diatonic scale	The term diatonic scale is commonly used to denote both major and minor scales. Diatonic scales have seven notes. Major scales include five steps of a tone and two steps of a semitone.

GLOSSARY OF MUSICAL AND MATHEMATICAL TERMS

diminution	A rhythmic device where note values are made shorter, often halved.
dissonance	Dissonant chords feel somewhat unstable or discordant.
divisive rhythm	A divisive rhythm system uses regularly repeated units (bars or measures) which can be divided into smaller parts (usually two, three or four beats).
dodecaphony	See serialism
dominant seventh	Dominant 7th chords are built on the fifth degree of the scale (the dominant). They are made up of four notes: the first, third and fifth notes of a given scale - plus a flattened 7th note from that scale.
drone	The extended sustaining or repetition of a note.
dynamics	The dynamics of a piece indicate the variations in loudness between notes or phrases.
enharmonic equivalent	Notes that sound the same but are written (or 'spelt') differently are said to be enharmonic e.g. E# and F where E# is the enharmonic equivalent of F
ensemble	A group of soloists, singers or instrumentalists, performing together.
figures or figuration	Short repeated patterns of notes with a distinctive shape (e.g. scales or arpeggio patterns), often used as decoration or accompaniment.
flat	A flat (b) placed before a note lowers its pitch by one semitone.
forte/fortissimo	Loud/very loud
four-on-the-floor	A rhythmic pattern where the bass drum accents each of the four beats in a 4/4 bar. Often found in disco music.
fugal	A contrapuntal style using a good deal of imitation.
fugue	A contrapuntal musical form which follows a detailed set of rules: two or more voices use the systematic imitation of a principal theme (the subject) an answer and (sometimes) a countersubject in simultaneously sounding melodic lines (counterpoint).
functional harmony	A term used to describe the relationships between chords in music and the idea that chords have specific functions within a key. There is a clear hierarchy between the chords; the tonic serves as the home base and each of the others has its own level of status, the three most important chords being the tonic, dominant and subdominant.
glissando	An instrumental or vocal slide.
ground	A recurring melody, usually in the bass, accompanied by continuous variation in the upper parts
happening	An artistic event that combines elements of theatre, performance art, music, and the visual arts, often within a loose structure and without a plot.

harmony	Harmony is produced when any combination of notes are sounded together.
hemiola	A pattern that occurs when three beats are performed in the time of two or two beats are performed in the time of three.
hexachord	A six note pattern.
imitation	Imitation occurs when an initial melody (or rhythm) is imitated at a specified time interval by one or more parts.
improvisation	A performance where the music (or part of it) is made up on the spot.
instrumentation	The particular instruments used in a piece of music.
integral serialism	See total serialism.
interval	The distance between two notes.
intro	The opening section of a song.
isorhythm	A rhythmic technique using multiple repetitions of the same rhythm against different pitch patterns.
key	When a piece of music is based on a particular scale it is said to be in the key of that scale.
key signature	A sign at the beginning of each stave of music indicating the key of the piece.
loops and looping	Where a short section or sample, often rhythmic in nature, is constantly repeated.
metre	The organisation of regular pulses into patterns of strong and weak beats.
metric modulation	Where there is a change in pulse rate or time signature wherein a note value from the first section is made equivalent to a note value in the second section.
microtone	An interval smaller than a semitone.
modes of limited transposition	A term first used by the French composer Olivier Messiaen to denote scales which can be transposed a limited number of times before the original set of pitches reappears. Examples include the whole tone scale and the octatonic scale.
modulation	The change from one key to another.
motif	A short melodic or rhythmic idea.

GLOSSARY OF MUSICAL AND MATHEMATICAL TERMS

note row	Note rows (also known as tone rows) form the basis of serialism. A note row uses all 12 notes of the chromatic scale and is the basis of the whole composition. There are four main permutations of the row. They are often referred to as the prime order, inversion, retrograde and retrograde inversion.
octatonic scale	The octatonic scale is made up of eight notes alternating tones and semitones
octave	The interval between the first and last notes of a major or minor scale. The two notes have the same letter name.
oral tradition	Where music is transmitted from one generation to another by word of mouth.
orchestration	The scoring of instruments used in an arrangement.
ostinato	A short musical pattern repeated throughout a section or complete piece. The plural is ostinati.
pentatonic scale	Pentatonic scales are made up of five notes. There are several different versions. They can be categorized as either hemitonic (with semitones) or anhemitonic (without semitones).
phase shifting or phasing	Where one part repeats constantly and another gradually shifts out of phase with it.
phrase	A subdivision of a melodic line.
piano/pianissimo	Quiet/very quiet
pitch	The word used to describe how high or low a sound is.
pizzicato	A string technique where the instrument is plucked with the fingers.
polymetric	Where different meters are combined simultaneously.
polyphony	A style of music that combines several distinct melodic lines simultaneously.
polyrhythm	Polyrhythms occur when two or more independent rhythms are heard together against the same pulse, such as one drum in triple time playing against another in quadruple time.
prime order or prime series	See note row.
pulse	The basic underlying beat in a piece of music to which we clap along or dance.
quintuple rhythm	Where rhythms are divided into five beats e.g. 3 + 2 or 2 + 2 +1.
range	The distance between the lowest and highest notes of a melody or composition.

register	A particular part of the range of a voice (e.g. chest or head voice) or instrument (e.g. high or low register).
retrograde	Where an existing melody or rhythm is played backwards.
rhythmic serialism	Where the principles of serialism are applied to rhythm.
riff	A short, repeated melodic or chordal pattern that may be heard at different pitches to fit in with the harmony.
sample	A recorded fragment of sound, newly recorded or from a pre-existing source.
scale	A pattern of notes arranged in order from low to high (or vice versa).
score	The written form of a musical composition.
semitone	A semitone is a measurement of pitch. There are semitones between all adjacent notes on a keyboard, whether black or white.
septuple rhythm	Where rhythms are divided into seven beats e.g. 3 + 4 or 4 + 3.
serialism (dodecaphony or 12-note system)	The twelve-note system of serialism (sometimes known as dodecaphony) follows strict mathematical rules in the form of an algorithm. First of all a note row (or series) is composed that is the basis of the whole composition. There are four main permutations of the row – often referred to as the prime order, inversion, retrograde and retrograde inversion.
set theory	In music a set is a group of pitch classes, usually a 12-note set, it may also be a set of other musical elements such as durations or dynamics. Music set theory categorises musical objects and analyses their relationships.
sharp	A sharp (#) placed before a note raises its pitch by one semitone
slendro	A five-note scale used in Javanese gamelan music.
solmization	A sight-singing system where a set of syllables is matched to the degrees of the scale - ut, re, mi, fa, sol, la.
song cycle	A group of songs designed to be performed together as one unit.
sruti	A microtonal interval used in Indian music.
syncopation	The effect created when off-beat notes are accented
tala	A repeated cyclical rhythm pattern used in Indian music.
tempo	The speed of a piece of music.
texture	The number of parts in a piece of music and how they relate to one another. The texture of a piece refers to the overall picture of the sound.
timbre	Tone colour. The characteristic quality of a musical sound.

time line	A short repeated rhythm which is either clapped or played by a single or double bell.
time signature	A numerical sign found at the beginning of a piece of music telling you the number of beats in each bar and the note-value of the beat.
tonal ambiguity	This occurs when it is not clear what key a passage is in.
tonal harmony	Where the harmony is centred on diatonic keys.
tonality	The key centre or mode of a piece of music.
tone colour	Timbre. The characteristic quality of a musical sound.
total serialism (integral serialism)	Where the procedures of serialism are extended to the other aspects of the music beyond pitch, such as rhythm, dynamics, tempo, timbre and note attack.
transposition	Where a passage of music is written or performed at a different pitch.
triple time	Three beats in a bar.
triplet	Where three notes are played in the time of two.
twelve-note system	See serialism.
unison	Two voices producing the same pitch are said to be in unison.
verse and chorus	A standard song form where the verse and chorus usually alternate. The verses have the same or similar music but different text. The choruses usually repeat the same words and music.
whole tone scale	The whole tone scale is made up of six whole tones starting on either C or Db (its only transposition).

Glossary of mathematical terms

$1/f$ distribution	In terms of noise, $1/f$ noise (or fractal noise) is a signal with a frequency spectrum such that the power per frequency interval is inversely proportional to the frequency (symbol f) of the signal.
$180°$ rotation	A function that moves each point of the plane through an angle of $180°$ about a fixed point.
phi – Φ	The Greek letter *phi* – Φ, an irrational number, is used to denote the value of the golden ratio.

algorithm	Where a set of precisely described instructions or routine procedures are designed to be applied systematically through to a conclusion in a number of steps.
Brownian motion	A continuous-time version of the random walk displayed by minute particles of solid matter when suspended in a fluid or a gas resulting from their collision with the fast-moving molecules in the fluid.
Butterfly Effect	The way a small change in one state of a deterministic system can bring about large differences in a later state with the potential to render long-term predictions impossible.
Cantor set	The Cantor set, sometimes known as the middle third Cantor set, is obtained by repeatedly removing the middle thirds of intervals. Each stage of the construction is obtained by removing the middle third of the previous stage.
cent	A logarithmic unit of measurement for the ratio between two frequencies.
chaos theory	Chaos theory (the science of dynamical systems) focuses on the behaviour occurring in a system under iteration and is the study of apparently random or unpredictable behaviour in systems governed by deterministic laws.
cipher	A cipher uses an algorithm, which usually replaces a letter or other single character with another, to convert the plaintext, a message, for example, into another text known as the ciphertext.
coding	Coding theory refers to the reliable transmission of data and to the detection of and correction of errors in its transmission.
combinatorics	The study of the enumeration, combination and permutation of sets of elements and the mathematical characteristics of their properties.
cryptogram	An enciphered message written in code. The original message is called the plaintext and the enciphered message is called the cryptogram.
cryptography	The practice of writing in code or cipher aiming to conceal information.
deterministic system	A system in which no randomness is involved in the development of future states of the system. If the initial state is known exactly then the future state could, in theory, be predicted. A model which incorporates random elements or processes is said to be stochastic, otherwise it is said to be a deterministic model.
devil's staircase	In mathematics a devil's staircase (sometimes referred to as the infinite staircase or the Cantor function) has unequal ascending steps constructed by using, for example the recursive 1/3 to 2/3 proportions of the most common middle-thirds Cantor set.
dynamical system	A dynamical system is a mathematical system whose state is uniquely specified by a set of variables and whose behaviour is described by predefined rules.
encryption	The process of converting the plaintext to ciphertext is called encryption, with decryption denoting the reverse process.

GLOSSARY OF MUSICAL AND MATHEMATICAL TERMS

Euclidean algorithm	The Euclidean algorithm is a systematic repetitive procedure used for computing the greatest common divisor (GCD) of two integers.
Euclidean rhythm	In the Euclidean rhythm $E(k,n)$, k is the number of ones (onsets), and n (the number of pulses) is the length of the sequence (zeroes plus ones).
Fibonacci series	A summation series in which each number is the sum of the two which precede it.
fractal	Fractals belong to a class of curves or complex geometric shapes where each part has the same statistical character as the whole, that is, it is made up of smaller scale copies of itself.
frequency	Frequency (f) is the number of occurrences of a repeating event per unit of time. Frequency is measured in hertz (Hz). A hertz is equal to one event per second. For cyclical phenomena such as sound waves frequency is defined as the number of cycles or repetitions per unit of time.
frequency analysis	Part of descriptive statistics which measures the number of times an event occurs.
frieze pattern	A repeating pattern of elements arranged along a line or in a strip.
Gaussian distribution	Gaussian distribution (often known as normal distribution) is a very common continuous probability distribution and is the basis of a large proportion of statistical analysis.
GCD	See greatest common divisor.
glide	A form of symmetry where a figure is reflected and then translated by being shifted horizontally.
Golden Section	The unequal division of a line into two parts such that the ratio of the smaller part to the larger is the same as that of the larger to the original whole. This ratio is approximately 1:1618.
greatest common divisor (GCD)	The GCD of two or more numbers is the greatest common factor number that divides them exactly.
group theory	A branch of abstract algebra, which looks at the main features of a group, from both the point of view of its elements and its group operations.
infinite	Having a size or absolute value greater than any natural number (positive integer).
integer	A whole number (not a fraction) that can be positive, negative or zero. Positive integers are sometimes known as natural numbers.
invariance	A property or quantity is said to be invariant if it is not changed by one or more specified operations or transformations.
irrational number	A real number which cannot be expressed as an integer or as a quotient of two integers. Irrational numbers have infinite, non-repeating decimals.
iteration	A method uses iteration if it yields successive values by repetition of a certain procedure.
Latin square	A square array of symbols arranged in rows and columns such that each row or column of the array contains each symbol precisely once.

LCM	See least common multiple.
least common multiple (LCM)	The LCM of two positive integers is the smallest integer that each number divides into evenly.
Lucas summation series	An integer sequence which has the same recursive relationship as the Fibonacci sequence, where each term is the sum of the two previous terms, but with different starting values.
magic square	A square matrix where a different positive integer is written in each cell, each occurs only once. The 'magical' quality is that each horizontal, vertical and diagonal row adds up to the same number.
Möbius strip	A 2-dimensional strip where one continuous side is formed by joining the ends of a rectangle after twisting one end through 180°.
modular arithmetic	A system of arithmetic for integers which gives the remainders in division.
Moiré patterns	Geometrical designs produced when a set of straight or curved lines is superimposed onto another set.
multiplier	The number or term by which another is multiplied in multiplication.
n factorial	The product of all positive integers less than or equal to n.
prime number	A number that can only be divided by itself and 1 without remainders. Numbers that are relatively prime have no common factors other than 1.
probability	The probability of an event is a measurement of the possibility of the event occurring.
randomness	Having no specific pattern, purpose or principle of organization.
random numbers	Random numbers have two main properties: all of the numbers or digits in the numeric sequence will, in the long run, occur equally often; and the occurrence of any one number or digit in a particular position in the sequence is no guide to the occurrence of the number or digit later in the sequence.
random walk	A process in which a sequence of discrete steps of fixed length is described in terms of the movement of a particle, so in a one-dimensional random walk the state of the process is described as a position on a straight line.
ratio	The quotient of two numbers or quantities giving their relative size. The ratio of x to y is written as x:y (or x/y) and is unchanged if both quantities are multiplied by the same quantity.
rational number	A rational number is one which is either an integer or can be written as a ratio (or quotient) of two integers e.g. 1, 7, 544 or 2/3.
recursive construction	Recursive construction involves repeating the same a simple step over and over again.
reflection	When an object has reflectional symmetry it can be divided into two pieces which are images of each other. The dividing line is known as the axis of symmetry. This could be the on the horizontal x axis (vertical reflection) or the vertical y axis (horizontal reflection).

GLOSSARY OF MUSICAL AND MATHEMATICAL TERMS

rotation	When an object has rotational symmetry it can be turned about a fixed point whilst keeping the same overall shape.
Sator square	An ancient palindromic 5 x 5 Latin square using the letters S A T O R that can be read horizontally, vertically and backwards.
scale symmetry	An object has scale symmetry when it can be expanded or contracted whilst keeping the same overall shape.
self-similarity	A self-similar object is one whose component parts resemble the whole.
set theory	A set is a well-defined collection of objects which are referred to as elements or members. Set theory is the study of the properties of sets and their relations.
stochastic process	A process in which the steps are governed by rules of probability. Stochastic processes are random and non-deterministic; the next state of the environment is not fully determined by the previous one
summation series	An infinite sequence in which each number is the sum of the two which precede it.
symmetry	A geometric object or shape is symmetric if it can be divided into two or more identical parts and is invariant under transformation. There are several different types of transformation; the main types are reflection, rotation, translation, and scale.
translation	When an object has translational symmetry it can be shifted a fixed distance in a fixed direction whilst keeping the same overall shape. This can happen in two ways. It can be shifted from left to right – horizontal translation or It can be shifted upwards or downwards – vertical translation.
variable	An expression, usually denoted by a letter that is defined for different values within a given set.
von Koch curve	A fractal curve, the main von Koch curve contains many tiny von Koch curves which are made up of smaller scale copies of itself. This property is known as self-similarity.
von Koch snowflake	The von Koch snowflake is developed from the von Koch curve. Instead of one line the snowflake begins with an equilateral triangle. The steps in creating the Koch curve are then repeatedly applied to each side of the equilateral triangle, creating a 'snowflake' shape.
x-axis	The horizontal axis of a graph.
y-axis	The vertical axis of a graph

General index

SONGWRITERS, ARTISTS AND their album titles will be found in the 'Popular music index' under the artist's name. Works by classical music composers will be found in the 'Index of composers and their works' under the composer's name.

acoustics 106, 107
Adams, Courtney 163-4, 166-7
additive rhythms 2, 6, 11, 26, 42, 49, 54, 257
African music VII, 5, 9, 17, 31, 35, 37, 38, 39, 41-5, 54, 88-9, 116, 210
   sub-Saharan Africa 9, 38, 42
   West African drumming VII, 5, 17, 35, 41-5, 54
   master drummer 43-4
Afro-Cuban music 44-5, 88
aksak (see Balinese monkey chant)
aleatoric music (see randomness in music)
algorithm (see also Euclidean algorithm) VIII, 125, 134, 137, 153, 155-7, 198, 212, 213, 256, 262, 264
Artificial Intelligence (AI)

Balinese monkey chant 37, 46-7, 152
Ballet Russes 89
Bjorklund, Erik 38
blues 87, 116, 161
boogie-woogie 14-15
Brownian motion 190, 264
Bulgarian rhythms 10-11, 40

canons VIII, IX, 21-2, 28, 65, 77, 85-6, 141-52, 193, 199-200, 212, 257
   canon by augmentation 148-9
   canon by diminution 149
   canon by inversion 144
   double canon 145
   mirror canon 147
   prolation canon IX, 142, 150-1, 193, 199-200, 212
   puzzle canon (see riddle canon)

retrograde canon 146
rhythmic tiling canon 151-2
riddle canon 146
tempo canon 21-2
Cantor, George 196
Cantor set (see 'fractals')
catches 142-3
chance music (see randomness in music)
chaos theory 193, 207-10, 212, 264
  Butterfly Effect 208-9, 264
change ringing X, 249-56
  Plain Bob Minimus 253-5
  Plain Hunt 252-4
  rounds 250, 253-4
circle of fifths VIII, 99, 103, 104-5, 107-8, 117, 118, 121
Code, David Loberg 218, 225
Cohen, David 242
Cohen, Joel E 155
combinatorics VIII, 127-8, 131, 134, 182-3, 264
Corbyn, Jeremy 91
Cross, Jonathan 137
cryptography IX, 213-27, 264
ciphers 213, 215-9, 221-6, 264
  codes 189, 213-4, 216, 218-9, 224-5, 241
  cryptograms 213-14, 219-25, 264
  encryption 213-14, 218, 222, 224-5, 264
Cunningham, Merce 23-4
  'Dromenon' 24
Cuban music 37, 39-40, 44-5, 88
  cinquillo 39-40
  clavé 37, 44-5, 88

Darmstadt School IX, 133-4, 137-8, 159, 172-5, 244
deterministic systems 188, 207-9, 212, 264
Diaghilev, Sergei 89
divisive rhythms 2, 26, 42, 49, 53, 54, 259
dodecaphony (see serialism)
Drabkin, William 64
Dürer, Albrecht 240
dynamical systems 207-8, 212, 264

EDM (see electronic dance music)
Einstein, Albert 136
electronic dance music (EDM) VII, X, 1, 15, 16-17, 35, 75, 88
  bigbeat 16
  DJs 16, 88
  drum 'n' bass 16-17, 35
  garage 16, 87
  hardcore 16
  house 16, 88
  loops 16, 31, 75, 88
  samples (see samples and sampling)
  techno 16
Ellis, Alexander 110
Euclid 38, 102n94, 159
  Elements 102n94, 159, 159n150, 160
Euclidean algorithm VII, 37-8, 265
Euclidean rhythm VII, 37-41, 265
Euler, Leonhard 107, 241

Fibonacci series IX, 159-60, 168-74, 175
flamenco VII, 51-4

bulerías 52-3
palmas 52
palos 52-3
Fluxus 184-6
Fox, Christopher 14, 137-8
fractals IX, 151, 193-212, 263, 265, 267
   Cantor set 193, 196-7, 198, 199, 202, 264
   devil's staircase 202-3, 264
   self-similarity IX, 193, 194-9, 201, 203-4, 206, 211-12, 267
   von Koch curve 193, 194-6, 204, 267
   von Koch snowflake 196, 267
frequencies (see tuning)
frieze patterns 79-96
   Conway, John 81, 94
   glide 79-81, 89-90, 95-6
   horizontal 79-81, 90-2, 94-5
   rotational 79-81, 93-6
   translational 79-96
   vertical 79-81, 94-6
fugues VIII, 68, 77-8, 141, 142, 152-7, 259
   and Artificial Intelligence 154-7

gamelan VII, VIII, 24, 28, 37, 45-7, 54, 92, 117, 262
   colotomic structure 47, 54, 258
   gongan 47
   gongs 24, 45-7, 117, 151, 262
   pelog 117
   slendro 117, 262
Gaussian distribution 188-9, 265
Golden Section !X, 159-75, 265

gospel music 16, 116
graphic notation 177, 186
greatest common divisor (GCD) 38, 265
Greece 40, 187
Griffiths, Paul 12, 131, 169
group theory X, 79, 132n121, 134, 249, 255, 256, 265

harmonics 105, 107, 118
harmonic series VIII, 99, 103, 105-6, 110, 119
hemiola 8-9
Hertz 109-110, 124, 265
Hertz, Heinrich 110
Howat, Roy 168-71
Huron, David 118
Huygens, Christiaan 119-20

indeterminacy 177, 184-5, 191
Indian music 25-6, 35
   22-note system 120-1
   bols 49-50
   instruments 48
   North Indian classical music VII, 35, 37, 48-51, 53-4, 120-1
   raga 48
   ragavardhana 25-6
   South Indian Carnatic music 48
   sruti (or shruti) 120-1, 262
   tabla 48-51
   tala (or tal) VII, 6, 25, 48-51, 258, 262
   theka 49-51, 54
Indonesian music 24, 28, 37, 45-7, 54
   gamelan (see gamelan)

intervals (see also tuning) 99-102
  consonance 99-101, 109, 118
  dissonance 11, 61, 99-101, 109, 118, 223, 259
  harmonic series (see harmonic series)
  microtones VIII, 34, 111, 113, 119, 121-4, 244, 260
  ratios of (see ratio)
irrational numbers VIII, 99, 108-9, 161, 265

Japan 47, 116
  gagaku 47
jazz 13, 14, 15, 21, 41, 87, 115
Julia set 204

katak (see Balinese monkey chant)
Kepler, Johannes 107, 124
Könnicke, Johann Jakob 108, 119

Latin squares IX-X, 229, 241-8, 266, 267
least common multiple (LCM) 4-5, 29, 266
Le Corbusier 173-4, 187-8
Lehrdahl, Fred 137
Lendvai, Ernő 168-9
Lucas, François Édouard 170n172
Lucas summation series 170, 266

magic squares IX-X, 134, 229-42, 246, 248, 266
  Lo Shu square 230
McPhee, Colin 45, 46
Maor, Eli 136
Melamed, Daniel 175

Mercator comma (see tuning)
Mercator, Nicholas 120
Mersenne, Marin 107, 109, 119, 124
  Harmonie Universelle 119
Meyer, Leonard B 137
Meyer, Max Friedrich 123
Middle East 13, 40, 44
minimalism 30-4, 87, 142, 185, 191, 209, 261
  phase shifting (or phasing) 30-4, 209, 261
Möbius strip 147, 266
modes of limited transposition (see scales)
modular arithmetic 237, 266
monochord 101
Moore, Gillian 11

Newbould, Brian 69-70
  'A Schubert palindrome' 69-70
New Complexity 34
Newton, Isaac 107, 124, 136
New York 21, 23, 3, 82-3, 156, 170, 185, 218
n factorial 135, 250-1, 253, 255, 256, 266

Odington, Walter 107
Orledge, Robert 83
Owens, Peter 236

Paynter, John 160, 161-2, 181
player piano 19, 21-2
polymeter 20, 24, 42, 43-4, 205, 261
polyphony 46, 106, 142, 143n138, 157, 214, 261

polyrhythms VII, 3-5, 11, 12, 14-15, 20, 21, 25, 35, 42n60, 43, 53-4, 202-3, 261
polytempo 20
Porta, Giovanni Battista della 215-16
  Furtivis Literam Notis 216
prepared piano 23, 23n29, 24
Pythagoras 101-3, 123-4, 159n150
Pyhtagorean comma (see tuning)
Pyhtagorean scale (see scales)

randomness in mathematics 177-81, 225, 264, 266, 267
randomness in music IX, 178-91, 266
  chance procedures 177-8, 182
  graphic notation (see graphic notation)
  happenings 184, 259
  I Ching 182-3
  random numbers IX, 177, 178, 225, 266
  rolls of dice IX, 177-181, 183-4, 191
  stochastic music (see stochastic processes)
random walk 189-90, 264, 266
ratios
  golden ratio 159-60, 161, 163, 266
  of intervals 101-9, 118, 121
  of rhythms 3
  square root form 9, 19, 22-4
of tempos 22, 150, 200
rational numbers 108, 266

reggae 15-16
Roberts, Gareth 208-9
rockabilly 41
Ross, Alex 29, 172
Rostropovich, Mstislav 221-2
rounds (see also change ringing) 142-3

Sacher, Paul 222
samples and sampling 16, 262
Sams, Eric 216, 219, 225-6
scales VIII, 60-1, 73-4, 99-124, 258, 260, 261, 262, 263
  19-note, 31-note and 53-note 113, 119-20
  43-note 122-3
  chromatic 83, 109, 125, 134-5, 136, 202, 258, 261
  diatonic 99-101, 103, 107, 137, 154, 258
  22-note system (see Indian music)
  modes of limited transposition VIII, 27, 113-16, 260
  octatonic VIII, 113, 114--16, 261
  pelog (see gamelan)
  pentatonic VIII, 116-18, 261
  Pythagorean scales VIII, 99, 101-6, 107, 108-11
  slendro (see gamelan)
  whole tone VIII, 113, 114-15, 128, 263
Scratch Orchestra 185-6
Second Viennese School 71-2, 125, 128, 244
serialism VIII, 72, 74, 78, 125-38,

142, 173, 235n272, 236n274, 238, 242, 244, 248, 262
combinatoriality 127-8, 131-2, 258
note rows VIII, 125-6, 128, 131, 133, 134-5, 238, 242, 244, 261
permutations of the row 126, 135, 261, 262
prime order (or prime series) 125, 126, 127, 135, 261, 262
rhythmic serialism 125, 131-3, 262
total serialism 125, 133-4, 238, 260, 263
set theory (mathematics) 134, 225, 267
set theory (music) 132, 134, 262
Shepherd, Alan 175
Smend, Friedrich 175
solmization IX, 214, 262
spiral of fifths 105
Stedman, Fabian 249, 255
Steinitz, Richard 190, 202-3, 204, 208
Stevin, Simon 108-9
stochastic processes IX, 177-8, 187-91, 267
symmetry VIII, 57-8, 113, 126, 128-9, 134-5, 147, 152, 194-5, 255, 267
frieze patterns (see frieze patterns)
reflection VII, 57, 58-72, 126, 134, 141, 147, 152, 266
rotation VII, 57, 72-4, 126, 134, 141, 263, 267

scale VII, 57, 76-8, 126, 141, 152, 194-5, 196-7, 203, 205, 212, 267
translation VII, 30, 57, 74-6, 134, 141, 209, 267

Tagg, Philip 42
Tatlow, Ruth 174-5
Thailand 47
  pi phat 47
Theinred of Dover 107
Theremin, Leon 20
  Rhythmicon 20-1
  Theremin (instrument) 20
Thicknesse, Philip 216-17, 218
  A Treatise on the Art of Deciphering 217
Tilley, Leslie 46
time line 37-8, 41-3, 45, 263
tonality diamond 123
Toussaint, G T 37-9
tuning 99-111
  Baroque tuning 110n101
  cents 110-11, 119n109
  equal temperament VIII, 99, 106, 108-11, 113, 119, 120
  frequencies 20, 101-2, 105-6, 109-11, 118, 157, 198n221, 263, 264, 265
  just intonation VIII, 99, 106-8, 111, 119, 120
  Mercator comma 120
  Pythagorean comma 104-5, 106
  Pythagorean scale (see scales)
  syntonic comma 108, 119, 121
  wavelengths 101

Wilkins, John 216-17
World War II 27, 187, 221

Zarlino, Gioseffo 215

Index of composers and their works

WORKS BY CLASSICAL music composers will be found in the 'Index of composers and their works' under the composer's name. The list includes both compositions and writings. Songwriters, artists and their works will be found in the 'Popular music index' under the artist's name.

Adams, John 87
Alkan, Charles-Valentin 7-8
   Air à 7 temps 7-8
Anonymous
'Sumer is Icumen In' 141

Babbitt, Milton 131, 132-4
   Second String Quartet 133
   Three Compositions for Piano 133
   Writings
   'Set Structure as a Compositional Determinant' 131-2
   'Some Aspects of Twelve-Tone Composition' 131
   'Twelve-Tone Invariants as Compositional Determinants' 131
   'Twelve-Tone Rhythmic Structure and the Electronic Medium' 132

Bach, C P E 66, 67, 69, 70, 71, 149, 178
   Minuet in C 66
   Miscellanea Musica 149
Bach, Johann Sebastian IX, 61-2, 72, 77, 109, 123-4, 142, 144, 146, 148, 150, 153-4, 159, 174-5, 219
   14 Canons 'Canon a 4 per Augmentationem et Diminutionem' 150
   Art of Fugue 142
   Brandenburg Concertos 174, 198
   Cello Suite No. 3 199
   English Suite No. 6 in D minor 61-2
   Goldberg Variations 142, 144, 150
   Musical Offering 142, 146-7
   Vom Himmel hoch 142
   Well-Tempered Clavier 153
   Well-Tempered Clavier Book I

Fugue No. 16 in G minor 154
Well-Tempered Clavier Book II
Fugue No. 2 in C minor 77
Well-Tempered Clavier Book II
Fugue No. 9 in E 77
Bartók, Béla IX, 10-11, 19, 40, 58-9, 61, 63, 93-4, 116, 153, 159, 168-70, 172, 175
Mikrokosmos No. 141 58, 116
Music for strings, percussion and celesta 63, 153n143, 168, 169
Six Dances in Bulgarian Rhythm 10-11
Sonata for Two Pianos and Percussion 166
String Quartet No. IV 93-4
Beck, Conrad 222
Beethoven, Ludwig van IX, 3-4, 29n40, 68-9, 75-6, 94-5, 142, 152, 153, 184, 219
Diabelli Variations 94-5
Grosse Fuge, Op. 133 153
Hammerklavier Sonata, Op. 106 68-9, 153
Piano Sonata, Op. 10, No 2 in G 3-4
Symphony No. 5 in C minor 75-6
Berg, Alban VIII, 72, 125, 128, 131, 151, 236n274
Lyric Suite 131
Violin Concerto 128
Berio, Luciano 131, 222
Nones for orchestra 131
Berlioz, Hector 7
Benvenutu Cellini 7
Boulez, Pierre
Structures 1a
Brahms, Johannes
Symphony No. 1 in C minor
Britten, Benjamin 222
Busoni, Ferruccio 219
Byrd, William 8-9, 65-6,
Diliges Dominum 65-6
'Though Amaryllis Dance in Green' 8-9

Cage, John VII, IX, 19, 23-4, 82-3, 178, 182-5, 191
4' 33" 184
Atlas Eclipticalis 183
Concert for Piano and Orchestra 183
First Construction (in Metal) 23
HPSCHD 183-4
Music for Piano 183
Music of Changes 182-3
Sonatas and Interludes 24
Theatre Piece No. 1 184
Three Dances for Two Prepared Pianos 23
Writings
Lecture on Something 182
Silence. Lectures and writings by John Cage 22, 182, 184
Cardew, Cornelius 184-6
Octet '61 for Jasper Johns 186
The Great Learning 186
Treatise 186
Cavalli, Francesco 6
Chopin, Frederic 4-5, 183-4
Nocturne in C# minor 4-5

INDEX OF COMPOSERS AND THEIR WORKS

Coleridge-Taylor, Samuel 8
   Fantasiestucke Op. 5 8
Cope, David 156
   Well Programmed Clavier, The 156, 157
   Writings
   Algorithmic Composer, The 156
   Experiments in Musical Intelligence 156
Copland, Aaron 5
Correa de Arauxo, Francisco 6
   Libro de tientos 6
Cowell, Henry 19-21, 22-3, 182, 191
   Banshee 23
   Fabric 19-20
   Mosaic Quartet 182
   Quartet Euphometric 20
   Quartet Romantic 20
   Rhythmicana (for piano) 21
   Rhythmicana (for rhythmicon and orchestra) 21
   Writings
   New Musical Resources 19, 20, 21

Davies, Peter Maxwell IX-X, 229, 231-8,
   A mirror of whitening light 231-8
   Ave Maris Stella 231
   Eight Songs for a Mad King 231
   'Farewell to Stromness' 231
Debussy, Claude IX, 7, 90, 92, 114, 115-6, 117-8, 159, 166, 168, 170-1, 175, 221
   Estampes 'Pagodes' and 'La soirée dans Grenade' 92, 114, 117

   Images 'Reflets dans l'eau' 170
   La mer 170
   L'isle joyeuse 170
Dufay, Guillaume 142
Dukas, Paul 221
d'Indy, Vincent 221
Dutilleux, Henri 222

Eastman, Julius 83-4
   Stay on It 83-4
Elgar, Edward 214, 225-7
   Enigma Variations 214, 225-7

Feldman, Morton 182
   Extensions 1 182
Ferneyhough, Brian 19, 34-5
Finnissy, Michael 34
Fortner, Wolfgang 222
Fux, Joseph 152, 155
   Writings
   Gradus ad Parnassum 152-3, 155

Gershwin, George 171n177
Ginastera, Alberto 222
Glass, Philip 10, 87
Grainger, Percy 9-10
   Lincolnshire posy 'Lord Melbourne' 10
   The Song of Solomon 'Love verses' 10

Hába, Alois 113, 122
   Matka 122
   Suite for string orchestra 122
Hahn, Reynaldo 221
Halffter, Cristobal 122
Handel, George Frederick 6-7, 95-6

Orlando 7
Suite No. 1 95-6
Haydn, Joseph 4, 66-7, 69, 70, 71, 125n117, 142, 152, 153, 178, 221
   Menuet al Reverso 66-7
   Piano Sonata No. 26 in A 66-7
   Symphony No. 47 in G 66
Henze, Hans Werner 222
Higgins, Dick 185
Hindemith, Paul 72-4, 153-4
   Ludus Tonalis 72-4, 153-4
Holliger, Heinz 222
Holst, Gustav 198-9
   The Planets 198-9
Honegger, Arthur 84
Huber, Klaus 222
Ives, Charles 10, 121-2, 182, 191
   Three Quarter- Tone Pieces 122

Janacek, Leoš 7
Johnson, Tom IX, 205-7
   Narayana's Cows 205-7
   Writings
   Self-Similar Melodies 206

Kirnberger, Johann 146n140, 178
   Der allezeit fertige Polonoisen und Menuettencomponist 178
Krenek, Ernst 173, 175
   Fibonacci Mobile 173
Ligeti, György IX, 29, 173, 193, 200, 201-5, 207, 208-10, 211, 218
   Etudes pour piano No. 1 'Désordre' 201, 203-4, 208-9
   Etudes pour piano No. 13

   'L'escalier du diable' 202-3
   Piano Concerto 204-5
   Poème Symphonique 29
Liszt, Franz 7, 219
Lutoslawski, Witold 222

Machaut, Guillaume de VIII, 57, 63, 141
   'Ma fin est mon commencement et mon commencement ma fin' VIII, 57, 63-4, 141
Maderna, Bruno 133, 172, 229, 244-8
   Serenata No. 2 244-8
Manoury, Phillipe 229, 240-1
   Melencolia (d'apres Dürer) 240-1
Messiaen, Olivier VII, 19, 24-8, 113-5, 124, 133, 151, 187, 213-14, 224-5, 238, 260
   Catalogue d'Oiseaux 28
   Les corps glorieux 26
   Méditations sur le Mystère de la Sainte Trinité 224
   Mode de valeurs et d'intensités 133, 238
   Quatuor pour la fin du temps (Quartet for the End of Time) 27
   Turangalîla-symphonie 28
   Visions de l' Amen 26
   Writings
   Technique of My Musical Language, The 24-6, 28
Monteverdi, Claudio 6
Morley, Thomas 64-5
   Writings
   A Plaine and Easie Introduction to

Practicall Musicke 64
Mozart, Wolfgang Amadeus IX, 3, 125n117, 142, 145, 152, 153, 159, 162, 163-4, 175, 178-81, 183-4
   Anleitung zum Componieren von Walzern (attrib.) 178-81
   Piano sonatas 3, 162, 163-4
   Serenade No. 12 in C minor 145

Nancarrow, Conlon 7, 19, 21-2
   Studies for Player Piano 21
Nketia, Joseph Kwabena 41-2
Nono, Luigi 133, 172-3
   Il Canto Sospeso 173
Nørgård, Per 173
   Iris 173, 175
Nyman, Michael 86, 184-5
   'An eye for optical theory' 86n90
   'Chasing sheep is best left to shepherds' 86

Ockeghem, Johannes IX, 141, 142, 150, 193, 200
   Missa prolationum 150, 200
Ono, Yoko 185

Pachelbel, Johanne 85-6
   Canon for three violins and continuo 85-6
Paganini, Niccolò 59
   Caprice for solo violin No. 24 59
Pärt, Arvo 150
   Cantus in Memoriam Benjamin Britten 150
Partch, Harry 113, 122-3
   U. S. Highball (A Musical Account of a Transcontinental Hobo Trip) 122-3
   Writings
   Genesis of Music 122-3
Pergolesi, Giovanni Battista 226
   Stabat Mater 226
Prez, Josquin des 9, 141, 193, 200, 213-15
   Missa Hercules Dux Ferrariae 213-5
Purcell, Henry 86-7, 143
   Dido and Aeneas 86
   King Arthur 86-7
   'Once, twice, thrice' 143

Rachmaninov, Sergei 60-1
   Rhapsody on a Theme of Paganini 60-1
Ravel, Maurice 75, 84, 116, 221
   Bolero 75, 84
   Menuet sur le nom d' Haydn 221
   Trois poèmes de Mallarmé 116
Reich, Steve VII, 19, 30-4, 187, 209
   Clapping Music 32-4, 209
   Come Out 31
   Drumming 31-2
   It's Gonna Rain 31
   Piano Phase 31
Riley, Terry 30, 184-5, 191
   In C 185, 191
Rimsky-Korsakov, Nicolai 219
Roads, Curtis 35
   Writings
   Rhythmic Processes in Electronic Music 35

Satie, Erik IX, 11, 82-3, 159, 163, 164, 166-8, 175
  Avant-dernieres pensees 166n163
  Gnossiennes 11
  Les Trois Valses 166n163
  Nocturnes 166n163
  Trois Gymnopedies 166n163
  Trois Mélodies 167
  Vexations 82-3
Scarlatti, Domenico 84-5, 92
  Keyboard Sonata K 27 85
  Keyboard Sonata K 514 in C 92
Scheidt, Samuel 143
  Tabulatura nova 143
Schillinger, Joseph 171
  Writings
  Mathematical Basis of the Arts, The 171
  Schillinger System of Musical Composition, The 171
Schoenberg, Arnold 57, 72, 82, 125-8, 130-1, 136-7, 142, 183-4, 236n274
  Five Piano Pieces Op. 23 131
  Variations for Orchestra, Op. 31 125-8
  Writings
  Fundamentals of Musical Composition 57, 82
Schubert, Franz 60-1, 69-71, 164-5
  Die Zauberharfe 69-71
  Du bist die ruh 164-5
  (Wanderer) Fantasia Op. 15 60-1
Schumann, Robert 7, 214, 219-20
  Carnaval 'Eusebius' 7
  Variations on the name "Abegg" 219-20
Sherlaw Johnson, Robert 193-4, 211
  Writings
  Messiaen 26
  'Composing with fractals' 211
Shostakovitch, Dmitri 150-1, 153, 154, 154n144, 200, 214, 222-4
  24 Preludes and Fugues 154
  Cello Concerto No. 1 in G 222
  String Quartet No. 5 in Bb 222
  String Quartet No. 8 in C minor 222-4
  Symphony No. 1 in F minor 222
  Symphony No 7 in C 'Leningrad' 154n144
  Symphony No. 10 in E minor 222
  Symphony No. 15 in A 150-1, 200
  Violin Concerto No. 1 in A minor 222
Spiegel, Laurie 155-6
  Three Sonic Spaces 156
Stockhausen, Karlheinz IX, 122, 133, 134, 172, 175
  Elektronische Studien 134
  Gruppen 134
  Klavierstuck IX IX, 172
  Kreuzspiel 134
  Schlagtrio 134
  Studie I 122
Stravinsky, Igor VII, VIII, 11-12, 40, 89-90, 116, 131, 142, 153n143
  Firebird 11
  In memoriam Dylan Thomas 131
  Petrushka 11, 89-90, 116

Rite of Spring 1, 11-13, 118
Symphony of Psalms 153n143
Threni 131
Writings
Poetics of Music in the Form of Six Lessons 90

Tavener, John 229, 243-4
Ikon of Light 229, 243
To a Child Dancing in the Wind 229, 243
Tchaikovsky, Pyotr Ilyich 7

Varèse, Edgar 188
Poème électronique 188

Wallin, Rolf 193, 200, 209-10, 212
Stonewave 210
Webern, Anton VIII, 72, 116, 125, 128-30, 131, 142, 146n139, 229, 242-3
Concerto Op. 24 128-30, 229
Fünf Canons, Op. 16 144-5
Ricercare Fuga (Ricercata) a 6 voci 146n139
Symphony Op. 21 130, 145
Variations Op. 30 131
Writings
Path to New Music, The 242
Weill, Kurt 75
'Mack the Knife' 75
Widor, Charles-Marie 221
Wolff, Christian 185
Wuorinen, Charles 193, 200, 210-11

Xenakis, Iannis IX, 173-4, 177-8, 187-91
Concret PH (originally titled *Interlude Sonore*) 188
Eonta 189
Metastaseis 173-4
Mikka 189-90
N'Shima 190
Pithoprakta 188-9
ST/4-1,080262 189
Writings
Formalized Music: Thought and Mathematics in Composition 187, 188